HEALING AT
THE PERIPHERY

Duke University Press Durham and London 2022

HEALING AT THE PERIPHERY

Ethnographies of Tibetan Medicine in India

LAURENT PORDIÉ AND
STEPHAN KLOOS, EDITORS

Printed in the United States of America on acid-free paper ∞
Designed by Courtney Leigh Richardson
Typeset in Garamond Premier Pro and Din
by Westchester Publishing Services

Library of Congress Cataloging-in-Publication Data
Names: Pordié, Laurent, editor. | Kloos, Stephan, editor.
Title: Healing at the periphery : ethnographies of Tibetan medicine
in India / Laurent Pordié and Stephan Kloos, editors.
Description: Durham : Duke University Press, 2021. | Includes
bibliographical references and index.
Identifiers: LCCN 2021012727 (print)
LCCN 2021012728 (ebook)
ISBN 9781478013525 (hardcover)
ISBN 9781478014454 (paperback)
ISBN 9781478021759 (ebook)
Subjects: LCSH: Medicine, Tibetan. | Traditional medicine—India. |
Traditional medicine—Himalaya Mountains Region. | Medical
anthropology—India. | Medical anthropology—Himalaya Mountains
Region. | BISAC: SOCIAL SCIENCE / Anthropology / Cultural &
Social | HISTORY / Asia / General
Classification: LCC R603.T5 H43 2021 (print) | LCC R603.T5 (ebook) |
DDC 610.954—dc23
LC record available at https://lccn.loc.gov/2021012727
LC ebook record available at https://lccn.loc.gov/2021012728

COVER ART: Eshe Kunzang (1938?–2003), Tibetan practitioner of
medicine who lived in Stok village in the Indus Valley, Ladakh.
Photograph taken in 2000. Courtesy of Rolex/Heine Pedersen.

To all amchi across the Himalayas

Contents

Afterword. WHEN "PERIPHERY" BECOMES CENTRAL · 197
SIENNA R. CRAIG

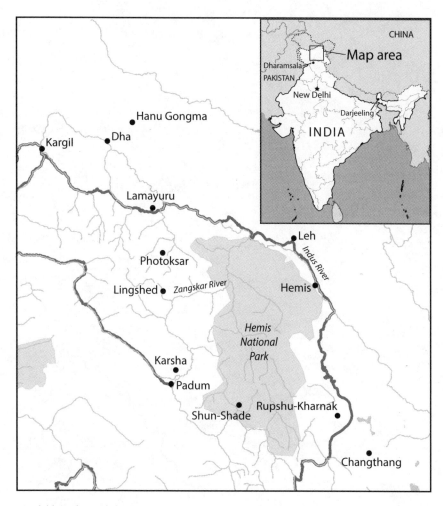

Ladakh, India, and the main sites covered in this book.

Introduction
The Indian Face of Sowa Rigpa
STEPHAN KLOOS AND LAURENT PORDIÉ

From its very beginnings, Tibetan medicine has had strong connections to *rgya gar*, that is, India. Tibetan medical historiographers report visits of eminent Indian physicians as early as the seventh century CE (Kilty 2010; Yang Ga 2014), an influence that only grew with the sustained influx of Indian Buddhism into Tibet from the eighth and, especially, tenth centuries CE onward. Although Tibetan Bon, Chinese, and Persian medical knowledge also contributed significantly to the Tibetan science of healing, also known by its Tibetan term Sowa Rigpa (*gso ba rig pa*), its partial Indian origins were privileged through an identification of the Buddha as the originator of Tibetan medicine. Besides numerous translations of Sanskrit medical texts into Tibetan, even Tibetan-authored texts such as Sowa Rigpa's standard treatise, the Gyüshi (*rgyud bzhi*, the Four Treatises), were presented as "Indian" to enhance their authority (Yang Ga 2014). Whether owing to India's status as the country of the Buddha, its highly developed medical traditions, or its strong historical connections of exchange with Tibet, it holds a special and well-documented place in the mythology, historiography, theory, and practice of medicine in Tibet. Tibetan medicine's place in India, by contrast, has begun to receive sustained scholarly attention only very recently, and this book constitutes the first collaborative effort to address the topic directly.

Tibetan medicine's history on the Indian subcontinent can be traced back to the establishment of the Western Himalayan kingdom of Ladakh in the tenth century CE and the consolidation of Tibetan cultural influence over the area (Norboo and Morup 1997, 206). Tibetan medicine has since then served as the prime—indeed, in many cases the only—professional health resource not only in Ladakh but also in other Himalayan regions that today belong to India, such as Zangskar, Lahaul, Spiti, Sikkim, and the Monpa areas of Arunachal Pradesh. Yet while Sowa Rigpa was one of Tibet's five major sciences and counts as one of Asia's great medical traditions, on par with Chinese medicine and Ayurveda, in the Himalayan periphery it resembled a folk medicine, transmitted in village lineages rather than prestigious state or monastic institutions. Indeed, until very recently Indian officials simply regarded Sowa Rigpa in the Himalayas as a "tribal medicine," and many exile Tibetan medical practitioners in India similarly consider it an unsophisticated folk variant of Tibetan medicine proper (Pordié 2016, 42).[1]

Over the past decades, however, Sowa Rigpa has achieved an unprecedented level of development in India. While Tibet was closed off to the world and subjected to heavy-handed political repression that also affected the traditional medical establishment there (Janes 1995), the Tibetan community in exile was free to reestablish, almost from scratch, their most important cultural, social, and religious institutions from 1959 onward, among them Tibetan medicine (Kloos 2008). Soon Tibetan medicine attracted considerable Indian and foreign interest, rendering it a central means of humanitarian engagement with India and the world (Kloos 2019). Thus, as exile Tibetan medical institutions became leading centers for Sowa Rigpa expertise and development, providing crucial training and support to Himalayan medical communities in lieu of their inaccessible or destroyed counterparts in Lhasa, Tibetans were able to reclaim some of their erstwhile cultural hegemony and political influence from exile (Kloos 2017). Furthermore, an ever-expanding network of Tibetan clinics began to operate not only in the Tibetan refugee settlements but also in India's Himalayan areas and megacities. The provision of affordable yet efficacious health care to all strata of Indian society, coupled with romantic images of Tibet and the popular figure of the Fourteenth Dalai Lama, ensured Tibetan medicine's growing popularity in India.

In 2010 the government of India legally recognized Sowa Rigpa, paving the way for its full integration into the Indian national health-care system (Kloos 2016). On the one hand, this was a direct consequence of several decades of exile Tibetan efforts to rebuild their medical institutions in India, coupled with the just-mentioned Tibetan humanitarian politics of providing development aid to Indian Himalayan communities. As Maling Gombu, a Himalayan official at the National Minorities Commission in New Delhi pointed out in 2008, "India is a big country, and the government is not aware of many things that are going on. It's thanks to the Tibetans that Sowa Rigpa came to the awareness of the government, because they developed it" (quoted in Kloos 2016, 30). On the other hand, this perspective hides from our view the essential social, political, and medical role that Indian Himalayan practitioners of Sowa Rigpa play at the local and the national levels. For example, it was only in coalition with Ladakhi practitioners (also known as *amchi*) that the exile Tibetan medical institutions managed to achieve their common goal of recognition (Blaikie 2016), and it was the Ladakhis who gained most from it in terms of prominence, financial support, and political power. Indeed, with the recognition of Tibetan medicine as an "Indian system of medicine" "practiced in the sub-Himalayan region" (Rajya Sabha 2010, 3), the Himalayan periphery has become central to this system's status and development in India.

It is thus time for a sustained look at Sowa Rigpa's social ecologies (Craig 2012) in the Indian Himalayas, with a specific focus on small social groups at the peripheries of modern India. What place does Sowa Rigpa hold in Indian Himalayan societies? What are the main issues involved in Sowa Rigpa's social and therapeutic transformations at the local level? And to what extent can an analysis of these transformations shed light on larger dynamics taking place in the Tibetan cultural area? The chapters of this volume address these questions from a variety of disciplinary perspectives: social and medical anthropology, qualitative economics, and development studies. They are connected by an ethnographic and analytic sensibility for how issues of power and legitimacy, religion, the dynamics of medical pluralism and institutionalization, and regional socioeconomic development come together to shape social and medical realities in the Indian Himalayas. Yet while the focus is squarely on Sowa Rigpa practitioners in rural and remote India, the contributors to this volume certainly do not bypass or ignore the larger-scale dynamics at play. They each address issues that affect the communities in question, which include complex social processes such as national and local government policies, global economic liberalization, biomedical development, and the shifting aspirations of the practitioners and their patients. These processes all contribute to the ongoing redefinition of Sowa Rigpa not only in the Indian Himalayas but also throughout the Tibetan world.

Besides this ethnographic focus, there is also a noteworthy historical dimension to the research presented in this volume. All chapters are based on fieldwork carried out in the late 1990s and early 2000s, capturing a unique moment of socioeconomic transformation impacting Sowa Rigpa and its communities in all locations. We know, for example, that a nascent Sowa Rigpa industry began to emerge in Tibet following Chinese economic and health-care reforms around the turn of the millennium (Saxer 2013) and that, at the same time, exile Tibetan medicine's success and growing commercialization in India (Kloos 2013) triggered the political processes that eventually led to its recognition in

2010. In the Indian Himalayas, however, the same large-scale social transformations of capitalism and modern development that fueled Sowa Rigpa's success elsewhere forced local amchi to reflect on, and renegotiate, their increasingly tenuous social and medical positions. By focusing mainly on Himalayan practitioners of Sowa Rigpa during this period of transformation in India, the chapters of this volume provide not only rare historical-ethnographic insights that enable us to better understand Sowa Rigpa's dynamics today but also a sharp lens through which larger social transformations in the Himalayas become visible.

The overall aim of this book, then, is to explore the reconfiguration of the therapeutic space and the sociopolitical reconstruction of Sowa Rigpa that took place during the key moment of the early 2000s. The emphasis is on a comparative approach, with research conducted among agriculturalist groups residing in remote mountainous areas of Ladakh and Zangskar; nomadic pastoralists of Ladakh's Changthang plateau; an amchi lineage in Sikkim; and exile Tibetans practicing in institutional contexts in the Himalayan foothills of Dharamsala and Darjeeling (northwestern and northeastern India respectively). Presenting a counterpoint to the success (commercial, cultural, political) of Tibetan medicine elsewhere during the 2000s, this volume specifically focuses on a moment of existential crisis, transformation, and renewal. It locates key questions about the proliferation and transformation of Tibetan medicine on the margins of so-called high Tibetan culture, grounding these inquiries specifically at the village level within the context of the Indian Union. In doing so, this book complements Theresia Hofer's (2018) subaltern account of Tibetan medicine in rural Tsang (Tibet Autonomous Region, China) and explicitly follows Sara Shneiderman (2015) in taking the village as a key site for the production of social meaning, negotiations of social change, and the mediation between the universal and the particular. It also responds to Ester Gallo's (2015) and Michael Herzfeld's (2015) calls for focusing on villages as integral parts of larger multisited research agendas. Far beyond their local and historical specificities, the case studies presented here approach a wide range of questions pertaining to scholarly Asian medicine and rural societies in the contemporary world and provide data of comparative value and broader relevance to the social sciences in general.

Before proceeding further, some clarifications on spelling and terminology are necessary. While we use the terms "Tibetan medicine" and "Sowa Rigpa" interchangeably in this introduction, most contributors to this volume refer to either "Tibetan medicine" or "amchi medicine." At the time of our research in the early 2000s, all interlocutors in the exile Tibetan community as well as Indian and Western experts spoke of "Tibetan medicine" in English, while among La-dakhis the term "amchi medicine" was more common, referring to the title of its practitioners. Among themselves, both Tibetan and Ladakhi practitioners used Sowa Rigpa (Tib. *gso ba rig pa*, the science of healing) or alternatively, in the case of the Tibetans, *bod sman* (Tibetan medicine) or, in the case of the La-dakhis, *amchi sman* (amchi medicine), and this is reflected in this volume's eth-nographic case studies. Since then, however, Sowa Rigpa's industrialization and expansion have created significant economic and cultural value, giving rise to multiple claims of ownership, often made through politics of naming (Blaikie 2016; Craig and Gerke 2016; Kloos 2016; Pordié 2008c), and Sowa Rigpa has become the official nomenclature in India since 2010. Hence, we use both terms in this introduction: "Tibetan medicine" as the best-known and established name internationally and Sowa Rigpa as the official Indian name, commonly agreed upon by both the Tibetan and Himalayan medical communities.

While the spelling of common Tibetan and Ladakhi terms like *amchi* (a Mongolian loanword that signifies practitioners of Tibetan medicine) or Gyüshi (*rgyud bzhi*, the title of the standard treatise of Tibetan medicine) and common personal names and place-names (Lobsang, Tashi, Lhasa, etc.) is angli-cized for convenience, we use the Wylie system of transliteration for less com-mon or more technical terms. This makes it easier for interested readers to look up their full meanings in Tibetan dictionaries and also leaves space for these terms' different pronunciations in Ladakhi and Tibetan language. However, for reasons of readability and ethnographic detail, simplified phonetic versions of the correct Wylie spellings are used in case of frequent repetitions of such terms. The suffix "-pa," as in Monpa, Hanupa, Changpa, and so on, although technically male, is commonly used to refer to male or female individuals or en-tire communities from a particular place: thus, Hanupa are people from Hanu, and Changpa are people from Changthang. In adjectival use, a Rupshupa amchi is a practitioner of Tibetan medicine from Rupshu.

Scholarly Literature on Sowa Rigpa in India

A brief overview of the scholarly literature on Tibetan medicine, or Sowa Rigpa, reveals three basic observations. First, despite counting among Asia's most important scholarly medical traditions by any definition, Sowa Rigpa was very late in attracting serious Western scholarship (Kloos 2013, 2015b; Pordié 2008c) and has long remained absent from fundamental collective works on Asian medicines (e.g., Bates 1995; Leslie 1976; Leslie and Young 1992). Sec-ond, the majority of research on Sowa Rigpa, from the 1980s until today, has focused on Tibetan medical orthodoxy, that is, on Sowa Rigpa's central institutions (mostly in Lhasa but more recently also in Xining and Dharamsala) and the textual theory and historiography produced by them. Third, considering the small size of Sowa Rigpa in India as compared to Tibet, a disproportionate number of studies and publications on Tibetan medicine have come out of India, many of them also dealing with village traditions. This is due to the relatively easy accessibility of the Tibetan exile community and culturally Tibetan areas in the Indian Himalayas to foreign researchers, and the international attention generated by the Dalai Lama and his exile government in Dharamsala (Kloos 2015a). While it would go beyond the scope of this introduction to discuss scholarship on Sowa Rigpa in its entirety, it is useful to situate the present volume within the context of scholarly literature on Sowa Rigpa in India.

As already mentioned, this literature can be roughly divided into two parts: one on Sowa Rigpa in the Indian Himalayas, predominantly focused on Ladakh and the surrounding mountain regions in northwestern India, and the other on Tibetan medicine among the Tibetan exile community, based in Dharamsala but operating a network of clinics all over India. Research in both contexts began in the 1970s and 1980s but remained a small fringe interest until the early 2000s, when a new generation of scholars—mostly medical anthropologists and most of them contributing to this volume—began a more sustained scholarly engagement with Sowa Rigpa in India that continues to grow today. While early publications based on interactions with the Tibetan medical establishment in Dharamsala focused on Sowa Rigpa's medical theory, literature, and history and thus represented an orthodox perspective, those coming out of Ladakh were mostly ethnographic descriptions of the heterodoxy found in Sowa Rigpa's periphery (although not presented as such for lack of a comparative approach). Only in the early 2000s did Tibetan medicine in exile become the subject of anthropological studies, and it took some more time before the relationship and interactions between the Himalayan and exile Tibetan fields of Sowa Rigpa began to be problematized in the late 2000s.

The first serious publications on Sowa Rigpa in English in the 1970s and 1980s were all based on engagements—either personal or textual—with Tibetan medicine in exile or were written by exile Tibetan practitioners or scholars themselves. Since, up to that moment, virtually no knowledge about Tibetan medicine existed outside small medical and scholarly circles in Asia and Russia, it is not surprising that these works mostly covered basic theoretical and historical information, either translating or summarizing key Tibetan medical texts that had found their way out of Tibet to India (e.g., Donden and Kelsang 1977; Emmerick 1975, 1977; Finckh 1975, 1978; Norbu 1976; Rechung Rinpoche 1973).

Christopher Beckwith (1979) offered a noteworthy challenge to the received wisdom of Sowa Rigpa's predominantly Indian origins, based on critical textual analysis. These early publications were followed by a number of works in the 1980s and 1990s that presented Tibetan medicine to larger audiences, still largely focused on the foundational Tibetan medical literature rather than actual medical practice in the Indian context (Clark 1995; Clifford 1984; Donden 1986; Dummer 1988; Jäger 1999; Meyer 1981, 1987; Parfionovitch, Meyer, and Dorje 1992).

After some early anthropological interest in health and healing among the exile Tibetan population in India (Calkowski 1986; Connor, Monro, and McIntyre 1996) that did not specifically focus on scholarly Tibetan medicine, the first ethnographic studies of Sowa Rigpa in Tibetan exile were conducted in the 1990s by Geoffrey Samuel (1999, 2001) and Eric Jacobson (2002, 2007, 2009) at branch clinics of the Dharamsala Men-Tsee-Khang in Dalhousie (Samuel) and Darjeeling and Gangtok (Jacobson). Established in 1961, the Men-Tsee-Khang—also known as the Tibetan Medical and Astrological Institute—is not only the oldest but also the largest and most prestigious institution of Tibetan medicine in exile. Having remained unexplored by social science scholars for almost four decades despite virtually embodying Tibetan medicine in exile for much of that time, the Men-Tsee-Khang emerged as a central site for anthropological studies once they finally commenced. After Samuel's and Jacobson's initial efforts, Audrey Prost conducted her doctoral research at the Men-Tsee-Khang's headquarters in Dharamsala, leading to a number of articles (Prost 2006a, 2006b, 2007) and the first book publication directly devoted to the topic (Prost 2008). Building on Prost's study and Vincanne Adams's work in Tibet (e.g., Adams 2001a, 2001b, 2002a, 2002b), Stephan Kloos further pursued critical anthropological research at the Men-Tsee-Khang and elsewhere, resulting in the first detailed historical account of Tibetan medicine in exile (Kloos 2008) as well as various papers on its contemporary role and development (Kloos 2011, 2012, 2013, 2015a, 2015b, 2016, 2017, 2019). Barbara Gerke's ethnography of Tibetan medicine in the Darjeeling Hills (Gerke 2010, 2011), as well as her meticulous work on the "subtle body" and longevity practices (Gerke 2007, 2012a, 2012b, 2012c, 2013a, 2017) and pharmaceutical traditions (Gerke 2013b, 2015a, 2015b, 2016, 2018, 2019), is likewise based on long-term research among the Tibetan exile community in India.

Not long after the first publications on Tibetan medicine based on texts and expertise in the Tibetan exile began to appear in the 1970s, Alice Kuhn pioneered ethnographic research on Sowa Rigpa in Ladakh in the mid-1980s (Kuhn 1988, 1994; Kuhn and Hoffmann 1985), thus initiating work on Tibetan medicine in the Indian Himalayas. Providing a comprehensive description of the therapeutic resources in the region, including Sowa Rigpa, she positioned this medical tradition in the wider context of increasing biomedical hegemony. During the same period, I. A. Navchoo and G. M. Buth (1989) gave a general, mainly technical description of Tibetan medicine in Ladakh, and a small number of other studies mentioned its existence (e.g., Ball and Elford 1994). Overall, however, after a brief period of initial interest, Sowa Rigpa in the region fell out of favor with social scientists, and it took about a decade before a revival of research on the topic took place around the turn of the millennium. This research locally coincided with a revival of traditional medicine itself, which mainly grew out of the urban context of Ladakh's capital, Leh.

This second generation of scholarship, initiated by Laurent Pordié, began by addressing the difficult social and medical transformations of Sowa Rigpa in a newly emerging socioeconomic environment (Kloos 2004; Pordié 2000, 2001a, 2002, 2015), touching also on issues of public health (Hancart Petitet 2005). This initial focus was gradually refined and expanded in a number of publications on the dialectical relationship between health development and power at the village level (Kloos 2005), the sociogeographical positioning and transformations of Tibetan medicine (Kloos 2006), the role of religion (Pordié 2003, 2007, 2008b, 2011, 2015), or the local impact of intellectual property regimes among Ladakhi amchi (Pordié 2005, 2008a). Florian Besch (2006, 2007) was the first to explore the modernization and institutional development of Tibetan medicine in Spiti, along Himachal Pradesh's border to Tibet, providing important insights into traditional health in an even more peripheral context than Ladakh. As Sowa Rigpa's existential crisis in India's Himalayan regions—which provided the background to all these studies in the early 2000s—abated, and the commercial and political value of Sowa Rigpa became noticeable even there, Calum Blaikie (2009, 2012, 2013, 2015, 2018, 2019) conducted crucial work on Sowa Rigpa pharmaceutical knowledge, practices, and materials in Ladakh (see also Pordié 2002, 2008c). Most recently, some authors also began to explore in some depth the ambivalent relationship between Ladakhi and exile Tibetan Sowa Rigpa communities (Blaikie 2016; Kloos 2016, 2017; Pordié 2008a; Pordié and Blaikie 2014) and between Ladakhi amchi and Tibetan medical globalization (Pordié 2011, 2016).

Although by no means comprehensive, this brief overview of the scholarly literature shows that despite the recent growth of studies on Sowa Rigpa in India, it remains a small field covered by an even smaller group of social scientists. Indeed, most scholars of the second generation are contributors to the present volume, which thus documents not only a crucial moment in the social transformation of health-care in the Indian Himalayas but also the very beginnings of renewed and sustained scholarly engagement with this topic (not to mention several individual academic careers). It was in the summer of 2001 in Leh, Ladakh's capital, that Pordié assembled a group of young scholars, including Florian Besch, Calum Blaikie, Pascale Hancart Petitet, and Stephan Kloos, to conduct original ethnographic fieldwork with rural amchi. This was part of an experimental approach by Nomad RSI (Recherche et Soutien International), an international nongovernmental organization (NGO) headed by Pordié, to revitalize amchi medicine in the region based on a sound understanding of local sociomedical realities gained through "pure" (as opposed to "applied") research (Pordié 2001b; see also Besch and Guérin in this volume). As it turned out, Nomad RSI revitalized not only amchi medicine on the Indian periphery but also anthropological scholarship on it through a concerted effort to bring together, in a comparative framework, a multiplicity of voices and perspectives. The strength of this volume lies precisely in this: although a collection of different case studies, it can be read as *one* ethnography of the role and place of amchi medicine at a moment of large-scale transformation in the Indian Himalayas, owing its anthropological wealth and breadth to the diversity and collegiality of its contributors.

Much has changed in the almost two decades since with regard to both amchi medicine in Ladakh and scholarship on it. When Nomad RSI began its work in Ladakh in 1999, between 110 and 140 amchi were practicing in the region (including Tibetan refugees), of whom 11 percent were monks and only 7 percent were women.[2] At the time of our research, the amchi tradition in Ladakh was thus almost exclusively male and carried a high social status (second only to monks), yet was undergoing a profound existential crisis linked to the region's accelerated socioeconomic and medical transformation.[3] Although gender is not an explicit analytic focus of the ethnographies in this volume, several chapters reveal how it was connected to Tibetan medicine's status and social role in ways that compounded this crisis, affecting (largely) male amchi and their predominantly female patients, as well as village communities more broadly. Difficulties connected to gender imbalance and social power were highlighted by both male and female villagers. When Nomad RSI started to organize a diploma course in Tibetan medicine, these insights resulted in the enrollment of an equal number of female and male students from medically underserved villages. These twenty-two students graduated in 2004 and 2005 and returned to their villages to establish clinics. Since 2010 they have constituted more than half of the Sowa Rigpa practitioners integrated into the public health-care system via the National Rural Health Mission, working as salaried government staff at primary health centers across Ladakh (Blaikie 2019). Today the majority of the National Rural Health Mission's amchi are female, as are the majority of students pursuing degrees in Sowa Rigpa at the Central Institute of Buddhist Studies near Leh. This indicates an increasing feminization of Tibetan medicine in Ladakh, something that has also been observed as part of Tibetan medicine's general modernization in other parts of Asia (e.g., Craig 2012; Fjeld and Hofer 2010–11; Hofer 2018, 81). Having lost some of its idealized and often problematic traditional status in the region, today Tibetan medicine has successfully overcome the crisis that formed the ethnographic context of this volume. Indeed, the upgrade of the research institute for Sowa Rigpa (established in 2014 in Leh) to the National Institute for Sowa Rigpa (the national administrative headquarters for Sowa Rigpa) in late 2020 moved Ladakh from the periphery to the center of contemporary Tibetan medicine in India.

In terms of scholarship, in contrast to ten or twenty years ago, today we have reasonably good insights into both the institutional exile Tibetan and the largely village-based Himalayan contexts of Sowa Rigpa in India, which has recently enabled some scholars to bring these two contexts together in a larger analytic frame.[4] Yet, especially as far as the Himalayan context is concerned, these studies remain too scattered to build up the critical mass needed to make a significant impact on social studies of Sowa Rigpa, the field of medical anthropology, and the overall effort to understand the Himalayan region in the larger context of rapid socioeconomic change in contemporary Asia. This is precisely the gap that the present volume addresses by bringing together case studies investigating the social foundations and transformations of Sowa Rigpa and its communities in India today. It does so with a particular focus on the periphery—from both the Tibetan and the Indian perspective and in both a social and geographic sense—not because of an imagined authenticity located in remoteness but because of the importance of the fringe in any endeavor to understand the center and indeed the whole. Thus, it is in fine-grained ethnographies of the social role of the amchi at the village level that the roots of Sowa Rigpa's most important current dynamics—commercialization and industrialization—can be traced, and their effects in society studied. This approach also provides a unique perspective on the role and functioning of the Indian nation-state at its territorial, medical, and social margins (Das and Poole 2004). By compiling seven such ethnographies in the present volume, we hope to offer not only new insights into Sowa Rigpa's overall development but also an essential comparative perspective and reference point for research on traditional medicine and contemporary rural societies in the Himalayas and beyond.

Chapter Outline

The chapters of this book can be roughly divided into two parts. While the first part focuses directly on the amchi—rural practitioners of Sowa Rigpa—as key figures and agents of Tibetan medicine's and Himalayan societies' transformations, the second section explores Sowa Rigpa as an apparatus of power that becomes particularly visible in liminal social situations. At the risk of invoking Sergio Leone's classic spaghetti western *The Good, the Bad and the Ugly*, one may sum up the chapters of the former as consecutively dealing with the good amchi (Pirie), the bad amchi (Kloos), no amchi (Blaikie), and the NGO amchi (Besch and Guérin). Similarly, the chapters of the latter—dealing with childbirth (Pordié and Hancart Petitet), mental illness (Gutschow), and institutionalization (Gerke)—may suggest a closer proximity to Michel Foucault's oeuvre than intended. Yet this casual summary offers a fundamental observation: in the early 2000s as much as now, Tibetan medicine in India straddled the fault lines between the agency of individual amchi (best represented by the "tragic hero" figure of Tashi Bulu in Kloos's chapter) and the impersonal dynamics of larger social apparatuses. It is precisely this tension—perhaps most explicitly illustrated by Gerke's chapter on the Men-Tsee-Khang clinic in the Darjeeling Hills—that is key to understanding Sowa Rigpa in the Indian Himalayas and that the contributors to this book collectively tackle.

Taking the individual agency of the healer as a starting point for analysis, the first section explores the social role of the amchi at the village level. A key theme recurrent in chapters 1 through 4 is the transformation of practitioners' social status into social power: while the status of amchi is generally high and directly related to their medical activities, it is not automatically consubstantial to social power. In other words, the influence of an amchi in village affairs may be no greater than that of a simple villager. However, differences in personal and familial histories, networks of influence, and economic affluence lead to remarkable variations in the role practitioners play beyond their direct medical functions. As the chapters in this section show, the success of an amchi's conversion of social status to actual power and influence depends on the consent of the group over which it is exercised. When this power is contested or considered problematic—or, conversely, when it is completely absent because there is no amchi—the very balance of the community is threatened.

Fernanda Pirie's chapter provides a good introduction to rural Ladakhi society, the social position of the amchi—at the turn of the millennium almost always male—within it, and the moral values that guide both. Against the backdrop of Ladakhi village society, characterized by a fundamental tension between hierarchical and egalitarian tendencies, as well as complex gender dynamics only alluded to here (but see Pirie 2007), Pirie describes the case of an amchi who successfully maintains the social equilibrium by *not* transforming his high status into power. In a Mahayana Buddhist microsociety that tends to eliminate asperities, the power of the therapist must be contained in and limited to medicine. Pirie here makes a strong case for using Tibetan medicine as a productive lens for social analyses of power, capitalism, and transformation at the village level, setting the stage for the chapters to follow.

Stephan Kloos's ethnography of amchi Tashi Bulu in Hanu serves as a counterpoint to Pirie's "good amchi." As in the previous case, here, too, the unity of the village is considered by its inhabitants as fundamental to social equilibrium (Vohra 1989). Yet Tashi Bulu, by converting his status into social power to improve the conditions of his family and ensure the continuation of quality medical care for the community, transgressed social and moral norms and thereby upset the village's social balance. Kloos cautions that such strategies cannot be ascribed to one man's character but need to be contextualized within the socioeconomic changes that directly impacted the sustainability of amchi medical practice. On a broader level, this case illustrates the political character of healing power, the moral character of social power, and the permeability of both. Thus, it was against the moral image of the ideal amchi that Tashi Bulu's political use of healing power was judged, resulting in conflicts that ultimately undermined both his social and medical roles.

Calum Blaikie's chapter, too, deals with the negative impacts of socioeconomic change and migration on Sowa Rigpa, in this case in nomadic communities on the remote Changthang plateau in northeastern Ladakh. Here, however, the figure of the amchi is noticeable mostly by its absence. Exploring the causes and consequences of there being no amchi, Blaikie shows how all attempts to reintroduce Sowa Rigpa into the community have failed. Again, the archetype of an ideal amchi—in this case formed by magnified recollections of a particular previous amchi—delimits the space in which the social role of healers is permitted, inevitably leading to their rejection. Although Tibetan medicines are available in Changthang from various sources, the absence of amchi exacerbates the nomads' risk perceptions regarding their way of living and contributes to the out-migration from the area. In Changthang, as much as in Hanu, rural amchi are thus perceived as playing a crucial social role beyond their medical functions but are simultaneously held accountable to sociomoral values that have become impracticable in modern Ladakh. Whether this leads to accusations of being a "bad amchi," as in the previous chapter, or to a complete lack of any amchi, as in Blaikie's case, the health of the village is affected in both a medical and social sense.

Against the background of such failed or problematic attempts at revitalizing Sowa Rigpa in rural Ladakh, Florian Besch and Isabelle Guérin present a case where the crisis of Tibetan medicine was successfully addressed through a development intervention by the international NGO Nomad RSI. Taking a socioeconomic analytic approach, the authors study the monetization of Sowa Rigpa in the context of the establishment of a health center in Lingshed, a remote village between Ladakh and Zangskar. After some initial setbacks, this led to a certain degree of professionalization of Tibetan medicine, effectively establishing a new system of reciprocity between amchi and community without transgressing the moral norms guiding an amchi's practice. While the amchi could still not charge money for their services, a community fund removed the economic insecurity that had until then made their practice unsustainable (Pordié 2002). Besch and Guérin illustrate well the centrality of the village community and its notions about an amchi's role as outlined by Pirie and the other authors, which ultimately determine the success or failure of any attempt to adapt amchi health care to the modern world.

If the first section's key subjects were individual amchi (or their absence) and their attempts to solve Sowa Rigpa's socioeconomic crisis, the second part of this book is organized around their patients' experiences with Tibetan medicine in different situations of sociomedical crisis. Thus, the chapter by Laurent Pordié and Pascale Hancart Petitet takes childbirth as a prism through which to read transformations of Ladakhi society. Moving their analysis from an isolated village in Zangskar to a modern hospital in Ladakh's capital, Leh, the authors reveal the existence of Sowa Rigpa emergency practices in childbirth as well as a specific treatment to assist delivery: the "butter fish." While traditional social norms strongly limit the (male) amchi's obstetric expertise in the village context, they are further marginalized—even declared illegal—in the presence of biomedical resources. In this case, then, the practice of Tibetan medicine must not simply conform to a defined social structure, as in the previous chapters; it is instead banished altogether from this structure. Despite the amchi's invisibility at the medical margins of urban society, however, Sowa Rigpa retains a central role—social, symbolic, and medical—for many patients.

A different scenario is presented by Kim Gutschow, who uses the example of "wind disorder" to analyze a patient's trajectory of treatment in a context of medical pluralism. In contrast to childbirth, amchi here emerge as more competent and valorized healers than their biomedical peers. Aside from the fact that wind disorder is a Tibetan medical concept, amchi have a profound knowledge of the village's social context, enabling them to socialize the (mental) illness and provide meaning. In this way, they restore not only the balance of the three "humors" (*nyes pa*) in the patient but also the social balance of their communities. Amid the pressures of capitalism and modern lifestyles, which elsewhere lead to the professionalization and standardization of Sowa Rigpa, the Zangskari amchi's local expertise and ability to interact with their patients in flexible and improvisational ways remain highly valued by the community. As healing practices reflect wider cultural and social practices, the amchi in this case are able to translate their social status and role into medical power.

In the last chapter, Barbara Gerke explores the effects of Sowa Rigpa's institutionalization in the Indian Himalayas, using the example of Men-Tsee-Khang branch clinics in the Northeast Indian Darjeeling Hills and Sikkim. Having its headquarters in Dharamsala and a network of dozens of branch clinics all over India and Nepal, this elite exile Tibetan institution is well known for its high quality of medical training and care. However, its doctors—who rotate between different clinics every few years—lack local knowledge and integration, which affects their social status and perceptions of their healing power. This shift from individual agency to institutional power, and from community-based to centralized/standardized health care, is well illustrated by Gerke, who describes the particular case of the transformation of a lineage amchi into an institutional amchi. If Gutschow's Zangskari amchi represent one end of the spectrum of Tibetan medicine in the Indian Himalayas, and Besch and Guérin's amchi health center is located in the middle, the Men-Tsee-Khang amchi in the Darjeeling Hills (and elsewhere) occupy the other extreme on the scale between individual agency and institutional power.

All chapters of this book capture Sowa Rigpa in a state of transition, at a crucial moment right at the beginning of its modern development. While each of them documents Tibetan medicine's local heterogeneity in great ethnographic detail, together they also offer an unprecedented overview of the larger social, moral, cultural, and economic context and dynamics that shape contemporary Sowa Rigpa in India. Much has been written about the traditional ideal type of Tibetan medicine, and even more about its professionalization, standardization, commercialization, and globalization in India and elsewhere. Yet this volume constitutes the first collective effort to study the liminal moment of social crisis and transformation that lies at the root of these processes, without which Sowa Rigpa's more recent official recognition and entrance into the lucrative market for herbal medicines would be unthinkable and impossible to understand. Meticulous ethnographic attention to local microprocesses at the village level thus serves not only as a powerful lens on larger social, cultural, and economic dynamics in the Indian Himalayas and the Tibetan world but also as an important foundation for engaging new global phenomena such as the Sowa Rigpa industry, whose remote Himalayan roots are all too easily forgotten.

Notes

1   This is in line with the Ladakhi's and Monpa's official status as Scheduled Tribes under Indian law.

2   These figures are the result of a region-wide empirical study carried out in 1998 (Pordié 2003). In official statistics (e.g., Rajya Sabha 2010, 10), the total number of amchi in Ladakh has been raised to four hundred for political and promotional reasons.

3   Sowa Rigpa has long been a male-dominated field not only in Ladakh but in all its locations, even if female amchi existed historically and exerted notable influences on the development of the tradition (Fjeld and Hofer 2010–11; Tashi Tsering 2005).

4   The European Research Council (ERC) Starting Grant project RATIMED (Reassembling Tibetan Medicine, 2014–19) at the Institute for Social Anthropology, Austrian Academy of Sciences, was the first comprehensive study of Sowa Rigpa in Asia, exploring the emergence of a transnational Sowa Rigpa industry across different regional contexts.

References

Adams, Vincanne. 2001a. "Particularizing Modernity: Tibetan Medical Theorizing of Women's Health in Lhasa, Tibet." In *Healing Powers and Modernity: Traditional Medicine, Shamanism, and Science in Asian Societies*, edited by Linda Connor and Geoffrey Samuel, 197–246. Westport, CT: Bergin and Garvey.

Adams, Vincanne. 2001b. "The Sacred in the Scientific: Ambiguous Practices of Science in Tibetan Medicine." *Cultural Anthropology* 16 (4): 542–75.

Adams, Vincanne. 2002a. "Establishing Proof: Translating 'Science' and the State in Tibetan Medicine." In *New Horizons in Medical Anthropology*, edited by Mark Nichter and Margaret Lock, 200–220. London: Routledge.

Adams, Vincanne. 2002b. "Randomized Controlled Crime: Postcolonial Sciences in Alternative Medicine Research." *Social Studies of Science* 32 (5–6): 659–90.

Ball, Keith, and Jonathan Elford. 1994. "Health in Zangskar." In *Himalayan Buddhist Villages: Environment, Resources, Society and Religious Life in Zangskar, Ladakh*, edited by John Crook and Henry Osmaston, 405–32. Delhi: Motilal Banarsidass.

Bates, Donald George, ed. 1995. *Knowledge and the Scholarly Medical Traditions*. Cambridge: Cambridge University Press.

Beckwith, Christopher I. 1979. "The Introduction of Greek Medicine into Tibet in the 7th and 8th Century." *Journal of the American Oriental Society* 99:297–313.

Besch, Florian. 2006. "Tibetan Medicine off the Roads: Modernizing the Work of the Amchi in Spiti." PhD diss., University of Heidelberg.

Besch, Florian. 2007. "Making a Medical Living: Discussing the Monetization of Tibetan Medicine in Spiti, Northwest India." In *Soundings in Tibetan Medicine: Historical and Anthropological Perspectives*, edited by Mona Schrempf, 155–70. Leiden: Brill.

Blaikie, Calum. 2009. "Critically Endangered? Medicinal Plant Cultivation and the Reconfiguration of Sowa Rigpa in Ladakh." *Asian Medicine* 5 (2): 243–72.

Blaikie, Calum. 2012. "Making Medicine: Materia Medica, Pharmacy and the Production of Sowa Rigpa in Ladakh." PhD diss., University of Kent.

Blaikie, Calum. 2013. "Currents of Tradition in Sowa Rigpa Pharmacy." *East Asian Science, Technology and Society* 7:425–51.

Blaikie, Calum. 2015. "Wish-Fulfilling Jewel Pills: Tibetan Medicines from Exclusivity to Ubiquity." *Anthropology and Medicine* 22 (1): 7–22.

Blaikie, Calum. 2016. "Positioning Sowa Rigpa in India: Coalition and Antagonism in the Quest for Recognition." *Medicine, Anthropology, Theory* 3 (2): 50–86.

Blaikie, Calum. 2018. "Absence, Abundance, and Excess: Substances and Sowa Rigpa in Ladakh since the 1960s." In *Locating the Medical: Explorations in South Asian History*, edited by Guy Attewell and Rohan Deb Roy, 169–99. New Delhi: Oxford University Press.

Blaikie, Calum. 2019. "Mainstreaming Marginality: Traditional Medicine and Primary Healthcare in Himalayan India." *Asian Medicine* 14 (1): 145–72.

Calkowski, Marcia. 1986. "Power, Charisma, and Ritual Curing in a Tibetan Community in India." PhD diss., University of British Columbia.

Clark, Barry. 1995. *The Quintessence Tantras of Tibetan Medicine*. Ithaca, NY: Snow Lion.

Clifford, Terry. 1984. *Tibetan Buddhist Medicine and Psychiatry: The Diamond Healing*. York Beach, ME: Samuel Weiser.

Connor, Linda, K. Monro, and E. McIntyre. 1996. "Healing Resources in Tibetan Settlements in North India." *Asian Studies Review* 20 (1): 108–18.

Craig, Sienna. 2012. *Healing Elements: Efficacy and the Social Ecologies of Tibetan Medicine*. Berkeley: University of California Press.

Craig, Sienna, and Barbara Gerke. 2016. "Naming and Forgetting: Sowa Rigpa and the Territory of Asian Medical Systems." *Medicine, Anthropology, Theory* 3 (2): 87–122.

Das, Veena, and Deborah Poole, eds. 2004. *Anthropology in the Margins of the State*. Santa Fe, NM: School of American Research Press.

Donden, Yeshi. 1986. *Health through Balance: An Introduction to Tibetan Medicine*. Ithaca, NY: Snow Lion.

Donden, Yeshi, and Jhampa Kelsang. 1977. *Ambrosia Heart Tantra*. Dharamsala: Library of Tibetan Works and Archives.

Dummer, Tom. 1988. *Tibetan Medicine and Other Holistic Health-Care Systems*. London: Routledge.

Emmerick, Ronald E. 1975. "A Chapter from the Rgyud-bzhi." *Asia Major* 19 (2): 141–62.

Emmerick, Ronald E. 1977. "Sources of the rGyud-bzhi." *Zeitschrift der Deutschen Morgenländischen Gesellschaft* (suppl. III) 2:1135–42.

Finckh, Elisabeth. 1975. *Grundlagen tibetischer Heilkunde*. Ülzen: Medizinisch-Literarische Verlagsgemeinschaft.

Finckh, Elisabeth. 1978. *Foundations of Tibetan Medicine*. London: Robinson and Watkins.

Fjeld, Heidi, and Theresia Hofer. 2010–11. "Women and Gender in Tibetan Medicine." *Asian Medicine: Tradition and Modernity* 6 (2): 175–216.

Gallo, Ester. 2015. "Village Ethnography and Kinship Studies: Perspectives from India and Beyond." *Critique of Anthropology* 35 (3): 248–62.

Gerke, Barbara. 2007. "Engaging the Subtle Body: Re-approaching *Bla* Rituals among Himalayan Tibetan Societies." In *Soundings in Tibetan Medicine: Anthropological and Historical Perspectives*, edited by Mona Schrempf, 191–212. Leiden: Brill.

Gerke, Barbara. 2010. "Tibetan Treatment Choices in the Context of Medical Pluralism in the Darjeeling Hills." In *Studies of Medical Pluralism in Tibetan History and Society; PIATS 2006: Proceedings of the Eleventh Seminar of the International Association for Tibetan Studies, Königswinter 2006*, edited by Sienna Craig, Mingji Cuomu, Frances Garrett, and Mona Schrempf, 337–76. Andiast, Switzerland: International Institute for Tibetan and Buddhist Studies.

Gerke, Barbara. 2011. "Correlating Biomedical and Tibetan Medical Terms in Amchi Medical Practice." In *Medicine between Science and Religion: Explorations on Tibetan Grounds*, edited by Vincanne Adams, Mona Schrempf, and Sienna Craig, 127–52. Oxford: Berghahn.

Gerke, Barbara. 2012a. *Long Lives and Untimely Deaths: Life-Span Concepts and Longevity Practices among Tibetans in the Darjeeling Hills, India*. Leiden: Brill.

Gerke, Barbara. 2012b. "Treating Essence with Essence: Re-inventing Bcud Len as Vitalising Dietary Supplements in Contemporary Tibetan Medicine." *Asian Medicine* 7 (1): 196–224.

Gerke, Barbara. 2012c. "'Treating the Aged' and 'Maintaining Health': Locating Bcud Len Practise in the Four Medical Tantras." *Journal of the International Association of Buddhist Studies* 35 (1–2): 329–62.

Gerke, Barbara. 2013a. "On the 'Subtle Body' and 'Circulation' in Tibetan Medicine." In *Religion and the Subtle Body in Asia and the West: Between Mind and Body*, edited by Geoffrey Samuel and Jay Johnston, 83–99. London: Routledge.

Gerke, Barbara. 2013b. "The Social Life of Tsotel: Processing Mercury in Contemporary Tibetan Medicine." *Asian Medicine: Tradition and Modernity* 8 (1): 120–52.

Gerke, Barbara. 2015a. "Moving from Efficacy to Safety: A Changing Focus in the Study of Asian Medical Systems." *Journal of the Anthropological Society of Oxford* 7 (3): 370–84.

Gerke, Barbara. 2015b. "The Poison of Touch: Tracing Mercurial Treatments of Venereal Diseases in Tibet." *Social History of Medicine* 28 (3): 532–54.

Gerke, Barbara. 2016. "When Ngülchu Is Not Mercury: Tibetan Taxonomies of 'Metals.'" In *Soulless Matter, Seats of Energy: Metals, Gems and Minerals in South Asian Religions and Culture*, edited by Fabrizio Ferrari and Thomas Dähnhardt, 116–40. Sheffield: Equinox.

Gerke, Barbara. 2017. "Tibetan Precious Pills as Therapeutics and Rejuvenating Longevity Tonics." *History of Science in South Asia* 5 (2): 204–33.

Gerke, Barbara. 2018. "The Signature of Recipes: Authorship, Intertextuality, and the Epistemic Genre of Tibetan Formulas." *Revue d'Etudes Tibétaines* 45:178–220.

Gerke, Barbara. 2019. "The Buddhist-Medical Interface in Tibet: Black Pill Traditions in Transformation." *Religions* 10 (4): article 282. https://doi.org/10.3390/rel10040282.

Hancart Petitet, Pascale. 2005. "Mortalité maternelle au Ladakh: De la santé publique à l'anthropologie." In *Panser le monde, penser les médecines: Traditions médicales et développement sanitaire*, edited by Laurent Pordié, 123–43. Paris: Karthala.

Herzfeld, Michael. 2015. "The Village in the World and the World in the Village: Reflections on Ethnographic Epistemology." *Critique of Anthropology* 35 (3): 338–43.

Hofer, Theresia. 2018. *Medicine and Memory in Tibet:* Amchi *Physicians in an Age of Reform*. Seattle: University of Washington Press.

Jacobson, Eric. 2002. "Panic Attack in a Context of Comorbid Anxiety and Depression in a Tibetan Refugee." *Culture, Medicine and Psychiatry* 26 (2): 259–79.

Jacobson, Eric. 2007. "'Life-Wind Illness' in Tibetan Medicine: Depression, Generalized Anxiety, and Panic Attack." In *Soundings in Tibetan Medicine: Anthropological and Historical Perspectives*, edited by Mona Schrempf, 225–45. Leiden: Brill.

Jacobson, Eric. 2009. "Panic Attack in Tibetan Refugees." In *Culture and Panic Disorder*, edited by Devon Hinton and Byron Good, 230–61. Stanford, CA: Stanford University Press.

Jäger, Katrin. 1999. *Nektar der Unsterblichkeit: Zwei Kapitel aus der Tibetischen Kinderheilkunde; Übersetzung aus dem Tibetischen Originalwerk und Kommentar*. Egelsbach, Germany: Hänsel-Hohenhausen.

Janes, Craig. 1995. "The Transformations of Tibetan Medicine." *Medical Anthropology Quarterly* 9:6–39.

Kilty, Gavin. 2010. "Translator's Introduction." In *Mirror of Beryl: A Historical Introduction to Tibetan Medicine*, translated by Gavin Kilty, 1–25. Somerville, MA: Wisdom.

Kloos, Stephan. 2004. *Tibetan Medicine among the Buddhist Dards of Ladakh*. Vienna: Wiener Studien zur Tibetologie und Buddhismuskunde.

Kloos, Stephan. 2005. "Le développement dans la négociation du pouvoir: Le cas de la médecine tibétaine à Hanu, Inde himalayenne." In *Panser le monde, penser les médecines: Traditions médicales et développement sanitaire*, edited by Laurent Pordié, 101–22. Paris: Karthala.

Kloos, Stephan. 2006. "Amchi Medizin zwischen Rand und Mitte." In *Der Rand und die Mitte: Beiträge zur Sozialanthropologie und Kulturgeschichte Tibets und des Himalaya*, edited by Andre Gingrich and Guntram Hazod, 55–77. Vienna: Verlag der Österreichischen Akademie der Wissenschaften.

Kloos, Stephan. 2008. "The History and Development of Tibetan Medicine in Exile." *Tibet Journal* 33 (3): 15–49.

Kloos, Stephan. 2011. "Navigating 'Modern Science' and 'Traditional Culture': The Dharamsala Men-Tsee-Khang in India." In *Medicine between Science and Religion: Explorations on Tibetan Grounds*, edited by Vincanne Adams, Mona Schrempf, and Sienna Craig, 83–105. Oxford: Berghahn Books.

Kloos, Stephan. 2012. "Die Alchemie exil-tibetischer Identität: Anmerkungen zur pharmazeutischen und politischen Wirksamkeit tibetischer Pillen." *Curare* 35 (3): 197–207.

Kloos, Stephan. 2013. "How Tibetan Medicine Became a 'Medical System.'" *East Asian Science, Technology and Society* 7 (3): 381–95.

Kloos, Stephan. 2015a. "(Im-)Potent Knowledges: Preserving 'Traditional' Tibetan Medicine through Modern Science." In *Fugitive Knowledge: The Loss and Preservation of Knowledge in Cultural Contact Zones*, edited by Andreas Beer and Gesa Mackenthun, 123–42. Münster: Waxmann.

Kloos, Stephan. 2015b. "Introduction: The Translation and Development of Tibetan Medicine in Exile." In *Das letzte Tantra, aus "Die vier Tantra der Tibetischen Medizin,"* translated by Florian Ploberger, 28–35. Schiedlberg, Austria: Bacopa.

Kloos, Stephan. 2016. "The Recognition of Sowa Rigpa in India: How Tibetan Medicine Became an Indian Medical System." *Medicine, Anthropology, Theory* 3 (2): 19–49.

Kloos, Stephan. 2017. "The Politics of Preservation and Loss: Tibetan Medical Knowledge in Exile." *East Asian Science, Technology and Society* 10 (2): 135–59.

Kloos, Stephan. 2019. "Humanitarianism from Below: Sowa Rigpa, the Traditional Pharmaceutical Industry, and Global Health." *Medical Anthropology* 39 (2): 167–81.

Kuhn, Alice. 1988. *Heiler und ihre Patienten am Dach der Welt: Ladakh aus ethnomedizinischer Sicht.* Frankfurt am Main: Peter Lang.

Kuhn, Alice. 1994. "Ladakh: A Pluralistic Medical System under Acculturation and Domination." In *Acculturation and Domination in Traditional Asian Medical Systems,* edited by Dorothea Sich and Waltraud Gottschalk, 61–73. Stuttgart: F. Steiner Verlag.

Kuhn, Alice, and C.-H. Hoffmann. 1985. "Buddhistische Heilkunst auf dem Dach der Welt." *Das Neue Universum* 103:359–70.

Leslie, Charles, ed. 1976. *Asian Medical Systems: A Comparative Study.* Berkeley: University of California Press.

Leslie, Charles, and Allan Young, eds. 1992. *Paths to Asian Medical Knowledge.* Berkeley: University of California Press.

Meyer, Fernand. 1981. *Gso-Ba Rig-Pa: Le système médical tibétain.* Paris: Éditions du CNRS.

Meyer, Fernand. 1987. "Essai d'analyse schématique d'un système médical: La médecine savante du Tibet." In *Etiologie et perception de la maladie—dans les sociétés modernes et traditionnelles,* edited by Anne Retel-Laurentin, 227–49. Paris: L'Harmattan.

Navchoo, I. A., and G. M. Buth. 1989. "Medicinal System of Ladakh, India." *Journal of Ethnopharmacology* 26:137–46.

Norboo, Tsering, and Tsering Morup. 1997. "Culture, Health and Illness in Ladakh." In *Recent Research on Ladakh 6: Proceedings of the Sixth International Colloquium on Ladakh, Leh 1993,* edited by Henry Osmaston and Nawang Tsering, 205–10. Delhi: Motilal Banarsidass.

Norbu, Dawa, ed. 1976. *An Introduction to Tibetan Medicine.* New Delhi: Tibetan Review.

Parfionovitch, Yuri, Fernand Meyer, and Gyurme Dorje, eds. 1992. *Tibetan Medical Painting: Illustrations to the Blue Beryl Treatise of Sangye Gyamtso (1653–1705).* 2 vols. New York: Harry N. Abrams.

Pirie, Fernanda. 2007. *Peace and Conflict in Ladakh: The Construction of a Fragile Web of Order.* Leiden: Brill.

Pordié, Laurent. 2000. "Tibetan Medicine: The Dynamic of a Biocultural Object in a Context of Social Change." In *Anthology of the International Academic Conference on Tibetan Medicine,* 935–36. Beijing: Chinese Medical Association of Minorities.

Pordié, Laurent. 2001a. "The Logics of Legitimization among the Amchi of Ladakh." Paper presented at the 10th Colloquium of the International Association for Ladakh Studies, University of Oxford, September 13, 2001.

Pordié, Laurent. 2001b. "Research and International Aid: A Possible Meeting." *Ladakh Studies* 15:33–45.

Pordié, Laurent. 2002. "La pharmacopée comme expression de société: Une étude himalayenne." In *Des sources du savoir aux médicaments du futur*, edited by Jacques Fleurentin, Jean-Marie Pelt, and Guy Mazars, 183–94. Paris: Éditions IRD–SFE.

Pordié, Laurent. 2003. *The Expression of Religion in Tibetan Medicine: Ideal Conceptions, Contemporary Practices and Political Use*. Pondy Papers in Social Sciences 29. Pondicherry: French Institute of Pondicherry.

Pordié, Laurent. 2005. "Claims for Intellectual Property Rights and the Illusion of Conservation: A Brief Anthropological Unpacking of a 'Development' Failure." In *Wise Practices in Sustainably Managing Himalayan Medicinal Plants*, edited by Yildiz Aumeeruddy-Thomas, M. Karki, D. Parajuli, and K. Gurung, 394–10. Kathmandu: IDRC, UNESCO, WWF Publications.

Pordié, Laurent. 2007. "Buddhism in the Everyday Medical Practice of the Ladakhi Amchi." *Indian Anthropologist* 37 (1): 93–116.

Pordié, Laurent. 2008a. "Hijacking Intellectual Property Rights: Identities and Social Power in the Indian Himalayas." In *Tibetan Medicine in the Contemporary World: Global Politics of Medical Knowledge and Practice*, edited by Laurent Pordié, 132–59. London: Routledge.

Pordié, Laurent. 2008b. "Reformulating Ingredients: Outlines of a Contemporary Ritual for the Consecration of Medicines in Ladakh." In *Modern Ladakh: Anthropological Perspectives on Continuity and Change*, edited by Marten van Beek and Fernanda Pirie, 153–74. Leiden: Brill.

Pordié, Laurent. 2008c. "Tibetan Medicine Today: Neo-Traditionalism as an Analytical Lens and a Political Tool." In *Tibetan Medicine in the Contemporary World: Global Politics of Medical Knowledge and Practice*, edited by Laurent Pordié, 3–32. London: Routledge.

Pordié, Laurent. 2011. "Accentuation et pragmatisme: Le savoir médical tibétain à destination des étrangers." *Revue d'Anthropologie des Connaissances* 5 (1): 99–130.

Pordié, Laurent. 2015. "Genealogy and Ambivalence of a Therapeutic Heterodoxy: Islam and Tibetan Medicine in North-Western India." *Modern Asian Studies* 49 (6): 1772–807.

Pordié, Laurent. 2016. "The Vagaries of Therapeutic Globalization: Fame, Money and Social Relations in Tibetan Medicine." *International Journal of Social Science Studies* 4 (2): 38–52.

Pordié, Laurent, and Calum Blaikie. 2014. "Knowledge and Skills in Motion: Layers of Tibetan Medical Education in India." *Culture, Medicine and Psychiatry* 38 (3): 340–68.

Prost, Audrey. 2006a. "Causation as Strategy: Interpreting Humours among Tibetan Refugees." *Anthropology and Medicine* 13 (2): 119–30.

Prost, Audrey. 2006b. "Gained in Translation: Tibetan Science between Dharamsala and Lhasa." In *Translating Others*, edited by Theo Hermans, 1:132–44. Manchester: St. Jerome.

Prost, Audrey. 2007. "Sa Cha 'Di Ma 'Phrod Na: Displacement and Traditional Tibetan Medicine among Tibetan Refugees in India." In *Soundings in Tibetan Medicine: Anthropological and Historical Perspectives*, edited by Mona Schrempf, 45–64. Leiden: Brill.

Prost, Audrey. 2008. *Precious Pills: Medicine and Social Change among Tibetan Refugees in India*. New York: Berghahn Books.

Rajya Sabha. 2010. *Forty-Sixth Report on the Indian Medicine Central Council (Amendment) Bill*. New Delhi: Rajya Sabha Secretariat.

Rechung Rinpoche. 1973. *Tibetan Medicine*. Berkeley: University of California Press.

Samuel, Geoffrey. 1999. "Religion, Health and Suffering among Contemporary Tibetans." In *Religion, Health and Suffering*, edited by John Hinnells and Roy Porter, 85–109. London: Routledge.

Samuel, Geoffrey. 2001. "Tibetan Medicine in Contemporary India: Theory and Practice." In *Healing Powers and Modernity: Traditional Medicine, Shamanism, and Science in Asian Societies*, edited by Linda Connor and Geoffrey Samuel, 247–68. Westport, CT: Bergin and Garvey.

Saxer, Martin. 2013. *Manufacturing Tibetan Medicine: The Creation of an Industry and the Moral Economy of Tibetanness*. Oxford: Berghahn Books.

Shneiderman, Sara. 2015. "Regionalism, Mobility, and 'the Village' as a Set of Social Relations: Himalayan Reflections on a South Asian Theme." *Critique of Anthropology* 35 (3): 318–37.

Tashi Tsering. 2005. "Outstanding Women in Tibetan Medicine." In *Women in Tibet*, edited by Janet Gyatso and Hanna Havnevik, 169–94. New Delhi: Foundation Books.

Vohra, Rohit. 1989. *An Ethnography: The Buddhist Dards of Ladakh; "Mythic Lore—Household—Alliance System—Kinship."* Ettelbruck, Luxembourg: Skydie Brown International.

Yang Ga. 2014. "The Origins of the Four Tantras and an Account of Its Author, Yuthog Yonten Gonpo." In *Bodies in Balance: The Art of Tibetan Medicine*, edited by Theresia Hofer, 154–77. New York: Rubin Museum of Art, in association with University of Washington Press.

1. THE AMCHI AS VILLAGER
Status and Its Refusal in Ladakh

FERNANDA PIRIE

"You should go and stay in the amchi's household. He's very active in village affairs, and you will learn a lot from him." This advice was offered by members of a Ladakhi development organization at the outset of my fieldwork in Photoksar.[1] They knew this remote village well, and their recommendation of the amchi's household was a good one. The family welcomed me with open arms, and Sonam Paljor, the only practitioner of Tibetan medicine in the village, became one of my best informants. Clever, thoughtful, and perceptive, he was an endless source of insights into local customs and events, including the sensitive subject of conflict resolution, which was the main focus of my research. As the development workers had promised, he was actively engaged in village affairs. They gave me the impression that Paljor had status and influence in this sphere. However, the issues of social status and hierarchy in village politics turned out to be highly complex. In this village, it transpired, there was a delicate balance among all forms of status, responsibility, and leadership, along with subtle methods for controlling and distributing power.

Issues of hierarchy have received considerable attention in the literature on Ladakh (Aggarwal 2004; Kaplanian 1981), as have the divisive effects of modernity (Kloos, this volume; van Beek 2000a, 2000b). This chapter illustrates some of the countervailing ideas and practices that have served to limit the effects of status and wealth and promote patterns of equality and inclusion within a village. The nature and effects of such practices are exemplified in the case of the Photoksar amchi and his position and activities within village politics. To illustrate these points, I return to the village as I approached it in the summer of 1999.

Photoksar

Photoksar is one of the remoter Ladakhi villages, lying on the main route from the Indus valley to the Trans Singe-la region. In 1999 it took two days to reach the village on foot from the end of the nearest road, including an ascent of the 4,900-meter Shi Shi La pass. The village consisted of around two hundred people, who still largely depended on their crops and animals for subsistence.

The amchi's household, in which I stayed, was one of the largest in the village, with many fields and a sizable number of livestock: yaks, sheep, and goats. His family consisted of four generations living together in the main house, the *khangba* (*khang ba*). It is common in Ladakh for older generations to move to a smaller, dependent household, the *khangu* (*khang bu*), but this family took pride in having all stayed together. Unusually, Paljor's younger brother had also married, and his wife and two sons were living in the khangba with the rest of the family. This represents a departure from the traditional systems of polyandry and primogeniture, which the villagers described as the practice of having only one wife per generation per household. This was still the norm in Photoksar, but with the increase in food security and a rise in population, five households had divided, with younger sons establishing families in independent khangu. In villages closer to Leh, the capital, division is more common.[2]

It was clear to me from the start that Paljor was respected within the village, not just for his medical training and skill, but also as a wise and knowledgeable member of the community. People would constantly come to the house to ask questions and consult him about village problems. He would, among other things, be asked to intervene in cases of conflict. An overheard quarrel was quickly the talk of the village. If two women were slinging insults from their rooftops or throwing stones, the details would soon be known to all. For the villagers, any public quarrel or, even worse, fight represented a problem that needed to be resolved by agreement between the parties, marked by the shaking of hands or, in more serious cases, a ceremonial restoration of good relations with beer and white scarves.[3] A fight, normally between men, was a serious affair, which often required a whole village meeting, but in the case of a shouting match, someone would generally come running to ask Paljor to intervene. "He's gone to make the women sit down, shake hands, and promise not to throw stones anymore," his mother explained to me on one such occasion.

When I learned that Paljor had an official position as the assistant (*membar*) to the headman, the *goba* (*'go ba*), I was not surprised. He was clearly eminently suitable for such a role. The goba himself was more of a puzzle. He was one of the shyest and most retiring men in the village. During the discussions that would ensue when any group of men gathered in our house, the goba would let other people talk over and around him. He intervened little in their discussions of village affairs. At the same time, the goba always sat near the top of the *dralgo* (*gral go*), the seating or dancing line that formed on every social occasion in the village. This is a ranking mechanism found throughout Ladakh, which places monks and aristocrats in the highest positions, above the majority commoner population. Photoksar had no members of the upper classes, nor of the small underclasses of musicians and blacksmiths, the *mon* and *garba* (*mgar ba*).[4] So, unless monks were present, the *onpo* (*dbon po*) would take the top seat. The onpo was the local ritual practitioner, who conducted minor rites when no monks were present. He was also the astrologer, who determined auspicious days for important agricultural and ritual events. The amchi sat next in the line, followed by the goba, and then the rest of the villagers, according to gender and age.

The onpo, amchi, and goba were all granted social status in this way, so when a conflict arose within our household, it only seemed natural that the onpo should be called in to mediate. Paljor's younger brother had been having marital problems, which culminated in a quarrel, during which he had hit his wife. In response, she had taken her children and returned to her natal household in the village. Their two fathers had tried to make them resolve their differences, to no avail, so the families called in the onpo. According to Paljor's wife, the onpo had "talked wisely," realized that reconciliation was unlikely, recommended a divorce, and brokered the resulting financial and practical arrangements.

The individuals most influential in village affairs appeared, therefore, to be those with social status. Moreover, two of them, the onpo and the amchi, also seemed to be respected for their wisdom and personal abilities to mediate conflict. However, just as the patterns of village politics were beginning to take shape in this way, they were destabilized by the occurrence of the big village meeting, which took place at the start of the new Ladakhi year, in February. Village meetings were attended only by the men, but Paljor and any others who attended from our house would always give a full report to the women around the stove afterward. On this occasion, they announced the appointment of a new goba and membar, along with several other village posts. These involved obligations such as being musician for the year (in the absence of a mon family in the village), protecting the fields from livestock, and organizing religious festivals. "So what about you?," I asked Paljor. "No, I am nothing anymore," he told me and smiled. "Every year we change the goba and his assistant," he explained. "These posts rotate between all the households of the village." It had just happened to be his turn the previous year. He also expressed an element of relief that his rather onerous tasks as the headman's assistant were over.

Not only did it thus transpire that there were no forms of permanent political status within the village, but over the coming weeks I saw Paljor make positive attempts to avoid continuing involvement in village politics. He would still attend village meetings, those that were called to resolve serious fights or make big decisions, for example. On one occasion this involved a resolution that every household with more than two sons should send at least one of them to join the monastery, a move that had major implications for many households. Paljor himself was one of the promoters of this idea. People also continued to ask him to intervene in minor conflicts, clearly acknowledging his skills in mediation. However, he always refused to get involved. "No, I am not the membar anymore, it is someone else's turn," he would protest. By this stage, it was also becoming apparent that the onpo had far less influence over village affairs than had at first appeared. He always sat at the top of the dralgo, but the conversation tended to flow around him, and, like the first goba, he rarely took an active part in discussions of village affairs.

Gradually, the logic of these seemingly fluid and paradoxical relations of status, power, and influence became clearer. There was a combination of structural methods of distributing power, similar to those found elsewhere in the Tibetan region, involving the hierarchy and symbolism of the dralgo and the rotation of positions of influence. These were matched by patterns of deference to, and distance from, centralized authority, which are typical of other Ladakhi villages. The villagers also feared the resentment and divisions that could be caused by wealth and status. Social capital was, in fact, lost by those who tried to dominate. In Photoksar the character of the amchi and the part he played in village affairs brought these contrasting processes into focus.[5]

The Social Hierarchy and Village Leadership in Historical Perspective

Ladakh, now with a population of around 250,000, was substantially an independent kingdom until it was conquered by the Dogras in 1842. Through long contact with Kashmir, a proportion of the Ladakhi population was converted to Islam, and Muslim communities now dominate the Kargil area, to the west of the region. However, the Ladakhi kings almost all patronized Buddhist monasteries, and the majority of the population of the east, where my fieldwork was conducted, are followers of Tibetan Buddhism.

The kings administered the region by elevating a number of Ladakhis into aristocrats who would act as their ministers, rewarding their families with land. These primarily acted as tax collectors but also mobilized the population to fight or provide labor in the many wars engaged in by the kings. There is little evidence that they exercised any significant administrative authority over the remoter villages, such as Photoksar, however. The villagers told me that they had always made their own decisions about internal matters, concerning agriculture, irrigation, the distribution of resources, festivals, the containment and settlement of disputes, and so on.[6] The status of the aristocracy, along with that of the monks, was symbolized in the dralgo, which is still observed today, as well as being expressed in the use of honorific language, food, and serving dishes. The same patterns also distance these outsiders from internal village affairs. Monks, aristocrats, and outsiders, although elevated in the dralgo, are not members of the village meeting.

In 1842 Ladakh was conquered by the Dogras and subsequently incorporated into the British Empire, via indirect rule, as part of the Princely State of Jammu and Kashmir. Since Indian independence, the region has been governed as part of the Indian state of Jammu and Kashmir, ruled by administrators appointed in Jammu. Taxation was largely abolished, and the urban center, Leh, came to represent a source of material benefits for the rural populations. Successive governments pursued modernizing agendas in the region, but officials remained reluctant to engage with the villagers in the distant areas. The remoter villages maintained a considerable measure of autonomy from the central administration. They continued to levy their own taxes, control their own resources, manage their own festivals, and impose order within their own boundaries.

The Photoksar villagers recounted that long ago, before the coming of "the kings' peace," and then again during the Dogra period, when the tax collectors' demands were onerous, they selected a strong and capable goba who occupied his post for a number of years. They needed someone skilled enough to deal with external threats and demands, they explained. However, almost all villages I inquired about had more recently initiated a system of selecting their goba by rotation. Selection by rotation is found widely throughout the Tibetan area— for posts within the administration of the Dalai Lamas in central Tibet, as well as within village politics (Pirie 2005; Ramble 1993; Sagant 1990; Samuel 1993). It means that leadership is impermanent and that power is distributed. When it works well, as it did in Photoksar, it ensures that power does not accumulate in the hands of any individuals or factions.[7]

In the late twentieth century, various attempts were made in Ladakh to alter these systems of village governance. The Ladakh Buddhist Association, a regional party that rose to power with its agitation for autonomy in the 1980s, tried to establish a more permanent form of leadership in the villages (Ahmed 1996; van Beek 1996, 323). This was largely abandoned, however. Later, the introduction of the Panchayat system of local government required the election of a member of each village (or group of villages, depending on size) to sit on a council that was supposed to take charge of funds for education, development, and so on. Although elections were held in April 2001, the system was only slowly implemented, and its effects on village politics were not dramatic.[8] Moreover, in most areas, the constituency of each member was a single village, and the Panchayat officer in Leh told me that the villagers simply selected a representative according to their own methods. In Photoksar they initially selected a young man, one of the few with some formal education, as their representative, and he was then honored, along with the goba and membar, at the festivities that mark the New Year. However, like other village posts, it was described to me as another burdensome tax for his household.

Elsewhere in Ladakh the availability of money and material benefits, which can be obtained for the village by those with skills and connections, resulted in newer and more permanent forms of headship and, often, factions and power struggles (Pirie 2007, chap. 9). In Photoksar they were not untouched by such developments, and as I have described elsewhere (Pirie 2006), the maintenance of a measure of autonomy from such influences is a continuing and creative process. Nevertheless, the villagers largely resisted the potentially disruptive effects of such developments on village politics. This chapter therefore gives insight into the operation and significance of a village system that, in the early 2000s, was still based on the principle of rotation for distributing power.

Village Structures

There were twenty-two main households, khangba, in Photoksar and eighteen khangu consisting of older generations or younger brothers who had set up on their own. To be a member of the village meant belonging to one of these households, either by birth or by marriage.[9] They were the basic organizational units of the village and formed various groupings for different purposes: life-cycle rites, agricultural events, festival organization, and neighborhood socializing. The full households also enjoyed equal status in village affairs, despite differences in wealth. The khangu paid fewer taxes and did not host all the rituals and festivals, which rotated between the khangba. However, moving to a khangu entailed no loss of personal status. The onpo, for example, although he sat at the top of the dralgo, lived in a tiny khangu. Having no children, he had allowed his khangba to be taken over by one of his younger brothers, who was married with children. The onpo had a hereditary position, and people told me that the current onpo would probably train a prospective husband for one of his two nieces in the main household to take over from him, thus keeping the link with the household. However, this khangba had no particular status in other aspects of village life.

The dralgo was observed on all social occasions in the village, even among informal groups of neighbors who might gather after a journey or an agricultural project or to finish up some beer after a festival. The Photoksar villagers were extremely sociable, and it was a rare day that any man in the village (as opposed to those tending livestock in the mountains) would not be involved in a dralgo several times. These lines place the Buddhist monks, aristocracy, and outsiders in separate, higher positions, and much has been made, in the literature, of the social hierarchy they exemplify (Aggarwal 2004, 154–55; Kaplanian 1981, 171–90). However, the line also arranges the villagers, who are all of the same class, solely according to age and gender. Inequalities between rich and poor and between elder and younger sons are ignored. In Photoksar, where there were no aristocratic families or members of the lower mon and garba classes, only the onpo, the amchi, and the goba took higher positions.

The goba's duties included the control of village funds, and he represented the community vis-à-vis outsiders, which often meant undertaking the long journey to Leh. He ensured that everyone was aware of the onpo's directions concerning the timing of agricultural events and made sure that festivals and rituals were properly organized, along with communal tasks such as the annual clearance of the irrigation system. He also called meetings, as and when necessary, and he was primarily responsible for settling disputes. The post rotated among all the full households of the village, as did that of his chief assistant, the membar, irrespective of the personal qualities of the member of the household who would undertake the role. As Martin Mills (1997) points out, it is the household, not the individual, that fulfills this position. Moreover, owing to the amount of time, travel, and expense involved, the villagers unequivocally regarded it as a burden and would say that their household had been "struck" by this obligation, as it was by any village tax. A household headed by a woman, in the case of a relatively young widow, for example, might ask to be excused from this obligation, but, if feasible, the villagers would encourage her to accept the role and send a male relative to the meetings.

In practice, the headman's power was also limited by the fact that all important and innovative decisions were taken at the village meeting. This gathering involved the *yulpa* (*yul pa*), literally "villagers." This was explained to me as consisting of "everyone," although in fact it included only the adult men.[10] Visitors and monks were always excluded, even if the latter were themselves from village households. In addition to the annual meeting, at which the next year's rotating village obligations were allocated, a meeting was called when any major decisions or changes were needed in the village. During my fieldwork, for example, development workers visited on a number of occasions to initiate or monitor projects, and meetings were called to discuss their proposals. Fights between members of the village and serious disputes that the goba was unable to resolve also required a village meeting. The yulpa, acting as a body in this way, exercised considerable authority over individuals, particularly when it came to resolving conflict. They could even threaten a social boycott, which occurred once during my fieldwork, to bring a recalcitrant party into line (Pirie 2006).

Procedurally, these meetings were relatively informal. Men tended to come and go, clustering around a small group consisting of the goba, his assistant, and a few other active participants. The dralgo was not observed here. Thus, even the superiority attributed to age and the statuses of the onpo and amchi, which were marked on all social occasions, were ignored during the meetings of the yulpa. Moreover, although only one man from each household was obliged to attend the meetings, very often more would do so. Paljor's father, brother, and eldest son very often accompanied him, for example. In fact, there was no obvious head of household in this khangba. Paljor explained his acceptance of the role of membar, when that obligation struck the household, by the fact that his father was getting old and he wanted to relieve him of the burden. At the yulpa's meetings, a vote could be conducted, in which one vote was counted from each household, but this was rarely necessary because, in practice, consensus was almost always reached. Differences of opinion might initially be expressed, but there was no question of opposing camps forming, and men never lobbied their neighbors to secure support for a controversial proposal. In practice, certain men, like Paljor and others who took an active interest in village affairs, did talk more than others and were listened to more respectfully. However, when people discussed the events of the meeting afterward, the influence of such individuals was never acknowledged. Paljor would come back and report what "we" had agreed or what fine "the yulpa" had decided on.

Similarly, the written reports of major decisions always referred to the yulpa as if they were a party to the agreement. There was an ideology of unity and agreement within the body of the yulpa that founded its authority over village affairs.[11] Both in practice, through the expectation of unity, and as a matter of ideology, individual influence was denied.

The Amchi in Village Politics

As a young man, Paljor was sent by his father to undertake amchi training at Ridzong monastery, where there was a respected teacher who had studied at the Mentsikhang (*sman rstis khang*), the famous college of Tibetan medicine in Lhasa. There was no other amchi in the village, and this was not a hereditary post—he was not a *gyudpa* (*brgyud pa*: lineage) amchi. Paljor was always modest when describing his status and skills to me. Although proud of his training, he claimed that he was not a really good or skilled amchi. At the top of his house was a room filled with pots, jars, and bags of medicinal ingredients, almost all unlabeled and seemingly in disarray. Yet whenever a villager came to consult him, he knew exactly where to find his medicines. Consultations were always informal. He would ask questions; as he explained to me, he took into account each person's individual circumstances, age, gender, and general health when deciding on a treatment; he would make recommendations about diet and prescribe medicines. Sometimes he gave out ready-made pills he had acquired in Leh, but more often he mixed up a powder from his ingredients, which he would wrap in a scrap of paper. Occasionally he used an external intervention, such as heat treatment. Paljor would go into the mountains to collect plants in a good year, when spring rains had carpeted the pastures with flowers. But he also needed to buy ingredients from Leh, which was costly. His patients could rarely afford to pay for treatment, but they offered services in return—a day's herding, the loan of implements, or a plate of meat.[12]

On quiet days in the winter, I would often go up to the roof and find Paljor reading through one of his medical texts. His training at Ridzong had involved considerable study of religious texts, as he often mentioned to me, and this brought him a particular respect from the other villagers.[13] To some extent, all the literate villagers in Photoksar, who, until recently, were exclusively men, possessed a certain status. Literacy allowed them to recite Buddhist texts, as they did both for their individual households and as part of a general *chossil* (*chos sil*), the communal reading of a long text, which took place at least twice a year. However, this status was not marked in any other way, either in the dralgo or during village meetings.

Paljor's household was also one of the richest in the village, in terms of land, livestock, and cash. Paljor's father had come as a *makpa* (*mag pa*), an in-marrying husband, from Nyeraks, a village two days' walk farther into the mountains. The older generation in the house had had no children, so both a husband and a wife were brought in from other households. This made no difference to the father's status within the village, however, and he was clearly ambitious for his household, being the first to install glass windows in his house, for example. Sending his eldest son to train as an amchi also increased the status of his household. Largely because there was a large family to cultivate the land and tend the livestock, the household became wealthy. This was noticeable during many events, when the food and drink provided was more lavish than that offered by other households. The villagers were acutely aware of differences in the size of landholdings and livestock herds, in monetary wealth, and in the grandeur of their houses. Members of the poorer households would always excuse their material circumstances when I visited. However, there were few occasions on which superiority in wealth was publicly acknowledged. It was many months into my stay before my host family would discuss these differences with me or even acknowledge them in response to my inquiries on the subject. Disparities in wealth are known to cause resentment and tensions, they eventually explained, which must be avoided at all costs.

In fact, the amchi's family was particularly sensitive to such issues because their own wealth, I came to realize, made them the object of a certain resentment in the village. Some villagers were also jealous of the contributions that my own presents to the family were making, and they subtly let their views be known to me, much to my embarrassment. It could be said that in denying differences in wealth, Paljor's family was merely trying to ignore such petty jealousies. At the same time, however, the parity between households that was represented in the dralgo and in village duties and decision-making effectively lessened the social impact of differences in wealth and ensured that they had no political significance. Paljor's own influence at village meetings had nothing to do with his household's wealth.

In fact, the ways in which one person or household was able to display any superiority over others were very limited. Social capital in the village was acquired by acting appropriately in each situation, not by setting oneself above others. There were set patterns and explicit village customs, *trims* (*khrims*), relating to agricultural practices, the preparation of food, the tailoring of clothes, and, above all, the conduct of hospitality. The margins for innovation were limited, and individuality was not a quality that was expressly valued. In one incident, Paljor's son, Gyaltsen, was aggressive toward the schoolteacher, a man from another village. The teacher told me later that he thought that Gyaltsen was trying to rely on his father's status. However, when Paljor heard about this incident, he disciplined Gyaltsen severely. Paljor was ambitious for his own sons, and we discussed the possibility of finding a sponsor for one of the younger boys so that he could attend a school in Leh. But the main advantage of this, Paljor told me, was not that he would be able to find a well-paid job in Leh but that he would be able to study the Tibetan texts well and become a good onpo or amchi. He could then become "better than I am," Paljor explained, with characteristic modesty. These are the only forms of social status that an individual can properly aspire to within the village, and Paljor's attitude was typical.

There was, therefore, an emphasis on knowing one's place, supported by a widely expressed set of moral norms, which valued helpfulness and cooperation in the village. The selfish were firmly, if quietly, criticized, along with those who got into too many quarrels. When some development workers visited the village to distribute toothbrushes, for example, some women were seen to take more than their fair share. "Some people always say, 'me, me,'" was the view of others around the stove that evening. In fact, there is social capital to be gained in denying one's status in the village. Although the age hierarchy was well established, anybody coming to take a place in the dralgo would first fight to sit lower than his or her proper place, in a performance of modesty, to howls of protest from others in the line. The women were delighted when I learned how to play this game, although they were also careful to ascertain my exact age, so they knew where my allotted place should be.

The case of the Photoksar amchi can be contrasted with that of the Hanupa amchi discussed by Kloos (this volume). As Kloos describes, this ambitious man used his status and connections to obtain wealth and land within his village. Even though this was motivated by his desire to continue his medical practice, it resulted in resentment and criticism from other villagers, some of whom even began to suspect him of abusing his medical power.[14] It is in a case of failure such as this that the villagers' expectations of helpfulness and selflessness from their amchi are most clearly articulated. By contrast, the Photoksar villagers had no cause to articulate such expectations to me. There were never any hints, within the village, that Paljor had ever threatened to withhold medicine or medical treatment, for example. His household's wealth, like that of all the rich khangba, was the cause of some resentment, but this was not attributed to any personal abuse of his status.

In contrast to the Hanupa amchi, therefore, Paljor was astute not to let either his own status or his ambitions for his children damage his relations with other villagers. His refusal to become involved in conflict resolution—after his time as the goba's assistant had ended—should undoubtedly be interpreted in this way. Moreover, to the puzzlement and frustration of the local members of

Nomad RSI, a nongovernmental organization (NGO) supporting amchi medicine in Ladakh, Paljor showed great reluctance to participate in the training sessions and medicine-provision programs they offered him.[15] When I mentioned these possibilities to him, he would always express enthusiasm and the intention to participate. However, for the most part, he simply did not turn up. His usual excuse was that he was too busy in the village or with household matters. It is true that Photoksar is far from Leh and his household was a big one, requiring considerable maintenance. However, this reluctance could also be seen as a positive decision on his part, either conscious or unconscious, to put his duties as a villager and householder before his medical practice. He did complain about not having enough money to buy medicines—the villagers simply could not afford to pay him significant amounts—and he was grateful to be recognized as a government amchi, which meant receiving a small salary. However, he was also reluctant to get involved with an external organization.

The reactions to conflict within the village, which always emphasized local resolution and ignored the authority of the police, were part of a general pattern of village autonomy (Pirie 2006). The yulpa, the principal political and judicial authority in the village, for instance, carefully excluded all outsiders. These dynamics were found in other Ladakhi villages, although Photoksar was particularly marked in the extent to which it distanced its internal organization from the influence of outsiders, including former aristocrats, monks, new government officials, and development workers.[16] They were all accorded the highest social and religious respect, but the directions of the latter on matters of village administration were routinely ignored when they left (Pirie 2002). In the same way, Paljor treated the Nomad RSI representatives with the greatest respect and was grateful for any financial benefits he could obtain from them, but he maintained his distance and independence from their organization. Unlike the Hanupa amchi, he regarded himself first and foremost as a member of the village and was careful not to let his status translate into any form of superiority that might be resented by the other villagers.

The dangers of acquiring undue status in the village were neatly illustrated by the case of one of the first young men in the village to pass his school-leaving exams. One development worker in Leh was promoting educational training for young people from the remoter villages, and together we secured a place for this man in a government training scheme, hoping that this would allow him to return to Photoksar later as a resident schoolteacher. The problems of absentee teachers bedevil all the remoter villages. However, shortly after the young man had started teaching in the village, on a temporary rather than a permanent basis, one of the villagers made a complaint about him to the education authorities. The grounds for the complaint were obviously spurious, and I and the development worker were dumbfounded. Did this man not appreciate the benefits of education for his own children? Paljor and other members of his family shrugged their shoulders over this incident, however. They were reluctant to criticize the man who had complained, although it was obvious that they thought that he was simply making trouble. The real reason for his action, I realized later, was a fear that the young teacher might return to the village with a new status that would place him above the other villagers. This was something that others could not tolerate.

Conclusion

Historians of Tibet have described conflicting tendencies toward equality and hierarchy within the polities that existed in the region before the 1950s. According to R. A. Stein ([1962] 1972, 94, 125), the two principles were "co-dependent and antagonistic": one favored hierarchy and hereditary power, while the other favored equality and cohesion within social and political groups. Geoffrey Samuel (1993, 153–54) has also identified "the deconcentration and distribution of authority" as a feature of social structures and processes found widely in the Tibetan region. What I have described in the Ladakhi village are similarly conflicting tendencies toward the concentration and deconcentration of power and status, albeit in a much more localized setting.

Ladakhi society, as a whole, is characterized by numerous forms of status and hierarchy. The social status of the aristocrats still allows them to prosper economically and politically. The monks enjoy religious status and respect, which enables some of them to achieve high political office. Within the village itself, status is enjoyed by the onpo, the amchi, and the goba; it is attributed to age and gender within the dralgo; respect is offered to the old, the knowledgeable, and the literate; significant differences in wealth are achieved and maintained. Nevertheless, the Photoksar villagers exclude outsiders from their internal systems of administration and deny them influence over village politics. This chapter further illustrates how forms of status and hierarchy that are internal to the village are also limited and counteracted by countervailing processes, ideas, and values.

Some of these patterns, such as the method of rotating positions of leadership, are found widely on the Tibetan plateau. Others serve directly to counteract the effects of status within the village. The relative equality represented in the dralgo, itself the main marker of social status for the aristocrats, is crucial among these factors. So is the rhetoric of unity and agreement that characterizes the meetings of the yulpa. These all serve to prevent power from accumulating in the hands of any individual or faction. Just as effective, and less visible, are the fear of the divisive effects of social inequality and the maintenance of local social capital, which is lost by those who try to dominate.

As anthropologists have found elsewhere, particularly in the context of South Asia, even within the most hierarchical societies many communities find ways of maintaining a measure of equality (Deliège 1992; Leach 1968; Obeyesekere 1967; Parry 1974). This is often done through the assertion of ideals of equality. In Photoksar, however, the maintenance of equality is not a matter of explicit ideology. Several writers have pointed out that an appearance or ideology of equality may be a mask for inequality (Cohen 1985, 33; Hayden 2002, 256).[17] In Ladakh, by contrast, an appearance of hierarchy and overt respect for status mask relations of equality and processes that limit the significance of status. The obvious recognition of status in the dralgo and the respect offered to outsiders belie the ways in which status is denied at village meetings and outsiders are excluded from village politics. The existing differences in wealth are counteracted by a fear of displaying superiority: the Photoksar villagers are fearful of the resentments and jealousies that wealth and status can inspire in the village and their potentially divisive consequences. The respect shown for Paljor's personal abilities and opinions is matched by the more general approval of knowing one's place in the village: the social capital to be gained from acting appropriately is lost by the individual who tries to set himself above others. Kloos's case study of the Hanupa amchi (this volume) is an excellent illustration of the consequences of doing so. There is thus a set of competing and conflicting processes in the village by which status, superiority, and influence are acquired and maintained but also denied and restricted, and their effects are limited. Neither the hierarchical nor the egalitarian tendency clearly dominates. Amchi Paljor, as one of the few villagers with ascribed status as well as respected personal qualities, skillfully negotiated a very delicate position in the village, aware of the resentment that his wealth and status could cause. His success in doing so, marked by his continuing popularity and respect among his fellow villagers, is a tribute to his individual qualities. However, it also throws into relief the fine balance that the villagers maintain, albeit not without a struggle, between power and social harmony and between status and equality.

How robust, we might ask in conclusion, are these dynamics? Elsewhere in Ladakh, in villages better connected to Leh, the activities of development organizations, along with new forms of wealth and influence, have caused factions and power struggles. Where men are regularly absent, women have become members of the village meetings, but employment, in turn, gives the men new forms of power and status. In 2012 the government built a road to Photoksar. Most villagers were delighted, but Paljor and his father expressed reservations during later visits. It gives opportunities to some, they explained, but transport is expensive—in 2018 there was still no bus service, and taxis charged heavily for the long journey to the village. The road thus offered new opportunities for the households that already had the wealth and labor to exploit them. And this risked unbalancing the fragile relations of status and power I have described here. The concerns of this perceptive and respected medical practitioner are easily overlooked by those who focus on the possibilities offered by the new road, amid the pervasive language of development. It will take time for the effects to become apparent, even to the villagers themselves.

Notes

The research on which this chapter is based was largely funded by the Economic and Social Research Council of Great Britain. My thanks are due to Marcus Banks, David Parkin, and Caroline Humphrey for their advice on the development of the ideas and to Laurent Pordié for his very helpful comments and suggestions on the chapter.

1   This article is based on eighteen months of fieldwork carried out in Ladakh between 1999 and 2003, followed by shorter visits up to 2018. It was concentrated on the village of Photoksar but also encompassed the capital, Leh, and a number of surrounding villages.
2   Household organization in other Ladakhi villages has been described in more detail by Maria Phylactou (1989) and Pascale Dollfus (1989).
3   I have described these processes of conflict resolution in greater detail elsewhere (Pirie 2006, 2007).
4   The aristocracy and the lower classes account for only a small proportion of the population, probably less than 10 percent.
5   Within these complex dynamics, gender is clearly an important factor, which I can only touch on here. As I have discussed in more detail elsewhere (Pirie 2007), women have far more influence in household and village affairs than their apparent exclusion from the village meetings would suggest.
6   This is supported by the report of the Land Settlement (Mohammad 1908).
7   The system can, of course, be manipulated, as the system of reincarnation almost certainly was in central Tibet (Goldstein 1973; 1989, 41).
8   The implementation of the Panchayati Raj Act 1989 was much delayed owing to the unrest in Kashmir.
9   When I would refer to Paljor's house as "mine," it would always cause amusement. Even though I was treated by the family as a member of the household, the term "my" suggested that I had married one of Paljor's younger brothers.

10 As I have described elsewhere (Pirie 2007), women have considerable influence in village affairs. Even if they do not attend the meetings, all members of a household express their views forcefully to those who attend and expect full reports of the discussions and debates afterward.

11 This ideology contrasts with the religious authority of monks, which is based on cosmological efficacy, scholarship, and the system of reincarnation (Mills 2003), and that of the modern political leaders, which is based on the economic power and democratic structures of the modern state.

12 That the system of reciprocity is still active in Photoksar distinguishes this village from many others in Ladakh (Besch and Guérin, this volume; Kuhn 1994; Pordié 2002).

13 Paljor was unusual because the in-depth study of religious texts is not a common element in amchi training in Ladakh (Pordié 2007). Neither was the study of medicine integrated into monastic training, even as a scholarly topic not intended to lead to practice, as was the case in Tibet (Meyer 1995). However, as Stephan Kloos (this volume) describes, the Hanupa amchi's knowledge of classical texts (both medical and religious) was partly constitutive of his status in the eyes of both the villagers and the wider amchi community.

14 I have discussed elsewhere (Pirie 2007) the factions and power struggles that have resulted from similar maneuvering by ambitious villagers in other Ladakhi villages and the disruption this can cause to the inclusive nature of village politics. Such events have almost always been associated with the funds or access to resources provided by government departments or development organizations, often with the best of intentions.

15 Nomad RSI was then a France-based international NGO; its project in Ladakh later became autonomous in the form of the Ladakh Society for Traditional Medicines.

16 The reasons for this are not entirely clear. Remoteness is certainly one factor, but even among the Trans Singe-la group of villages, which includes several farther from the road, Photoksar is noted for its inhabitants' unwillingness to engage with outsiders.

17 In Photoksar the fact that women do not attend village meetings is, for example, masked by the insistence that the yulpa includes "everyone." But this, along with the gender separation marked in the dralgo, in turn masks the practical influence that women have in household affairs and the positions taken by their men at the meetings.

References

Aggarwal, Ravina. 2004. *Beyond Lines of Control: Performance and Politics on the Disputed Borders of Ladakh, India*. Durham, NC: Duke University Press.

Ahmed, Monisha. 1996. "'We Are Warp and Weft'—Nomadic Pastoralism and the Tradition of Weaving in Rupshu." DPhil diss., University of Oxford.

Cohen, Anthony. 1985. *The Symbolic Construction of Community*. London: Routledge.

Deliège, Robert. 1992. "Replication and Consensus: Untouchability, Caste and Ideology in India." *Man* 27:155–73.

Dollfus, Pascale. 1989. *Lieu de neige et de genévriers: Organisation sociale et religieuse des communautés bouddhistes du Ladakh*. Paris: Éditions du CNRS.

Goldstein, Melvyn. 1973. "The Circulation of Estates in Tibet: Reincarnation, Land and Politics." *Journal of Asian Studies* 32:445–55.

Goldstein, Melvyn. 1989. *A History of Modern Tibet, 1913–1951: The Demise of the Lamaist State.* Berkeley: University of California Press.

Hayden, Brian. 2002. "Comments on Wiessner, P.: 'The Vines of Complexity.'" *Current Anthropology* 43:256–57.

Kaplanian, Patrick. 1981. *Les Ladakhis du Cachemire.* Paris: Hachette.

Kuhn, Alice S. 1994. "Ladakh: A Pluralistic Medical System under Acculturation and Domination." In *Acculturation and Domination in Traditional Asian Medical Systems*, edited by Dorothea Sich and Waltraud Gottschalk, 61–74. Stuttgart: F. Steiner.

Leach, Edmund. 1968. *Pul Eliya, a Village in Ceylon: A Study of Land Tenure and Kinship.* Cambridge: Cambridge University Press.

Meyer, Fernand. 1995. "Theory and Practice of Tibetan Medicine." In *Oriental Medicine: An Illustrated Guide to the Asian Arts of Healing*, edited by Jan Van Alphen and Anthony Aris, 109–42. London: Serindia.

Mills, Martin. 1997. "Religious Authority and Pastoral Care in Tibetan Buddhism: Ritual Hierarchies of Lingshed Monastery, Ladakh." PhD diss., University of Edinburgh.

Mills, Martin. 2003. *Identity, Ritual and State in Tibetan Buddhism: The Foundations of Authority in Gelukpa Monasticism.* London: Routledge Curzon.

Mohammad, Chaudri Kushi. 1908. *Preliminary Report of Ladakh Settlement.* Jammu, India: Ranbir Prakash Press.

Obeyesekere, Gananath. 1967. *Land Tenure in Village Ceylon: A Sociological and Historical Study.* Cambridge: Cambridge University Press.

Parry, Jonathan. 1974. "Egalitarian Values in a Hierarchical Society." *South Asian Review* 7:9–121.

Phylactou, Maria. 1989. "Household Organisation and Marriage in the Ladakh Indian Himalayas." PhD diss., London School of Economics.

Pirie, Fernanda. 2002. "Doing Good Badly, or at All?" *Ladakh Studies* 17:29–32.

Pirie, Fernanda. 2005. "The Impermanence of Power: Village Politics in Ladakh, Nepal and Tibet." In *Ladakhi Histories: Local and Regional Perspectives*, edited by John Bray, 379–94. Leiden: Brill.

Pirie, Fernanda. 2006. "Legal Autonomy as Political Engagement: The Ladakhi Village in the Wider World." *Law and Society Review* 40:77–103.

Pirie, Fernanda. 2007. *Peace and Conflict in Ladakh: The Construction of a Fragile Web of Order.* Leiden: Brill.

Pordié, Laurent. 2002. "La pharmacopée comme expression de société: Une étude himalayenne." In *Des sources du savoir aux médicaments du futur*, edited by Jacques Fleurentin, Jean Marie Pelt, and Guy Mazars, 183–94. Paris: Éditions IRD–SFE.

Pordié, Laurent. 2007. "Buddhism in the Everyday Medical Practice of the Ladakhi Amchi." *Indian Anthropologist* 37:93–116.

Ramble, Charles. 1993. "Rule by Play in Southern Mustang." In *Anthropology of Tibet and the Himalaya*, edited by Charles Ramble and Martin Brauen, 287–301. Zürich: Ethnological Museum of the University of Zürich.

Sagant, Philippe. 1990. "Les tambours de Nyi-shang (Nepal)." In *Tibet: Civilisation et société; Colloque,* edited by the Fondation Singer-Polignac, 151–70. Paris: Éditions de la Fondation Singer-Polignac.

Samuel, Geoffrey. 1993. *Civilized Shamans: Buddhism in Tibetan Societies.* Washington, DC: Smithsonian Institution Press.

Stein, R. A. (1962) 1972. *Tibetan Civilisation.* Stanford, CA: Stanford University Press.

van Beek, Martijn. 1996. "Identity Fetishism and the Art of Representation: The Long Struggle for Regional Autonomy in Ladakh." PhD diss., Cornell University.

van Beek, Martijn. 2000a. "Beyond Identity Fetishism: 'Communal' Conflict in Ladakh and the Limits of Autonomy." *Cultural Anthropology* 15:525–69.

van Beek, Martijn. 2000b. "Lessons from Ladakh? Local Responses to Globalization and Social Change." In *Globalization and Social Change,* edited by Johannes Dragsbaek Schmidt and Jacques Hersh, 250–66. London: Routledge.

2. GOOD MEDICINES, BAD HEARTS

The Social Role of the Amchi in a Buddhist Dard Community

STEPHAN KLOOS

For much of the twentieth century, the trans-Himalayan region of Ladakh was located at the cultural, political, and economic periphery of Tibet, the British Empire, and, after independence, the Indian state. Particularly in the wake of China's occupation of Tibet and the subsequent closure of its borders in 1959, Ladakh's geographic and political remoteness delayed modern developments; only in the late 1990s and early 2000s did fundamental socioeconomic change begin to be felt in rural Ladakh. The cumulative impact on Ladakhi society of several armed conflicts between India on one side and Pakistan and China on the other; heavy militarization and infrastructure development; a combination of local, national, and global politics; and an increasing influx of foreign tourism has been examined in a number of studies on continuity and change in Ladakh (e.g., Aggarwal 2004; Gutschow 1998; Mills 1999; Pirie 2006, 2007). Together with and as a result of these developments, Ladakh's growing exposure to capitalism overall and the monetization of local economies in particular had rendered many long-established practices, norms, and values problematic and in need of renegotiation by the late 1990s. One of the domains most affected by this was Tibetan medicine (Tib. *gso ba rig pa*, commonly called "amchi medicine" in Ladakh), which had been the main professional health resource in Ladakh until the establishment of rural biomedical primary health centers in the 1970s (Norboo and Morup 1997). Consequently its practitioners, the amchi, stood at the forefront of their communities' struggle to ensure social stability and cultural continuity in times of change, thus playing an important social role beyond the provision of their medical services.

Medical anthropological work on the social dimensions and modern transformations of Tibetan medicine in South Asia (e.g., Craig 2007, 2008; Kloos 2013, 2017; Pordié 2008b; Samuel 2001) as well as in Tibet (e.g., Adams 2001a, 2001b, 2002, 2007; Craig 2012; Hofer 2018; Janes 1995, 1999, 2001; Saxer 2013) highlights the amchi's position at the interface between tradition and modernity, individual and society, center and periphery. All these studies agree on the structural factors influencing change in Tibetan medicine, such as political reforms, environmental degradation, the entanglement of traditional social systems with the capitalist market and the resultant transformations of social ties and reciprocal relations, and the structural, material, and intellectual hegemony of biomedicine. However, despite such growing academic interest, Vincanne Adams's (1988) argument for an increased focus on microlevel ethnographic analyses had, in the early 2000s, hardly been answered in the form of in-depth studies focusing on the amchi's practice and role at the village level. Although since then more such work has come out (e.g., Blaikie 2009, 2013, 2018; Craig 2012, 2013; Hofer 2008a, 2008b, 2012, 2018; Kloos 2004, 2005, 2006; Pordié 2008b), we still have an incomplete picture of the social mechanisms of Tibetan medicine in Himalayan village communities.

This chapter offers a local perspective on the multiple forces shaping the practice of Tibetan medicine in the remote and ethnically unique village of Hanu Gongma. It is based on five months of field research in Hanu as well as in Ladakh's capital and administrative center, Leh, and the Zangskar valley (where I accompanied this study's main character on a plant collection trip) between July and December 2001, carried out in cooperation with the nongovernmental organization (NGO) Nomad RSI. During that time I conducted over a hundred qualitative interviews with five Hanupa amchi (all male, as in most of rural Ladakh at that time) and sixty interlocutors from Hanu Gongma and surrounding villages (thirty-three male, twenty-seven female). I argue that the organization of amchi medicine has, in the noninstitutionalized setting of rural Ladakh, the amchi's social role at its core. The expectations, norms, and pressures of society on the amchi, and their connected behavior, relate not only to their medical practice but also to all their social dealings and relations around and beyond it. Examining the social role of one Hanupa amchi, Tashi Bulu, the following ethnography shows that not only the amchi's social role but also, consequently, the condition of amchi medicine in the context of the rapid changes that took place in Ladakh in the early 2000s can be explained by a dialectic between medical and social power, shaped by both local and larger-scale processes.

Hanu Gongma

Hanu Gongma is the uppermost of the three villages in Hanu, a side valley to the north of the Indus River in the Khaltsi Block of Ladakh, bordering the Line of Control with Pakistan.[1] Hanu, like the nearby villages of Dha, Byema, Garkun, and Darchiks, is populated by an Indo-Aryan group of Buddhist Dards, related to the first settled inhabitants of Ladakh two millennia ago (Francke [1907] 1999; Petech 1977; Vohra 1989a, 1989b). With the Tibetanization of Ladakh in the tenth century CE and the later Islamization of Baltistan, Dardic language and traditions survived only in the remote valleys at the border zone between the two, which continued to be the destination of Dardic migrations until the fifteenth or even sixteenth century (Vohra 1989a, 1989b). As a consequence of an agreement with King Tsewang Namgyal in the sixteenth century (Kaul and Kaul 1992; Phuntsog 1999; Vohra 1989a), the Hanupa adopted the Ladakhi language as well as Tibetan medicine, and today they form a group identifying completely with neither the Ladakhi nor other Buddhist Dards. Hanu has been significantly affected by the Kargil conflict of 1999 and the subsequent militarization of the region, which involved considerable infrastructural development of the valley. In 2000 a road was completed linking Hanu Gongma with Leh; biomedical subcenters were set up in each of the three villages, providing basic health care and medicines for free; and new ration stores began selling supplies like kerosene, rice, cooking oil, and liquor. As a further consequence of Indo-Pakistani tensions as well as the area's further sensitization following September 11, 2001, the area was also declared strictly off-limits to foreigners for well over a decade, effectively cutting it off from tourism and foreign research alike.

According to a census conducted in 2000, Hanu Gongma had 478 inhabitants living in seventy-seven households and belonging to twenty-nine families, including five families who were not originally of Dardic origin.[2] The social organization of the Hanupa was largely the same as elsewhere in Ladakh (see Dollfus 1989, 1996), but underneath institutions testifying to central Ladakhi influence, such as the *pha spun*, the *lha bdag pa*, or the social hierarchy with monks and amchi at the top and musicians and blacksmiths at the bottom, older Dardic elements were still tangible.[3] Thus, in spite of there being a few Hanupa monks in the nearby Drigung monastery of Lamayuru, Hanu society had remained essentially nonmonastic, with some religious functions being carried out by amchi versed in Buddhist scriptures. Indigenous features of ancestor worship and animism were evident in village festivals, and Dardic restrictions on the consumption of cow-milk products were still adhered to by the older generation. Furthermore, the pha spun had relatively weak social importance in Hanu, and the individual household's independence and self-sufficiency were emphasized (see Vohra 1989a).

In 2001, however, the connection of Hanu with the rest of Ladakh and the improvement of facilities were changing the area's cultural, socioeconomic, political, and health-care situation profoundly. With central Ladakhi influences and the "reformed" Buddhism propagated by the Ladakh Buddhist Association (Mills 1999), the remnants of Dardic traditions were increasingly perceived as "backward" and "against Buddhism" and consequently began to be abandoned. At the same time, economic developments reinforced other local features, like the strong independence of individual households. The market economy, which had spread to the valley only slowly and superficially before the arrival of the army and the road, was now rapidly replacing older structures of reciprocity, subsistence agriculture, and the connected social organization. By the time the Panchayat Raj Act (1989) was belatedly implemented in Hanu in July 2001 through the local election of a *sarpanch* representing the three villages in regard to administrative and budgetary matters vis-à-vis the Leh administration, better communications and links with Leh had actually long necessitated this new political function.[4] All this had considerable significance for the unique establishment of amchi medicine in this non-Tibetan community and for its most important representative, amchi Tashi Bulu.

In the absence of written sources, oral histories permit us to trace the practice of amchi medicine in Hanu back to at least the late nineteenth century, possibly even to the seventeenth century, when members of an amchi family lineage (*gyudpa*) from Hemis Shukpachan—the Abapa—occasionally visited the area. Around 1910 a lineage amchi from Zangskar settled in Hanu Gongma, following a request from the villagers; by passing on his knowledge to local apprentices, he founded the local establishment of amchi medicine. About twenty-five years later, a member of the Abapa family also settled in Hanu Gongma. From then on, Hanu had a constant number of four to five practicing amchi. In 2001 there were four practicing amchi in Hanu Gongma and one in the neighboring village of Hanu Yogma, who, together with one *lhamo* (*lha mo*: female oracle healer), represented the traditional sector of health care in Hanu.[5] In addition, two local *onpo* (*dbon po*: male ritual astrologers) were sometimes consulted for the prevention or cure of spirit-related illnesses.[6] Two of the amchi received, through their position as government amchi, some government support in the form of a nominal monthly salary and a yearly allowance for medicinal raw materials (see Tondup 1997).[7]

Like elsewhere in Ladakh but for a much longer time, owing to the remoteness of the area, the amchi of Hanu had an almost complete monopoly on medical care until 2000. However, the situation quickly changed with the construction of a road link and the introduction of the biomedical subcenter. Staffed by a local male nurse orderly with two weeks' training and a female pharmacist from a nearby village, and stocked with an assortment of around fifty medicines, the subcenter quickly became the most popular first resort for minor illnesses, which constituted the majority of cases in Hanu. In 2001 the four amchi together received only one-third of all patients seeking medical treatment in Hanu Gongma (Kloos 2005), and the trend clearly continued in favor of the subcenter. Interestingly, while the subcenter was more or less equally popular among male (48.5 percent) and female (51.5 percent) patients, almost three-quarters (74.6 percent) of the amchi's patients were women.[8]

Amchi Tashi Bulu

One of the first things I noticed upon my arrival in Hanu Gongma was the predominance of Tashi Bulu. He was the amchi with the biggest stock of medicines, the most experience, and the most patients, and he was a government amchi as well as a member of the Ladakh Amchi Sabha.[9] As I spent more time with him, it became clear that he was an intelligent, widely traveled, eloquent man who was keenly interested in amchi medicine and who knew how to talk to foreigners. Although he looked much younger than his sixty-one years, in the social hierarchy of the village Tashi Bulu occupied the highest position in terms of status, social importance, and power. He was quick to point out his superiority over the other amchi in Hanu and, with the exception of his son Skarma Stamphel and his former student Tsering Thundup in neighboring Hanu Yogma, his disapproval of them. Indeed, in 2001 he was the only Hanupa amchi to have trained any students, which underscored his dominant role in the local sector of amchi medicine.[10]

Tashi Bulu was born in 1940 in Hanu Gongma and at the age of thirteen commenced his amchi training in the village of Teah, then a three-day journey from Hanu. His grandfather belonged to the first generation of Hanupa amchi, and his family felt that the tradition should be continued. During the eight years that Tashi Bulu stayed with his teacher in Teah, he often had the opportunity to travel to Leh—something that was unusual for Hanupa at that time. He passed the traditional amchi exam (*thit*) in Hanu Gongma in 1961 and four years later, at the age of twenty-five, married his wife, Sonam Dolma, with whom he had five children. After passing another, official exam in the 1970s, Tashi Bulu was among the first thirty amchi in Ladakh to be awarded the position of government amchi, which came with the responsibility to provide health care to all the villages in the Dha-Hanu area. In an event that was to be of major importance for his social role, he built a glass room (*shel khang*) as an extension of his house in 1985, which, just like the amchi exam and the position as a government amchi, was a first in Hanu.[11] In the mid-1990s, Tashi Bulu divided his land between his two sons, keeping only some grassland and a few goats, in order to have more time for his medical work, to which he was seriously committed.

When I talked to the other Hanupa about Tashi Bulu, my first impression appeared to be confirmed. Initially, the majority readily stated that Tashi Bulu had the most medicines and the most experience and was therefore the best and most popular amchi in the area. Besides being an amchi, he also served as an astrologer who was consulted to determine auspicious days for the major rituals and ceremonies of the agricultural and pastoral year, such as the ceremonial first plowing of the fields. He also performed rituals in case a ceremony could not be performed on an auspicious day. In this way, the benevolence of the *lha* (deities), who played an important role in local etiologies for sickness and misfortune, was ensured (see Dollfus 1996; Kaplanian 1995). Tashi Bulu's social role therefore appeared in the positive light often shone on traditional healers, contributing not only to the physical but also the material and mental well-being of the village. This was, however, only the surface layer of social reality in Hanu Gongma.

Beyond such general explanations, I noted a persistent reluctance by the Hanupa to talk about amchi medicine and especially Tashi Bulu. In interviews and informal conversations alike, few people expressed their opinions openly (even if these increasingly seemed to be the majority's opinion) and even then only if no one else was present. As they explain much of Tashi Bulu's social role and indeed make a deeper analysis possible, I quote two statements, each given by a different informant, as representative of much of the data gathered in interviews and observations:

> People don't say bad things about Tashi Bulu, because he's powerful and they are scared. Maybe one day they will get a serious disease—then they will need him.

> Now Tashi Bulu has no power anymore, because there is the hospital [the subcenter] and the road. . . . Now nobody is afraid of him anymore.

Social and Medical Power

Several issues are revealed by these statements: on the one hand, most obviously, they emphasize the importance of power both as a local concept and as an analytic tool in the study of Tashi Bulu's social role. They explain much of the amchi's as well as the villagers' behavior in relation to each other. On the other hand, a comparison between the two statements, or indeed the fact that they were made at all, indicates that the amchi's power was decreasing, with the second statement already presenting some locally perceived reasons for this development. Some of the most central issues of amchi medicine's social dimension, such as the amchi's social role and status, and the factors in and effects of their transformations in a changing clinical and socioeconomic environment are contained here. Power emerges as the key to understanding Tashi Bulu's case and the relationship between medicine and society in the changing context of Hanu Gongma.

The following analysis is based on a distinction between social and medical power. While the concept of medical power—the power to heal—seems straightforward enough, social power in Hanu needs to be strictly distinguished from political power. The Hanupa were, without exception, very clear that neither Tashi Bulu nor any other amchi had any particular political influence or carried out duties of the village headman (*'go ba*), such as mediating conflicts (see Pirie 2006, this volume). Indeed, Tashi Bulu's wife, in her role as the village schoolteacher, was considered to wield significantly more influence than her husband. What power, then, did the informants quoted above mean, if it was neither political power nor medical power nor, for that matter, the high symbolic status of amchi in general? In the context of Hanu, Tashi Bulu's alleged power referred neither to politics nor to his uncontested medical skills, but to the basic ability—described by Max Weber (1969, 117)—to pursue his own interests against those of the majority of the Hanupa. In other words, Tashi Bulu's power pertained first and foremost to the ability to generate enough income to continue his medical practice and support his family.

There are two principal avenues to social power for a Hanupa amchi, namely, fear and popularity, even though in reality such a clear-cut distinction does not exist. Still, it is possible to determine the relative predominance of one or the other, and in Hanu Gongma Tashi Bulu's power derived to a large extent—although not exclusively—from fear. This fear among the population was based on his ability to sanction his opponents by not visiting a patient, not giving medicine, or giving only "bad medicine." Although there is no evidence that he ever used this power to sanction, this actually amounted to a fear for one's life in case of sickness, owing to a lack of medical alternatives to the amchi and the resulting dependency on their goodwill. With the biomedical subcenter and the road connection to the hospitals in Khaltsi and Leh, the dependency was only partially broken. Not only were local health beliefs often at odds with biomedical diagnosis and therapy, but the subcenter's poor equipment, the frequent absence of its staff, and its inconvenient location and opening times were unfavorably compared to the amchi's services. With regard to the better-equipped hospitals in the bigger towns, despite the new road the journey there was still long and uncomfortable. Although on the wane, the perceived reliance on amchi medicine and Tashi Bulu remained in 2001, especially in respect to more serious cases. As one Hanupa told me, "Earlier, everybody went to the amchi. Then they set up the hospital [subcenter], so we went there, but they don't have much, also not in Hanu Yogma. Therefore, we mostly go to the amchi now. For coughs and headaches, the hospital's medicine is better, and also for first aid we go there. But for most other diseases, like internal diseases, heart problems, etc., amchi medicine is better. . . . The amchi has more medicines, and they are better quality than those from the hospital." His wife added, "The amchi is nearer to my house, and the subcenter here doesn't have many medicines. They also don't have any instruments for diagnosis, while the amchi checks the pulse and can give the right medicine."

With the presence of more than one practicing amchi, public medical dependency and thus also social power varied among individual amchi. The number of patients an amchi received was a good indicator of this, which could also be a direct factor for social power in itself through popularity and gratitude. An amchi's popularity could depend on his charisma but more so on his actual medical skills and stock of medicines, the latter being the single most frequently mentioned reason for the choice of an amchi in Hanu Gongma. However, social factors such as strong family links or strong animosity in some cases overrode all other considerations. While directly influencing his popularity, an amchi's medical skills also depended on the number of patients, since the more people he treated, the more experience and skills he could accumulate.

In relation to the number of patients, a second factor determining an amchi's stock of medicines and skills was important: his mode and level of income, which traditionally depended on reciprocal relations with his patients and the villagers as a whole (see Adams 1988; Kuhn 1988; Pordié 2002). The collection, exchange, or buying of medicines and raw materials requires time and material resources, both of which are, in today's context, money. The more favorable the reciprocal relations were for the amchi—or in any case the more favorable his financial situation—the easier it was for him to devote time to the practice and study of medicine. Besides the reciprocal patterns or the amchi's wealth, which were in turn dependent on the prevailing socioeconomic situation and the community's medical dependency on the amchi, the environmental situation increasingly affected an amchi's stock of medicines (Janes 1999). This included the natural availability of medicinal plants in the amchi's region, ongoing environmental degradation in Ladakh and the rest of the Himalayan region (Blaikie 2009, 2018; Craig 2012), and the increasingly stringent enforcement of environmental regulations and restrictions (Pordié 2008a).

The amchi's social power thus emerged from a complex combination of cultural values, social practices, economic processes, politics, and the environment and was made and unmade with the alliances he managed to create and maintain through medical dependency, gratitude, or family relations (see Latour 1988). To fully understand its relevance not only in the specific case of Tashi Bulu but also for the institution of amchi medicine in Ladakh more generally, it is necessary to contextualize Tashi Bulu in a brief history of the area's socioeconomic transformation since the 1970s.

Socioeconomic Change, Amchi Medicine, and Tashi Bulu

Even though socioeconomic change accelerated drastically only in the wake of the 1999 Kargil conflict, it had begun to affect amchi medicine much earlier than that. In the 1970s the old reciprocal system of *bsod snyoms* (alms) fell from favor. Traditionally, amchi not only received gifts from their patients upon cure but also collected bsod snyoms (mainly barley) regularly from every household in their village. This practice, as implied in the literal meaning of the word, was theoretically a voluntary act of gratitude and support on the part of the villagers and even an opportunity to create Buddhist merit (see Adams 1988). In practice, bsod snyoms in Hanu appear to have been given out of a sense of duty mixed with fear arising from the people's medical dependency on the amchi, whose goodwill they did not dare to lose. Tsering Samjor, age seventy-four, recalls, "Earlier the amchi wanted more. . . . If the patients didn't give enough, then the next time the amchi would give less medicine. So the people were scared for their lives and gave a lot." Although this was perceived as greed and therefore was a moral issue even then, there was not much the people could do about it except accept it as a fact of life. An old joke in Hanu about how the amchi were happier the more people fell sick further underscores the amchi's ambivalent moral status in the public perception. The collection of bsod snyoms therefore served not only as the primary source of income for the amchi, enabling them to spend time practicing medicine rather than laboring in the fields, but also as an assertion of their social power.

However, with the introduction of the government amchi scheme and the gradual rise of the market economy, this system of mutual dependency and reciprocity broke down and gradually disappeared. In concert with the idea behind the provision of a government salary for the amchi, the Hanupa began to see it as not only the amchi's moral duty but also his official duty to provide them with medicine. At the same time, their own sense of duty to provide the amchi with the necessary means to practice diminished, since this was now carried out by the government. In other words, the amchi started to be seen as dependent on outside agencies and not on their community anymore—a trend that increased with the involvement of international NGOs and was further aggravated by the fact that the locals did not discriminate conceptually between those amchi who received government support and those who did not. Consequently, the amchi's power to sanction changed from being accepted as a fact of life to being criticized as the moral shortcoming that, in the eyes of the community, it had been all along. In 2001, of course, it was rendered all the more obsolete by the presence of the biomedical subcenter and its free provision of medicines.

These developments were much the same as elsewhere in Ladakh (see Besch and Guérin, this volume; Pordié 2002) and shattered the very foundations of amchi medicine in Hanu. These foundations consisted in precisely the connection between practice and income—based on the amchi's power—as exemplified by the tradition of bsod snyoms. Owing to an unfavorable overlapping of traditional and new aspects of the amchi's social roles (see also Kloos 2004, 2005), the amchi became increasingly trapped in a dead-end situation where they had to distribute medicines almost for free (see Pordié 2002) and lacked the ability to establish new systems of exchange. As Tashi Bulu put it, "In Leh the amchi earn money, so they want more patients. But here patients cost money, so it is actually good that there is the subcenter now and half the patients go there." As a consequence, the amchi were now forced to generate their income elsewhere, to the certain detriment of their medical practice, on which they were able to spend less and less time and which they might even have to discontinue. Thus, the lineage of the Abapa had stopped, and two more amchi were hardly practicing at all owing to a lack of money and/or time. Accordingly, the usual competition between amchi shifted from attracting more patients to attracting more income, which were now two entirely separate, and indeed conflicting, issues. Given this existential crisis of amchi medicine, how did Tashi Bulu manage to not only continue his practice but actually improve and expand it? How, in other words, could he acquire, in radically changed circumstances, a degree of social power sufficient to generate income while practicing medicine and thus ensure the continuity of his practice?

As already mentioned, Tashi Bulu was one of the first Hanupa of his time to live and travel extensively outside Hanu during his amchi education in the village of Teah between 1953 and 1961. During that time he was exposed to new developments in Leh, which proved important with regard to establishing himself as a harbinger of change to Hanu. Two main influences from his apprenticeship and travels around Ladakh stand out: one was his interest in gaining the position of government amchi and generally in getting involved with regional developments concerning amchi, later also propagated by foreign NGOs. The other main influence was his wish to build a glass room (shel khang) in Hanu Gongma, just like the ones he had seen as a student, when they were nonexistent in Hanu and new even in Leh.

In the local political situation then, which lacked adequate structures and responsibilities for dealing with officials in Leh, the appointment as a government amchi and further involvement with organizations, as well as the construction of the shel khang, served as the foundations of Tashi Bulu's rise to power.[12] While the introduction of the government amchi scheme was, as already described, at least partially connected with the temporally coinciding breakdown of the old reciprocal system, the government position also raised Tashi Bulu's social status and importance considerably. With the completion of the shel khang, there was, for the first time, an adequate room in Hanu for official and other important guests to stay in. This made official visits possible and thereby enabled the Hanupa to meet administrative officers without having to go to Leh. Tashi Bulu, already one of the handful of Hanupa known in Leh as a result of his government position, naturally took advantage of his role as host and room owner and further extended his good relations with the administrative officers. Owing to the absence of modern political structures in Hanu, he quickly came to be seen, both by the officials and by his community, as an unofficial representative of Hanu Gongma, thus filling a political gap. He consequently used these contacts to get well-paid and much-coveted government jobs for his wife and sons, thereby securing the family's wealth. In addition to this, through his friendship with a *patawari* (land officer), he was able to register some newly created community land under his name, as well as more than his share of the family land, to the disadvantage of the villagers and his elder brother, respectively. Thus, Tashi Bulu was able to consolidate his wealth in both the old (land) and new (government jobs) ways, just as he established his family's medical dominance in both the old and new systems by training his eldest son as an amchi and getting his younger son the position as nurse orderly in the local subcenter.[13] We can see here how Tashi Bulu had preempted the changes underway and introduced them to Hanu himself.

The relationship between Tashi Bulu's social and medical power now becomes visible. On the one hand, his involvement with organizations brought him benefits, such as support in the form of medicinal raw materials, further education, and an exchange of experience with other amchi at seminars.[14] On the other hand, he also used his wealth for the practice of amchi medicine. He could now easily afford to hire Nepali laborers to work in his fields, insofar as the labor offered by the villagers was not sufficient. Furthermore, he could afford the time to collect medicinal plants in the mountains, as well as the costs of buying some of the more expensive ingredients for his medicines. Thus, while the other amchi became increasingly marginalized owing to the effects of the breakdown of traditional reciprocal patterns, Tashi Bulu gradually monopolized the community's medical dependency, thereby transforming his medical superiority into social power. The strategy closely follows the classic "big man" principle described by Marshall Sahlins (1963): "big men" need not only superior skills in a certain field—in this case medicine—but also, crucially, the ability to amass wealth and redistribute it, as Tashi Bulu did by giving medicines without demanding any material return.[15] Further, big men arise only in acephalous societies (i.e., societies consisting of clans or, in this case, organized in pha spun, however weak they may be in the case of Hanu) without hereditary chiefs, which do not (yet) have permanent institutions for dealing with other distant social and political entities (Godelier 1986, 163). According to the theory, big men in such situations serve as the "provisional mediums for supralocal political relations" (164). Indeed, Tashi Bulu displayed special skills not only in practicing medicine but also in amassing and redistributing wealth. He also could be seen as a provisional medium—before that function was taken over by the sarpanch—for relations with the bureaucrats in Leh, even though it has to be emphasized again that he never held any official political functions. Just like big men, Tashi Bulu used his acquired wealth to further extend his power, up to the point where the instability of the big-man principle became evident and the growing centralization and monopolization of power undermined his social base (Godelier 1986). As the consideration of socioeconomic and political developments is relevant for explaining Tashi Bulu's rise to power, a focus on the public expectations and perceptions of the amchi's practice is necessary to understand the mechanism that later destabilized Tashi Bulu's social power and gave his social role a problematic aspect.

The Ideal Amchi

Power, as well as the amchi's social role and status in relation to the other villagers, is explained and legitimized by the Hanupa in two fundamental ways, referring to practice on the one hand and to representations of an ideal amchi on the other. According to the common explanation, amchi deserve respect and high status because they give medicine and thereby "save our lives." Besides, they are also literate in Tibetan, which enables them to recite Buddhist prayers and perform certain rituals in the place of monks. In this explanation one can identify dependency, gratitude, and popularity, as well as the stratifying effects of scripturalism in a largely nonliterate society (Gingrich 1996; Goody 1968, 1986) as the sources of power and status. However, the same explanation also hints at local expectations of what makes an amchi a good amchi. In the context of the prevailing value system in Hanu Gongma as well as in much of Buddhist Ladakh, local notions of the ideal amchi are fundamental to the actual social legitimacy of an amchi's power.[16] Although this may have been a minor issue in the old days of amchi medicine in Hanu, by the 1990s and 2000s it had come to be of major importance for the stability of an amchi's power—and therefore practice—in the long run.

What, then, were the local representations of the ideal amchi that the real amchi were expected to live up to? According to the Hanupa, a good amchi "thinks only about his patients, like a mother loves her only son. He doesn't mind touching pus or blood and always gives good medicine" (Tashi Thundup, age forty-two). "A good amchi treats everyone; it doesn't matter if the patient is a relative or not, or if he has money or not. . . . He only thinks about others, not himself" (Stanzin Dorje, age fifty-seven). In comparison to these common explanations by the villagers, the five amchi strongly emphasized knowledge of the classical texts but, like the villagers, also noted the importance of having enough good-quality medicines. Thus, Tashi Bulu explained, "A good amchi is one who studies well. Knowledge is important, but there also has to be interest—the two should go together. . . . It's also good to have a lot of medicine. If one has good knowledge but no medicine, what can one do?" Similarly, amchi Smanla Rigzin said, "A good amchi has good knowledge of the scriptures, of medicines, the pulse, and different sicknesses." While these statements seem to follow a different line of argument than the lay Hanupa's, the amchi's further explanations make clear that they refer to a practitioner's qualities as described in the classical texts, constituting an ideal that is identical to the villagers'. Thus, according to the Gyüshi (*rgyud bzhi*), the Four Treatises of Tibetan medicine, the amchi is defined as being compassionate and mindful and as having a pure motivation to help the sick, without regard to sympathy, social status, or financial return (see Finckh 1985; Kuhn 1988; Men-Tsee-Khang 2008). Amchi Smanla Rigzin specified, "If an amchi knows the scriptures, he knows how to act well." Also, Tashi Bulu pointed out, "We are taught that it's important to love our patients, because otherwise the medicine will not be successful." Clearly, in the amchi's discourse, both the knowledge of the texts and the concept of "good medicines" imply a correspondence to the ideal.

As far as reality or its perception is concerned, the Hanupa amchi of the past did not necessarily conform to this ideal. However, given the Hanupa's absolute dependency on the amchi at that time, the latter did not need this kind of legitimation. In a context of medical pluralism, government subsidies, and a market economy, however, the image of the ideal amchi and the related issue of legitimation had moved to the center stage of public discourse, especially in the case of Tashi Bulu. While the community's expectations were increasingly shaped by a traditional ideal, in the modern socioeconomic and clinical context this very ideal created conflicting obligations for the amchi, leading to social disharmony. Tashi Bulu had managed to establish the foundations of his medical practice anew in response to the changing circumstances and indeed had risen to the top of the social hierarchy not only in a formal but also in a practical sense, but his strategy was not approved by the Hanupa and earned him a bad reputation as a "power-man" (*mi mkhar bdag*). He no longer corresponded, in the public perception, to the ideal picture of an amchi, and his social power was no longer seen as legitimate.

Good and Bad Hearts: The Power-Man's Dilemma

Given Tashi Bulu's uncontested status as the most experienced—and therefore, in a clinical sense, best—amchi in Hanu, how did such a discrepancy between his public image and the ideal amchi arise? What were the implications both for himself and for Hanu Gongma? The growing instability of Tashi Bulu's power and the resultant social disharmony have already been mentioned, but to understand the mechanisms behind this process as well as its wider implications for the village, it is necessary to examine the much-used local concept of "good hearts" and "bad hearts" (*sems bzang* and *sems ngan*, respectively).[17]

As in the English language, the concept generally refers to a person's character: the qualities of a "good-hearted" amchi have already been described. In the classical texts, amchi by definition have a "good heart," a view that was naturally supported by Tashi Bulu, who called this quality *dam tshig*—the inner connection between guru (teacher) and disciple. The amchi's guru in this

context is Sangye Smanla (*sangs rgyas sman bla*: the Buddha Master of Remedies, or Medicine Buddha), and the amchi can maintain this connection only
if he has all the qualities of a "good heart." Indeed, in line with the classical theory, some Hanupa categorically denied the possibility of an amchi with a "bad
heart." Most, however, could describe "bad-hearted" amchi in detail: they are
greedy and miserly, therefore giving "good medicine" only to their friends and
relatives and refusing to give medicine—or giving only "bad medicine"—to
others. In turn, just as the amchi's quality of dam tshig was considered important, so was the patients' trust in the amchi, called *dad pa* (faith). Both are
social concepts in so far as they link the efficacy of medicine to not only the
amchi's character and the patient's devoutness but also the personal relations
between amchi and patient. The quality and efficacy of medicine, regardless of
its actual ingredients, thus correspond to dam tshig and dad pa. Not only was
medicine considered less effective if an amchi had moral flaws, a patient lacked
trust, or unfriendly relations existed between amchi and patient, but a lack of
efficacy in the first place could lead to accusations of a "bad heart," especially
in a tense social context like Hanu. A similar lack of efficacy in the case of a
less controversial amchi's medicine, however, would usually be interpreted as
an astrological or karmic incompatibility (*khams*) between amchi and patient
without sociomoral implications.

When I asked about the possible combinations of the two concepts, all informants concluded that dad pa was more important, in the sense that it did
not matter whether an amchi had a "good" or "bad heart," as the medicine's
efficacy was determined only by the patient's faith. Tashi Thundup, age forty-
two, summed up the whole concept:

> As long as the amchi has a good heart, even if the medicine is not much
> or not so good, the patient will be helped. There is a story. One day there
> was a good-hearted amchi, to whom a patient came. The amchi had no
> medicine but was too shy to say so and therefore took some old wood
> instead, ground it, and gave it to the patient with prayer. The patient was
> cured. However, if one day the same good-hearted amchi gives medicine,
> but the patient has a bad heart and doesn't trust him, then even good
> medicine would not work. On the other hand, if an amchi has a bad
> heart but the patient has a good heart and trusts him, then the medicine
> will still work.

Thus, in principle, the Hanupa acknowledged the subjectivity of accusing an
amchi of having a "bad heart" by laying the blame for a medicine's inefficacy
on the patient's lack of trust instead. In practice, however, far from blaming

the patients, many Hanupa accused Tashi Bulu of having a "bad heart" quite categorically. He himself made this point: "Whichever amchi the people like, they say he has a good heart. Whichever amchi the people don't like, they say he has a bad heart."

There are three interlinked reasons for these accusations, which mostly reflect local perceptions of reality rather than Tashi Bulu's actual behavior. The most common line of explanation concerned Tashi Bulu's path to power, focusing on the land issues and the way he secured government jobs for his family. A second reason was a backlash of his power to sanction, which, as already mentioned, was more readily criticized as a moral shortcoming in 2001 than some decades earlier. Any refusal to give medicine, whether because the amchi was busy and told the patient to come back tomorrow or because he really did not have the required medicine, was interpreted in Tashi Bulu's case as a sanction, punishing a patient's earlier misbehavior (identified or not), or simply as miserliness and greed. Why it was interpreted in this way only in the case of Tashi Bulu and not the other Hanupa amchi becomes clear with the third explanation, given by Tsewang Dorje, age twenty-nine: "The people think a rich amchi has more medicine because he goes to other places. So they go to him rather than to one who only has few medicines. But if a medicine [raw material] is very expensive, the amchi doesn't want to give much of it and makes weaker medicine. Then there is no effect, and the people think badly of the amchi. . . . If an amchi is rich, there is jealousy, especially if he shows his power." The paradox of this situation did not escape the Hanupa. Said Tashi Sonam, age eighty-one: "The people don't like it if an amchi is rich. But they like it if an amchi has a lot of medicine." Tashi Bulu had fallen victim to his own success.

Such accusations, however, were not the only side effect of Tashi Bulu's strategy, nor are they in themselves the most pertinent. Even though they indicate the beginnings of the decline of Tashi Bulu's social power, the majority of Hanupa still felt dependent on him. Thus, while he may not have been popular, he remained powerful and respected for the time being. Above all, Tashi Bulu's social role, as a medium for the ongoing structural changes, had a problematic impact on the local situation of amchi medicine and public health. While his strategy assured him the power and wealth needed for his medical practice, it was not socially accepted and disturbed what social and health-care balance there was in the village. As a result, public trust in Tashi Bulu and his medicine's efficacy was undermined. At the same time, those amchi in Hanu who were not associated with him were increasingly marginalized, as they were unable to afford more than a bare minimum of medicines. A situation of unequal access to amchi medicine thus arose, where only one well-stocked but controversial amchi remained, whose services were avoided by part of the community and who, despite his relative wealth, would have been unable to meet the entire village's demand for amchi medicine anyway. The result was a rapidly increasing demand for the qualitatively inferior but socially less problematic biomedicine delivered in the subcenter.[18] Furthermore, since people who did resort to Tashi Bulu—especially those cured from serious diseases—took sides and defended him against accusations from those who did not resort to him, the unity of the village was damaged. Thus, the social tensions around the amchi, arising from a combination of regional, structural changes and local factors, caused the decline of amchi medicine in Hanu.

Conclusion: The Dialectic between Medical and Social Power

What would the situation have been without Tashi Bulu? A look at the Hanupa amchi not associated with him, as well as at rural Ladakh in general (see the chapters by Blaikie and Besch and Guérin in this volume; or Pordié 2002), suggests that amchi medicine was bound to face a crisis with or without a character like Tashi Bulu. From this perspective, it becomes possible to see a brighter side of Tashi Bulu's role emerging from behind the veil of local animosities (pertinent though they are) and to situate the unique case of amchi medicine among a non-Tibetan minority community within the larger context of Ladakh and the Himalayas more broadly.

At a time when in most parts of Ladakh the numbers of practitioners and the quality of amchi medicine had decreased, Tashi Bulu ingeniously tackled the crisis at its root and single-handedly reestablished the connection—albeit indirectly—between medical practice and income. Until the onset of socioeconomic changes in the 1970s, medical power was automatically transformed into social power through the amchi's monopoly on medical care and the people's dependency on them. Social power in turn ensured the necessary income for medical practice. The connection between an amchi's practice and income can therefore be regarded as the manifestation of a dialectic between medical and social power, which is of fundamental importance to the condition of amchi medicine. When the older form of this dialectic broke, Tashi Bulu actively pursued a new, more indirect strategy of transforming medical into social power and vice versa, thus becoming Hanu's most powerful amchi both in a medical and a social sense.

Through the success of his strategy, he not only improved the clinical quality of amchi medicine but also ensured its continuity by training two apprentices. Certainly, the support he received from regional and international organizations (including Nomad RSI) was crucial in this endeavor. Still, Tashi Bulu deserves credit for connecting the local establishment of amchi medicine, despite the area's inaccessibility, to the positive developments these organizations propagated. In 2001 both of his former students were practicing and benefited from Tashi Bulu's social connections, large stock of medicines, and the example their teacher had set at the cost of his reputation. In contrast to him, the Hanupa considered both as having "good hearts." In the almost two decades since then, the situation in Hanu and that of amchi medicine in Ladakh more generally has undergone dramatic changes, reminding us that ethnography is always an artifact of a particular time, place, and social setting. Hanu Gongma has been inaccessible for outsiders for more than ten years and is a completely changed place today; Tashi Bulu passed away in 2005, his early death constituting a major shift in Hanu's social and health-care situation; and the official recognition of Sowa Rigpa (Tibetan medicine) by the government of India in 2010 (Blaikie 2016; Kloos 2016) effected major socioeconomic improvements for amchi medicine in Ladakh.

Tashi Bulu's social role thus emerges as highly ambivalent in its consequences, which is not surprising considering its multifaceted nature. It was the product of supralocal forces as well as local power struggles, representations of ideal amchi as well as perceptions of reality, and the actions of Tashi Bulu himself in the setting of Hanu society. Certainly, Tashi Bulu's case is unique in several respects. However, the dynamics described in this chapter are by no means limited to the exceptional establishment of Tibetan medicine among a non-Tibetan community but highlight larger processes of socioeconomic change that affected amchi medicine throughout the rural Himalayas. Despite—or perhaps because of—the extremeness of Tashi Bulu's case, it may thus serve to generate insights into, and present a particular analytic framework for, the subtler social processes and conceptual structures that underlie the relationship between medicine and society in a changing social context. These processes and structures continue to determine the problems as well as the scope of possibilities for amchi in much of rural, noninstitutionalized Ladakh and other Himalayan regions, as Tibetan medicine continues to occupy a central—albeit transformed—place in Tibetan Buddhist societies on the Indian periphery.

Notes

This chapter is dedicated to the memory of amchi Tashi Bulu, without whose generous and patient help this study could not have happened. I am also indebted to the following people: Laurent Pordié for his initiative and support on all levels; Tsering

Thundup, who was the kind of field assistant every anthropologist wishes for; Sonam Phuntsog for valuable information on the history of Hanu; Calum Blaikie, Ursula Wagner, and several anonymous reviewers for their helpful comments; Andre Gingrich for academic support back home; then chief amchi Tsering Phuntsog, Tashi Namgyal (Amchi Medicine Research Unit), and Dawa Tsering for their crucial support—bureaucratic and otherwise—in Leh; and last but not least, the people and amchi of Hanu Gongma, for all their patience and hospitality. This study was generously funded and supported by the Nomad Research Unit, the University of Vienna, and Land Steiermark.

1   For detailed background information on Hanu, the history of amchi medicine in this area, and its development and current situation, see Kloos (2004).

2   The census was taken by Nawang Dorje, the then *sarpanch* and *numberdar* of Hanu, in the autumn of 2000 at the request of the Leh administration.

3   In Ladakh, a pha spun is an association of families that plays a role in ritual or ceremonial occasions like birth and death. For more information, see Crook (1994). The lha bdag pa is an inheritable office, in Hanu Gongma rotating every year between the families of a certain pha spun. Their original function was to act as the "representatives of the palace" (i.e., the king) during ceremonies (Dollfus 1996). Nowadays in Hanu they serve as village priests and, in an interesting inversion of their original role, uphold pre-Buddhist Dardic religious practices (Kloos 2004).

4   For more information on the implementation of the Panchayat Raj Act in Ladakh, and its considerable delay, see Pirie (2007).

5   Even though there are a growing number of female amchi in Ladakh, in Hanu all amchi are men.

6   For more information on lhamo (*lha mo*) and onpo (*dbon po*), refer to Kuhn (1988).

7   A government amchi receives a nominal monthly salary as well as a yearly allowance for medicines from the government and is assigned to serve a number of villages besides his own. While one idea behind this institution is to utilize existing health-care resources in biomedically neglected areas, it also brings these amchi under a certain amount of state control. Some local ramifications of governmentalizing amchi medicine are discussed later in this chapter.

8   Several months of epidemiological data were gathered from the patient register books of the biomedical subcenter and amchi Tashi Bulu as part of this research.

9   The Ladakh Amchi Sabha is the oldest and most influential association of amchi in Ladakh. It was created in 1978 and has since represented a majority of Ladakh's amchi both in regional politics and vis-à-vis international NGOs.

10 That he was the only amchi who had trained students is due to several factors, discussed in more detail in the following. Chief among them is Tashi Bulu's comfortable financial situation, which allowed him to give more time to his medical practice—and thus to training apprentices—than the other amchi could. Another factor is simply his senior position among Hanu's amchi; that is, his younger colleagues' sons, for example, had not reached the age to learn medicine yet. Last but not least, Tashi Bulu's genuine interest in perpetuating the tradition of amchi medicine as well as his own lineage needs to be mentioned.

11 In Ladakh a "glass room" signifies a room with large glass windows on three sides, allowing the sun to heat the room even in winter. Such rooms were, especially in remote areas, expensive to build owing to the high costs of transporting glass (Tashi Bulu cited a cost of twenty thousand Indian rupees—which especially in the 1980s was a very high sum). As the best and most representative room of the house, a glass room is therefore a status symbol showing off its owner's economic success.

12 Dealing with officials is now the function of the sarpanch and a higher representative of the area in Leh.

13 Government jobs mean a regular income and employment for life and are therefore highly prized in Ladakh.

14 Tashi Bulu was regularly invited by the organizations Ladakh Amchi Sabha and the Ladakh Society for Traditional Medicines (an Indian organization embodying the autonomy of the Nomad RSI project in Ladakh) to attend regional seminars on amchi medicine in Leh. He received some support in kind (raw materials) from Nomad RSI in 1998, 2000, and 2001, as well as from the Leh Nutrition Project (LNP) in the early 1990s. The LNP support was unofficial, however, because the organization did not include the amchi north of the Indus. Tashi Bulu used his connections to benefit from the LNP program in spite of his geographic location.

15 This is remarkable especially because Ladakhi villages are not big-man societies, and also otherwise have few, if any, parallels to Papua New Guinea.

16 Similar to the findings of this study, Pordié (2003) also shows for the urban, institutionalized context that social power is possible without this kind of legitimation. See Pordié (2007) for a more detailed discussion of this issue and generally the role of religion in the practice of amchi medicine.

17 The usual translation of *sems* is "heart-mind." However, since the English phrase "good/bad heart" conveys the correct meaning in the present context and is closer to common understanding, this rather than the literal translation is used in the title as well as throughout the chapter. To avoid misunderstandings, "heart" is put in quotation marks when used in the sense of "heart-mind."

18 The fact that Tashi Bulu's younger son runs the subcenter does not seem to impede this trend.

References

Adams, Vincanne. 1988. "Modes of Production and Medicine: An Examination of the Theory in Light of Sherpa Medical Traditionalism." *Social Science and Medicine* 27 (5): 505–13.

Adams, Vincanne. 2001a. "Particularizing Modernity: Tibetan Medical Theorizing of Women's Health in Lhasa, Tibet." In *Healing Powers and Modernity: Traditional Medicine, Shamanism, and Science in Asian Societies*, edited by Linda Connor and Geoffrey Samuel, 197–246. Westport, CT: Bergin and Harvey.

Adams, Vincanne. 2001b. "The Sacred in the Scientific: Ambiguous Practices of Science in Tibetan Medicine." *Cultural Anthropology* 16 (4): 542–75.

Adams, Vincanne. 2002. "Establishing Proof: Translating 'Science' and the State in Tibetan Medicine." In *New Horizons in Medical Anthropology*, edited by Mark Nichter and Margaret Lock, 200–220. London: Routledge.

Adams, Vincanne. 2007. "Integrating Abstraction: Modernising Medicine at Lhasa's Mentsikhang." In *Soundings in Tibetan Medicine: Anthropological and Historical Perspectives*, edited by Mona Schrempf, 29–43. Leiden: Brill.

Aggarwal, Ravina. 2004. *Beyond Lines of Control: Performance and Politics on the Disputed Borders of Ladakh, India*. Durham, NC: Duke University Press.

Blaikie, Calum. 2009. "Critically Endangered? Medicinal Plant Cultivation and the Reconfiguration of Sowa Rigpa in Ladakh." *Asian Medicine* 5 (2): 243–72.

Blaikie, Calum. 2013. "Currents of Tradition in Sowa Rigpa Pharmacy." *East Asian Science, Technology and Society* 7:425–51.

Blaikie, Calum. 2016. "Positioning Sowa Rigpa in India: Coalition and Antagonism in the Quest for Recognition." *Medicine, Anthropology, Theory* 3 (2): 50–86.

Blaikie, Calum. 2018. "Absence, Abundance, and Excess: Substances and Sowa Rigpa in Ladakh since the 1960s." In *Locating the Medical: Explorations in South Asian History*, edited by Guy Attewell and Rohan Deb Roy, 169–99. New Delhi: Oxford University Press.

Craig, Sienna. 2007. "A Crisis of Confidence: A Comparison between Shifts in Tibetan Medical Education in Nepal and Tibet." In *Soundings in Tibetan Medicine: Anthropological and Historical Perspectives*, edited by Mona Schrempf, 127–54. Leiden: Brill.

Craig, Sienna. 2008. "Place and Professionalization: Navigating Amchi Identity in Nepal." In *Tibetan Medicine in the Contemporary World: Global Politics of Medical Knowledge and Practice*, edited by Laurent Pordié, 62–90. London: Routledge.

Craig, Sienna. 2011. "From Empowerments to Power Calculations: Notes on Efficacy, Value and Method." In *Medicine between Science and Religion: Explorations on Tibetan Grounds*, edited by Vincanne Adams, Mona Schrempf, and Sienna Craig, 215–40. New York: Berghahn Books.

Craig, Sienna. 2012. *Healing Elements: Efficacy and the Social Ecologies of Tibetan Medicine*. Berkeley: University of California Press.

Craig, Sienna. 2013. "The Many Faces of a Teacher: Portrait of a Himalayan Healer." In *Les nouveau guérisseurs contemporains: Le néo-traditionalisme thérapeutique en biographies*, edited by Laurent Pordié and Emanuelle Simon, 155–80. Paris: Éditions de l'EHESS.

Crook, John. 1994. "Social Organization and Personal Identity in Zangskar." In *Himalayan Buddhist Villages*, edited by John Crook and Henry Osmaston, 475–518. Delhi: Motilal Banarsidass.

Dollfus, Pascale. 1989. *Lieu de neige et de genévriers: Organization sociale et religieuse des communautés bouddhistes du Ladakh*. Paris: Éditions du CNRS.

Dollfus, Pascale. 1996. "No Sacred Mountains in Central Ladakh?" In *Reflections of the Mountain: Essays on the History and Social Meaning of the Mountain Cult in Tibet and the Himalaya*, edited by Anne-Marie Blondeau and Ernst Steinkellner, 3–22. Vienna: Verlag der Österreichischen Akademie der Wissenschaften.

Finckh, Elisabeth. 1985. *Grundlagen tibetischer Heilkunde*. Uelzen: Medizinisch Literarische Verlagsgesellschaft.

Francke, A. H. (1907) 1999. *A History of Western Tibet*. Delhi: Pilgrims Books.

Gingrich, Andre. 1996. "Hierarchical Merging and Horizontal Distinction: A Comparative Perspective on Tibetan Mountain Cults." In *Reflections of the Mountain: Essays on the History and Social Meaning of the Mountain Cult in Tibet and the Himalaya*, edited by Anne-Marie Blondeau and Ernst Steinkellner, 233–62. Vienna: Verlag der Österreichischen Akademie der Wissenschaften.

Godelier, Maurice. 1986. *The Making of Great Men: Male Domination and Power among the New Guinea Baruya*. Cambridge: Cambridge University Press; Paris: Maison des Sciences de l'Homme.

Goody, Jack. 1968. *Literacy in Traditional Societies*. Cambridge: Cambridge University Press.

Goody, Jack. 1986. *The Logic of Writing and the Organization of Society*. Cambridge: Cambridge University Press.

Gutschow, Kim. 1998. "An Economy of Merit: Women and Buddhist Monasticism in Zangskar, North West India." PhD diss., Harvard University.

Hofer, Theresia. 2008a. "Socio-Economic Dimensions of Tibetan Medicine in the Tibet Autonomous Region, China: Part 1." *Asian Medicine: Tradition and Modernity* 4 (1): 174–200.

Hofer, Theresia. 2008b. "Socio-Economic Dimensions of Tibetan Medicine in the Tibet Autonomous Region, China: Part 2." *Asian Medicine: Tradition and Modernity* 4 (2): 492–514.

Hofer, Theresia. 2012. *The Inheritance of Change: Transmission and Practice of Tibetan Medicine in Ngamring*. Vienna: Wiener Studien zur Tibetologie und Buddhismuskunde.

Hofer, Theresia. 2018. *Medicine and Memory in Tibet: Amchi Physicians in an Age of Reform*. Seattle: University of Washington Press.

Janes, Craig R. 1995. "The Transformations of Tibetan Medicine." *Medical Anthropology Quarterly* 9 (1): 6–39.

Janes, Craig R. 1999. "The Health Transition, Global Modernity and the Crisis of Traditional Medicine: The Tibetan Case." *Social Science and Medicine* 48 (12): 1803–20.

Janes, Craig R. 2001. "Tibetan Medicine at the Crossroads: Radical Modernity and the Social Organization of Traditional Medicine in the Tibet Autonomous Region, China." In *Healing Powers and Modernity: Traditional Medicines, Shamanism, and Science in Asian Societies*, edited by Linda Connor and Geoffrey Samuel, 197–221. Westport, CT: Bergin and Harvey.

Kaplanian, Patrick. 1995. "L'homme dans le monde surnaturel du Ladakh." In *Recent Research on Ladakh 4&5: Proceedings of the Fourth and Fifth International Colloquia on Ladakh*, edited by Henry Osmaston and Philip Denwood, 101–8. Delhi: Motilal Banarsidass.

Kaul, Shridhar, and H. N. Kaul. 1992. *Ladakh through the Ages: Towards a New Identity*. New Delhi: Indus.

Kloos, Stephan. 2004. *Tibetan Medicine among the Buddhist Dards of Ladakh*. Vienna: Wiener Studien zur Tibetologie und Buddhismuskunde.

Kloos, Stephan. 2005. "Le développement dans la négociation du pouvoir: Le cas de la médecine tibétaine à Hanu, Inde himalayenne." In *Panser le monde, penser les médecines:*

Traditions médicales et développement sanitaire, edited by Laurent Pordié, 101–22. Paris: Karthala.

Kloos, Stephan. 2006. "Amchi Medizin zwischen Rand und Mitte." In *Der Rand und die Mitte: Beiträge zur Sozialanthropologie und Kulturgeschichte Tibets und des Himalaya*, edited by Andre Gingrich and Guntram Hazod, 55–77. Vienna: Verlag der Österreichischen Akademie der Wissenschaften.

Kloos, Stephan. 2013. "How Tibetan Medicine Became a 'Medical System.'" *East Asian Science, Technology and Society* 7 (3): 381–95.

Kloos, Stephan. 2016. "The Recognition of Sowa Rigpa in India: How Tibetan Medicine Became an Indian Medical System." *Medicine, Anthropology, Theory* 3 (2): 19–49.

Kloos, Stephan. 2017. "The Politics of Preservation and Loss: Tibetan Medical Knowledge in Exile." *East Asian Science, Technology and Society* 10 (2): 135–59.

Kuhn, Alice. 1988. *Heiler und ihre Patienten am Dach der Welt: Ladakh aus ethnomedizinischer Sicht*. Frankfurt am Main: Peter Lang.

Latour, Bruno. 1988. *The Pasteurization of France*. Translated by Alan Sheridan. Cambridge, MA: Harvard University Press.

Men-Tsee-Khang. 2008. *The Basic Tantra and the Explanatory Tantra from the Secret Quintessential Instructions on the Eight Branches of the Ambrosia Essence Tantra*. Dharamsala: Men-Tsee-Khang.

Mills, Martin. 1999. "Belief and the Priest, Religious Reform and Ethnical Self Determination in Buddhist Ladakh." *Scottish Journal of Religious Studies* 19 (2): 167–85.

Norboo, Tsering, and Tsering Morup. 1997. "Culture, Health and Illness in Ladakh." In *Recent Research on Ladakh 6: Proceedings of the Sixth International Colloquium on Ladakh, Leh 1993*, edited by Henry Osmaston and Nawang Tsering, 205–10. Delhi: Motilal Banarsidass.

Petech, Luciano. 1977. *The Kingdom of Ladakh c. 950–1842 AD*. Rome: Istituto Italiano per il Medio ed Estremo Oriente.

Phuntsog, Sonam. 1999. "Hanu Village: A Symbol of Resistance." In *Ladakh: Culture, History, and Development between Himalaya and Karakoram*, edited by Martijn van Beek, Kristoffer Brix Bertelsen, and Poul Pedersen, 379–82. New Delhi: Sterling.

Pirie, Fernanda. 2006. "Legal Autonomy as Political Engagement: The Ladakhi Village in the Wider World." *Law and Society Review* 40 (1): 73–103.

Pirie, Fernanda. 2007. *Peace and Conflict in Ladakh: The Construction of a Fragile Web of Order*. Leiden: Brill.

Pordié, Laurent. 2002. "La pharmacopée comme expression de société: Une étude himalayenne." In *Des sources du savoir aux médicaments du futur*, edited by Jacques Fleurentin, Jean-Marie Pelt, and Guy Mazars, 183–94. Paris: Éditions IRD–SFE.

Pordié, Laurent. 2003. *The Expression of Religion in Tibetan Medicine: Ideal Conceptions, Contemporary Practices and Political Use*. Pondy Papers in Social Sciences 29. Pondicherry: French Institute of Pondicherry.

Pordié, Laurent. 2007. "Buddhism in the Everyday Medical Practice of the Ladakhi Amchi." *Indian Anthropologist* 37 (1): 93–116.

Pordié, Laurent. 2008a. "Hijacking Intellectual Property Rights: Identities and Social Power in the Indian Himalayas." In *Tibetan Medicine in the Contemporary World: Global*

Politics of Medical Knowledge and Practice, edited by Laurent Pordié, 132–59. London: Routledge.

Pordié, Laurent, ed. 2008b. *Tibetan Medicine in the Contemporary World: Global Politics of Medical Knowledge and Practice*. London: Routledge.

Sahlins, Marshall D. 1963. "Poor Man, Rich Man, Big Man, Chief: Political Types in Melanesia and Polynesia." *Comparative Studies in Society and History* 5 (3): 285–303.

Samuel, Geoffrey. 2001. "Tibetan Medicine in Contemporary India: Theory and Practice." In *Healing Powers and Modernity: Traditional Medicine, Shamanism, and Science in Asian Societies*, edited by Linda Connor and Geoffrey Samuel, 247–68. Westport, CT: Bergin and Garvey.

Saxer, Martin. 2013. *Manufacturing Tibetan Medicine: The Creation of an Industry and the Moral Economy of Tibetanness*. Oxford: Berghahn.

Tondup, Stanzin. 1997. "Health Activities in Leh District, Ladakh." In *Recent Research on Ladakh 6: Proceedings of the Sixth International Colloquium on Ladakh, Leh 1993*, edited by Henry Osmaston and Nawang Tsering, 297–302. Delhi: Motilal Banarsidass.

Vohra, Rohit. 1989a. *An Ethnography: The Buddhist Dards of Ladakh; Mythic Lore—Household—Alliance System—Kinship*. Ettelbruck, Luxembourg: Skydie Brown International.

Vohra, Rohit. 1989b. *The Religion of the Dards in Ladakh: Investigations into Their Pre-Buddhist 'Brog-pa Traditions*. Ettelbruck, Luxembourg: Skydie Brown International.

Weber, Max. 1969. *Basic Concepts in Sociology*. Translated by H. P. Secher. New York: Greenwood.

3. WHERE THERE IS NO AMCHI
Tibetan Medicine and Rural-Urban Migration among Nomadic Pastoralists in Ladakh

CALUM BLAIKIE

Relationships among socioeconomic change, medical representations, and health practices are some of the central concerns of medical anthropology.[1] How people experience, classify, and respond to illness is shaped by complex processes that, although centered in the field of health, also extend far beyond it. This chapter uses ethnographic data collected in the Changthang region of western Ladakh in 2002 to examine the interactions among Tibetan medicine, social change, and rural-urban migration. In particular, it focuses on the Rupshupa, a community of Changpa nomadic pastoralists residing in the Samad Rokchen area of Rupshu-Kharnak, who had already been subject to far-reaching social transformations for several decades. Beginning in the 1980s, a stream of rural-urban migration carried large numbers of people from the Changthang plateau to the densely populated Indus valley and the regional capital of Leh (Ahmed 2003; Chaudhuri 1999; Goodall 2004). As part of this out-migration, five practitioners of Tibetan medicine, known as amchi, permanently left the region over a twenty-year period, causing continual disruptions to medical services and leaving the community lacking an established traditional medical practitioner. Over the same period, biomedical services became much more frequently utilized, despite their consistently poor quality. Under these conditions, medical pluralism was shaped by changes in the modality—and ruptures in the availability—of its indigenous component, alongside increasing use of a basic form of biomedicine.

In exploring the causes and implications of this, I focus on the changing social and economic relations of therapy (Adams 1988; Besch 2006, 2007; Besch and Guérin, this volume; Hofer 2008a, 2008b, 2012; Kloos 2004, this volume), while specifically addressing the relationship between traditional healers and migration processes.[2] Following a brief overview of the sustainable livelihoods framework, I review existing research on rural-urban migration among the Changpa (Blaikie 2001; Chaudhuri 1999; Goodall 2004). I then consider the processes that led to the out-migration of the Rupshupa amchi, examining different logics of legitimacy and forms of practice in relation to the wider shifts that have taken place over recent decades (Kloos 2004, this volume; Pordié 2000, 2002, 2007). The relative weights of medical and non-medical factors in the migration of the amchi are then assessed, before a more widely studied topic relating to the dynamics of medical pluralism is considered (Dignes 2014; Ernst 2002; Janes 1999, 2001; Leslie 1976, 1992; Samuel 2001; Sujatha and Abraham 2012). Here the responses of the Rupshupa to the circumstances prevailing around the turn of the millennium and the early 2000s are examined, particularly with regard to shifts in treatment-seeking behavior and modalities of diagnosis and drug administration. The latter part of the chapter considers the effects of discontinuous and unreliable amchi services in Samad, as well as attempts to reintroduce amchi to the area. I finally consider the extent to which the absence of a socially and medically accepted amchi contributes to a heightened sense of risk and hardship, and the implications that this may hold for the community more broadly.

Social Change, Migration, and Livelihoods among the Changpa

For many centuries, the Changpa nomadic pastoralists have moved with their herds of sheep, goats, and yaks around the Changthang plateau, which lies between four thousand and six thousand meters above sea level.[3] Extremely cold winters, poor soils, and scarce water ensure that the Changthang cannot support settled agricultural populations except on its very lowest edges.[4] Survival in this unforgiving environment would be impossible without continuous and sophisticated adaptation of the Changpa socioeconomy, in both its internal dynamics and its interactions with neighboring agricultural communities, economic actors, and political structures. The livestock, wool, *pashm* (fine goat wool), and meat they produce have long been sold or exchanged with settled populations and traders, and they remain products with thriving local and regional markets (Ahmed 1999, 2003; Darokhan 1999; Rizvi 1996, 1999). In spite of this demand and the considerable profits that can be made from it, a steady trickle of people leave the Changthang every year to join the unskilled, casual labor force of the Indus valley.

While there is a distinct lack of research into "new" forms of population movement among nomadic pastoralists, particularly in Asia, work within the sustainable livelihoods framework offers a productive approach to it (Ashley and Carney 1999; de Haan 2000; Ellis 2000; McDowell and de Haan 1997; Scoones 1998).[5] This literature highlights the multidimensional nature of migration activity and "goes beyond, on the one hand, studies that isolate individuals as rational decision makers in explaining migration; and on the other hand theories that focus only on macro-economic or political developments as explanatory factors" (McDowell and de Haan 1997, 3). The framework employs a multidisciplinary approach and a selection of analytic lenses to examine the factors affecting household survival and the strategies employed to secure it. A number of strategies are identified through which households can strengthen their livelihoods or respond to changes in the availability of resources, among which migration and diversification are key. This approach provides a broad typology of migration causality and form, while drawing attention to the considerable intracommunity variations that pertain to these factors.[6] It is well suited to the current study as it facilitates analysis of the shared and divergent factors influencing the migration behavior of different amchi, as well as differences between practitioners and nonpractitioners.

Although Changpa society has never been static or isolated, the socioeconomic changes of the postindependence era had a profound effect on the community, reducing livelihood resilience and rendering the continuation of pastoralism untenable for many families (Ahmed 1999, 2003; Rizvi 1996). At the time of my research in 2002, there were seventy-five households, or *drongpa* (*grong pa*: a family unit living together in one tent and collectively managing livestock), in Samad. When I asked people how many drongpa had permanently left the community over the preceding twenty years, the average answer was sixteen.[7] Although this was proportionally less than was reported for the nearby Kharnak Changpa group, the Samad community was in danger of reaching critically small proportions if this rate of out-migration continued for much longer (Blaikie 2001; Chaudhuri 1999).

Both migrants and those who remained mentioned the hardships and risks associated with winter as the primary cause of out-migration. Indeed, the winter months constitute a yearly period of hardship for the Changpa (Miller 2000), occasionally exacerbated by potentially ruinous and even life-threatening weather conditions in particularly severe winters.[8] While these risks are not new, from the 1980s onward they have led some households to leave, while others have remained despite facing similar circumstances. To understand this, it is necessary to consider not only livelihood change but also underlying shifts in attitudes and perceptions, as these, too, play a large part in migration behavior.

By 2002 rapid infrastructural and socioeconomic change had altered relationships within Changpa communities, as well as between them and the other inhabitants of the region. The construction of roads rendered transportation and travel much more rapid, bringing the Changpa closer to their neighbors and to more distant groups and forces, both practically and psychologically. The main Leh-Manali road officially opened in 1989, but sections of it were in use for several years before that. It passes right through the middle of Rupshu-Kharnak, in sight of many Changpa campgrounds, and its effects on their lives cannot be overestimated. Travel times from Samad to the nearest large towns of Leh and Manali have been cut from a week's hard trekking each way to a few hours by bus during summer (May–October). During winter, travel in either direction is hazardous and often impossible owing to snow blocking the passes. Nevertheless, the relatively circumscribed and largely self-contained social world formerly inhabited by the Changpa is gone. They often come into contact with Indian Army personnel, trekking groups, and truck drivers in their range areas, and visits to Leh are much more frequent than in former times. Among many other effects, this greater exposure to outsiders has heightened a sense of backwardness and inferiority among Changpa. Some cover it up with bravado and change their appearance so as to look more like "ordinary" Ladakhis, but most deride themselves for their lack of education, social sophistication, and access to facilities. One old woman even told me, "We are just like animals: moving here and there, dirty and stupid."

The road also facilitated the introduction of government-subsidized rations, hastening the ascendancy of the cash economy and weakening relations of reciprocity and barter. These relations were formerly central components of the subsistence economy and strongly linked the Changpa to one another and to neighboring agricultural communities. Polyandry had virtually disappeared in Samad by 2002, with the vast majority of marriages conforming to the monogamous pattern enshrined in law and popular practice elsewhere in Ladakh.[9] This had significant implications for Changpa livelihoods because labor demands are high throughout the year for pastoralists, unlike the highly seasonal pattern of settled agriculture. A Changpa drongpa comprising two or more men of working age is much better able to fulfill the continuous labor demands of pastoralism than one that includes only a single adult man. The growing number of children studying at boarding schools far from their families added further to these labor pressures, leaving fewer hands to care for the herds.

At the same time, many older Changpa referred to the increasing individualism of drongpa over this period: "Before, each large or wealthy drongpa had a small drongpa to look after them, to care for their animals and help them when the time came to move camp. Now every drongpa has its own animals and looks after its own affairs" (Tashi Phuntsog). Although this quote reflects the viewpoint of a wealthier pastoralist now required to manage his own herd without assistance from a poorer "client" drongpa, these relational shifts had implications for the whole community. Wealthy but labor-short drongpa had fewer options to bring in labor than before, while poorer drongpa increasingly opted to struggle on alone rather than seek the patronage of wealthier neighbors. The decline of patron-client arrangements roughly equalized labor availability and reduced disparities in flock size and income. Although considerable variations in herd size and wealth remained, this was more a function of labor availability than enduring social stratification. No longer a privilege of wealthier families, the expansion of herds was widely accepted as a route open to any drongpa with the human capital to follow it.

Reduced labor power had severely eroded the coping strategies of drongpa vis-à-vis the stresses and shocks they faced. This led to numerous cases of distress migration, in which drongpa no longer had the minimum amount of labor required to continue pastoralism. Such cases make up the majority of instances when complete drongpa migrated to Leh (Blaikie 2001; Chaudhuri 1999; Goodall 2004). A smaller group consisted of relatively wealthy drongpa who decided to sell their livestock (exchanging natural capital for financial capital), settle in the Leh area, and start small businesses such as shops and transport companies. This kind of investment was possible owing to the enormous sums that could be made if all of a drongpa's sheep, goats, horses, and yaks were sold at one time.[10] This represents the migration form with the highest degree of agency and forward planning.

Roughly 40 percent of the drongpa that remained in Samad followed "straddling" strategies, in which some members (often older people and young children) set up a base in the Indus valley and the rest continued to pursue pastoralism. This was a flexible diversification strategy that could take a variety of forms but was feasible only for larger extended-family groups. Some drongpa straddled the two realms for many years and bolstered their livelihoods significantly. Others used straddling as a form of gradual sedentarization and yet others used it as a form of insurance in case conditions became untenable in the Changthang. Many individuals left, too, including elderly people no longer able to support themselves, young men seeking work as laborers or with the army, and children of both sexes enrolled in schools.[11]

There was considerable diversity of opinion regarding migration among those who remained in Samad. Several people I spoke to were already in the process of moving away and argued that life would be easier for them in the Indus valley. Others were resolute about their wish to remain, speaking in largely negative terms about the expense and restrictions of urban life: "There is no land in Leh. You cannot keep animals, your hand is always in your pocket, and you need money for everything, yet there is no work. Mutton costs 100 rupees per kilo, and here it costs nothing!" (Urgyen Tseten). While all stated that the danger of a bad winter was very real, risk itself was subjectively constructed. Some did not see the risks as grave enough to leave, while others felt pastoralism to be increasingly impossible.

All Rupshupa pointed to the absence of effective health services as contributing to the risks they faced and as playing a significant part in migration decisions. Visits to doctors, hospitals, and pharmacies in Leh put into sharp contrast the absence of health services in Samad, fixing in people's minds their marginalized position. Many Rupshupa had firsthand experience of serious illnesses or deaths in the family that they believed could have been avoided had an amchi been present or a biomedical doctor reliably accessible. Vulnerability was assessed in relation to structural conditions but depended on individuals' perception of those conditions, their past experiences, and their current circumstances, which together shaped views of the costs and benefits of migration.

Livelihoods analysis can certainly take us much further toward an understanding of Rupshupa migration than more static and income-oriented approaches. However, the framework reaches its limit of utility when understandings of the actual decision-making process are required, such as when divergent choices are made by households whose circumstances appear very similar in livelihood terms. Underlying the structural changes that took place were myriad processes of psychosocial, personal, and cultural transformation, including encounters with the Indian education system, awareness of a possible "easy life" elsewhere, feelings of backwardness and marginalization, altered perceptions of the self in the world, and narratives of aspiration, risk, and loss. To explore such questions of identity, personality, and worldview, we need to turn to ethnography.

Tibetan Medicine in Ladakh

Tibetan medicine underwent a great deal of change in Ladakh during the latter part of the twentieth century, and its practitioners faced significant challenges in the early years of the new millennium (Besch and Guérin, this volume; Blaikie 2011, 2013; Kloos, this volume; Kuhn 1994; Pordié 2000, 2002, 2008; Pordié and Blaikie 2014). Ideally, the practice of Tibetan medicine was an additional role carried out by men (and occasionally women) who were also engaged in farming, animal husbandry, or wage labor.[12] The time and money required for medical practice were offset by reciprocal arrangements, such as the giving of gifts or informal payments on behalf of patients. In return for advice, diagnosis, and treatment, villagers worked in the amchi's fields, cared for their livestock, and offered gifts of animals, produce, or small amounts of money known as *sman yon* (medicine fees).[13] These arrangements varied from place to place depending on the popularity of the amchi, the respective wealth of the villagers, the local *trims* (*khrims*: customary rules), and the personal relationships connecting amchi to individual patients.[14] Although some Ladakhi amchi remained embedded in such relations at the turn of the millennium, the idealized reciprocal arrangements of former times had become severely undermined or obsolete in most places.[15]

The growth of the cash economy and the decline of reciprocity in structuring relations at the village level shifted the modalities of community support for amchi, rendering medical practice financially unsustainable for many. As reciprocal relations faded, the establishment of new, mutually agreed systems of cash payment became necessary. These arrangements needed to provide sufficient income for amchi to both purchase the required medicines and supplement their livelihoods, while remaining socially and morally acceptable to the community. Although there have been successful adaptations in some villages (see Besch and Guérin, this volume), major disjunctures remained in many rural areas (Blaikie 2014; Kloos, this volume; Pordié 2002). While these transformations affected all Ladakhi amchi in some way by the early 2000s, change was not uniform and played out differently according to geographic, financial, social, and practical specificities.

At the time of my research, Tibetan medicine in Ladakh had not been actively standardized, professionalized, secularized, industrialized, or integrated into public health care as it had been in the Tibet Autonomous Region of China.[16] There was a small amchi section in the Leh District Health Department, but its influence was severely limited both financially and practically. Two small clinics in Leh received government support, but there were no government-funded hospitals of Tibetan medicine and no formal clinics serving the rural areas where the majority of Ladakhis reside. Approximately forty "government amchi" were living in villages across Ladakh and Zangskar, but they received no standardized training, were subject to limited supervision, and were provided with only minimal financial support.[17] Apart from a slight increase in the number and salary of government amchi during the 1980s, there had been little change in the form or extent of state support since the 1960s. This had led to difficulties between amchi and their communities in many places, as this quote illustrates:

> I was to be the government amchi for the villages of Photoksar, Wanla, and Kanji, but I had only 50 rupees salary and 30 to buy medicines each month. I pointed out that it is very difficult to provide medicines for three villages with so little money. I told them that this money was insufficient even to fill one *kyal bu* [small leather bag], so I could not possibly help the people in all of these villages. People doubted me and thought it was not good to ask them for money, saying, "He is getting a salary and medicines free of cost from the government." This was a big misunderstanding by the villagers in my area and all the people of Ladakh.

Over the years, inflation seriously eroded the real value of the government stipend, yet villagers continued to expect free treatment, assuming that the government money would cover the costs as it had in the past. Thus, a once helpful state intervention later gave rise to serious problems in amchi therapeutic economics. Expectations of amchi selflessness, founded in idealized traditional relations and backed by once effective government support, clashed with emerging financial realities to create misunderstandings and mistrust, as shown in more detail in the following.

The training of amchi also underwent significant changes during this period. In 1989 the Central Institute of Buddhist Studies (CIBS) became the first central government-supported institution to offer standardized training in Tibetan medicine in Ladakh, although the course was assessed and the certificates granted by the Men-Tsee-Khang in Dharamsala. The CIBS course required students to have graduated from secondary school (twelfth grade), which was rare in Ladakh and almost unheard of in the remote areas. This restriction, combined with the considerable cost of supporting students during six years of training, meant that the CIBS took a very small number of students and that most of these originated from Leh or the Indus valley.[18] Although most graduates from the CIBS and the Men-Tsee-Khang went on to find full-time work as amchi, the vast majority of rural practitioners, including those receiving government support, had no institutional training and practiced without certification, regulatory frameworks, or legal rights. They could not, therefore, be described as medical professionals according to the standard criteria (e.g., Last 1986, 6).

Encounters between Tibetan medicine and biomedicine were comparatively limited and indirect in Ladakh. The tradition had not been subject to strong governmental influence and lacked a unifying institutional entity such as the Men-Tsee-Khang to drive professionalization. Changes in the modality of amchi training and practice took place more in response to socioeconomic shifts and emergent ideologies of modernity and development than to focused institutional action or state intervention (Pordié and Blaikie 2014). The rapid increase in the availability of biomedicine affected the social position of the amchi, ending their medical monopoly and challenging the logic of socially embedded, reciprocal medical practice. Alice Kuhn (1994, 71) suggests that the dominance of biomedicine in Ladakhi villages reduced the ability of rural amchi to support themselves in their places of origin, causing many of them to migrate to Leh. My research does not support this argument, suggesting a wider range of factors at play in the migration activity of the amchi and a need to consider the finer points of therapeutic economics as well as elements beyond the medical realm before reaching conclusions regarding their migration behavior.

Migration of Rupshupa Amchi

Understanding the relationship between migration activity and Tibetan medicine in Samad is pertinent for a number of reasons. First, out-migration affected the entire community, implying a need to examine the shared and divergent features of this phenomenon for amchi and their patients. Second, the absence of amchi and the continuing presence of local biomedical services, albeit in a highly unreliable form, shaped medical pluralism, treatment-seeking behavior, and health outcomes in specific ways. Third, the out-migration of the amchi and the consequent difficulties of access suggested to the community (and to others) the need to replace them, but reintroduction attempts faced significant problems. Finally, these issues impinged directly on the well-being and resilience of the Rupshupa and thus fed back into migration-related thought and action. I begin my approach to these matters by considering each of the Rupshupa amchi in turn, focusing on their form of training, their legitimacy and practice, their relationship to the community, and the processes that contributed to their departure.

Ngawang Namgyal, Idealized Amchi

Ngawang Namgyal was a highly respected and appreciated lineage (*gyudpa* or *brgyud pa*) amchi who practiced in Samad between the 1950s and the 1970s.[19] All those old enough to remember him did so fondly, commenting—in somewhat idealized terms—on his high levels of knowledge, skill, and compassion.

He was well integrated into the community and lived much as other Changpa did: relying entirely on the sale or exchange of his animal products, staying in Samad year-round, and fulfilling the usual social functions. In addition, he practiced Tibetan medicine, which he had learned from an uncle over many years of oral and practical instruction. In return for his services, he was afforded high social status and was exempt from the responsibilities usually shared among all drongpa, significantly easing the labor and financial burdens borne by his family.[20] Therapeutic interactions were based in principles of reciprocity, and there were no set fees for consultation or medicine. Other drongpa would regularly assist the amchi by grazing his livestock and would offer small amounts of money or gifts in kind following treatment, even offering a sheep or goat in cases where long courses of medicine were required.

These arrangements conform to the ideal relationship between amchi and community and are said to have worked well. They enabled Ngawang Namgyal to live his life as a highly integrated and valued part of the community. However, his wife was not Changpa by birth, originating from the village of Saboo in the Indus valley. This fact, combined with their relative wealth, led to their children being educated at schools in Leh. Their two sons showed no interest in following in their father's footsteps or in returning to Samad after their long period of absence, so the drongpa lost labor power and the family lineage died out. As an old man in the late 1970s, despite pleading and offers of further assistance from the community, Ngawang Namgyal left the Changthang to settle in Saboo. He returned a few times after his departure and offered treatment to those who needed it but was no longer a dependable source of medical care.

Tenzin Sherab, Tibetan Refugee Amchi-Lama

Tenzin Sherab was a lama (*bla ma*: spiritual teacher, monk) in western Tibet until the Chinese took control in 1959. While at the monastery, he had studied Tibetan medicine for seven years under two renowned amchi-lama.[21] Following his flight from Tibet, he spent one year in a transit camp before being allowed to enter Ladakh in 1961. Although not originally from a nomadic family, he found himself in the Changthang without possessions or money and decided to settle in Samad until his options became clearer. Ngawang Namgyal was already a well-established and popular amchi by this time, whereas Tenzin Sherab had fled Tibet without any of his equipment or medicines and was unknown in his new surroundings. Because he lacked resources, social networks, and a reputation, it was some years before he began working as an amchi again. However, by building links with medicinal plant traders from Himachal Pradesh and gaining assistance from the renowned amchi Urgyen Chosphel of Kerey, he gradually gathered enough medicines to begin treating patients.

By the mid-1960s, Tenzin Sherab was treating the Tibetan refugee families that had established themselves in the Samad area, many of whom remember him as skillful and compassionate.[22] A decade later, he was treating Ladakhi patients from Samad and Tibetans from other communities also, becoming well known throughout the region. However, he never fully adopted the pastoralist lifestyle and kept only minimal livestock. He therefore relied largely on his medical practice for his livelihood, charging patients an average of twenty Indian rupees (INR) per treatment and receiving milk, butter, cheese, and meat on an occasional basis. Although based much more firmly on money than the system within which Ngawang Namgyal practiced, these arrangements appear to have been widely accepted by the people, and he continued to expand his patient base throughout the 1970s.

Unused to the extreme conditions of life in the Changthang, however, Tenzin Sherab suffered chronic health problems, culminating in a severe case of tuberculosis in 1979. Having spent six months in a hospital and the winter in Choglamsar, he returned to Samad in 1980.[23] As Ngawang Namgyal had recently left and the Rupshupa were without health services of any kind, they were very keen for him to return permanently. They expressed this support strongly and managed to secure a monthly stipend for him from the health department. However, that winter Tenzin Sherab fell ill again. In spite of appeals from the people and an offer from the deputy commissioner to build him a house in Samad, he left the area finally in 1982 to settle in Choglamsar.

For the next few years, Tenzin Sherab returned to Samad during the summer months and brought his medicines with him. He also collected larger amounts of medicinal plants to send to the Men-Tsee-Khang in return for other raw materials and ready-made medicines. Two key developments took shape during this period. First, he began to provide medical treatment in a new way: giving medicines to the family members of patients in Choglamsar, who then returned to Samad to administer the treatment themselves. Second, he began making medicines in larger quantities and selling them to other amchi, joining an emerging group of cottage-industry pharmacists producing Tibetan medicines commercially for the first time in Ladakh (Blaikie 2011, 2013, 2015). His health remained poor, however, so his visits to Samad became rarer and eventually stopped altogether in the 1990s, although many Rupshupa visited him whenever they were in need or were in the Leh area for other reasons.

Sherab Singe, Amchi and Ritual Specialist

Sherab Singe, also of Tibetan origin, began his medical practice in the early 1980s, around the time that Tenzin Sherab moved away. His father, the Tibetan Rinpoche Churpa Tulku, was a well-respected religious figure who had an enormous impact on his life. The Rinpoche encouraged his son to become both an *onpo* (*dbon po*: astrologer and ritual specialist) and an amchi, as well as playing a crucial part in his decision to finally leave the area. Throughout his childhood and youth, Sherab Singe accompanied his father on tours of Ladakh and beyond, gradually accumulating textual, ritual, and astrological knowledge and becoming a well-known onpo in his own right.

In the late 1970s, Sherab Singe spent several winters studying with a senior amchi in nearby Khorzok, building on the basic theoretical knowledge that he had acquired from the Gyüshi (*rgyud bzhi*: the standard treatise of Tibetan medicine) and from his father. Following the departure of Tenzin Sherab, Tibetan refugees living in Samad began asking him to treat their afflictions, and by the mid-1980s, he had established a substantial patient base. He never learned how to make his own medicines, however, instead purchasing them from the Men-Tsee-Khang in Dharamsala, which was more expensive than producing his own. He always asked patients to give him the exact cost of the medicine and nothing more, stating, "I treat all the people equally, and they know this. . . . If I did not treat them fairly, they would not come back to me. Some amchi charge a lot of money, more than the cost of the medicine, which is not good as the people are very poor." In the 1980s he traveled widely throughout the Changthang region assisting his father while himself becoming a popular onpo, first among the Tibetan refugees and later among Ladakhi families also. The cash payment he received for these astrological and ritual services formed the basis of his livelihood. Holding a position of considerable social status and generating a reasonable income from his work as an onpo, Sherab Singe was able to offer medicine at cost and thus establish his reputation as a compassionate and fair amchi.

The bad winter of 1986 killed the majority of his livestock, and his father's health began to deteriorate, leading Sherab Singe to construct a house on the edge of Leh. Out of respect for the aged Rinpoche and his son, the local people granted them a plot of land and helped them build their house. For three years Sherhab Singe followed a straddling strategy, spending winter in the town and summer in the Changthang. He practiced Tibetan medicine in both places, but his family lived in Leh, and the advantages of sedentary living became increasingly apparent: "I had children, and they began to go to the school in Leh.

I became part of the community, I got used to the settled life, and the people here asked me to stay all the time. Now I cannot move back there [Samad]."

In the early 2000s, Sherab Singe lived most of the year in Leh and returned to Samad for just a few weeks each summer. He kept a small flock of sheep and goats in Samad, cared for by relatives and friends, which was forbidden for ordinary Changpa and thus underscored his special position: "It is only because I am an amchi and the people need me that I can keep these animals and live in Leh. Others cannot do as I do." Many Rupshupa visited him when they were in Leh, and he traveled to Samad a number of times specifically to treat seriously ill patients, but this was costly and beyond the means of most families. He therefore continued to be an amchi of significance for the Rupshupa, but because he was present only for short periods each year, this distant relationship was quite different from the dependable, permanent presence of his predecessors.

Ngawang Gilak, Controversial "New Amchi"

Ngawang Gilak was the next amchi to practice in Samad. He was not a lineage amchi but claimed to have studied for three years as an apprentice in Choglamsar during the early 1980s. Tenzin Sherab refuted this, stating that he himself had trained Ngawang Gilak for just one winter and that his student did not return to complete his training. Discrepancies such as this surround Ngawang Gilak. Although originally Rupshupa, he had traveled widely in his youth and, when he returned to Samad in 1986, had not lived with the community for many years. Between 1986 and 1991, he managed to secure support both from the government amchi program and from the Leh Nutrition Project, a local nongovernmental organization (NGO) that offered training and financial support to rural amchi. The NGO support was limited to a small grant for medicine and transportation costs, while the government assistance amounted to a salary of 300 rupees per month plus 1,500 rupees annually for raw materials between 1989 and 1994. This support reflected the value placed on amchi as health providers for rural areas at the time, but also gave rise to considerable misunderstandings between the amchi and the community.

Accounts of Ngawang Gilak's time in Samad vary. Although several people recalled him providing *sman rgyala* (good medicine), most spoke of serious problems. Some suggested that he was too involved in politics and interested in money, that he "was a friend of the strong but no friend of the weak" (Urgyen Dorje). In the eyes of most, he abused his position, seeking social power and financial gain and putting his own benefit before that of his patients (see Kloos 2004, this volume). This clashed strongly with the ideal image of the amchi as a fair and selfless person; as Sonam Targais commented, "Amchi Ngawang Gilak was too strong, he did not have compassion as an amchi should." Ngawang Gilak himself played down these problems, claiming that he was unable to support himself with the money provided to him and that the community's inability to accept the need to pay for medicine was the main cause of tension.

From all viewpoints, Ngawang Gilak again represented a new kind of amchi for the Rupshupa. Their expectations appear to have been colored by their idealized representation of lineage amchi and of those with religious or ritual functions (lama and onpo) in addition to their medical practice. The people were used to amchi living closely among them, with established relationships of reciprocity and mutually defined roles. Trained and supported financially from outside the community, Ngawang Gilak expected the same level of respect as his predecessors received but demanded payment for each consultation on top of the money he was known to be receiving from the government and the NGO. A lack of clarity over the amount and purpose of this external funding appears central here, as people assumed that it was sufficient for his medical needs and thus that supplementary demands for payment demonstrated greed and a lack of compassion. In this way, unfamiliar and vague forms of external support created mistrust and tension at the meeting point of health care, economics, and morality.

In 1991 Ngawang Gilak left Samad, purchased land in Upshi, and set up a small restaurant. He gave three reasons for this move: he was unable to support his family on the income he was receiving, he did not have sufficient livestock to augment his livelihood, and he wanted his children to receive a good education. He continued to receive government support until 1994 and during these three years returned to Samad sporadically, but his relationship with the community deteriorated. Many felt that by residing elsewhere he was receiving payment for a service he was not actually providing and that by asking for cash payment for what little he did provide, he was asking too much in return. This combination of an unfamiliar form of practice, the absence of religious or social legitimacy, financial demands, and personal mistrust proved unsustainable, resulting in the permanent out-migration of the third amchi in fifteen years. Ngawang Gilak started working full time at his tea stall in Upshi, rarely returned to Samad, and ceased practicing Tibetan medicine altogether. He was sometimes referred to as a successful businessman, an example of what sedentarized Changpa could achieve, but references to him were always tinged with disappointment or outright hostility whenever medical matters were mentioned.

Karma Targais, NGO Amchi

Next in line was Karma Targais, a young Rupshupa chosen by the Leh Nutrition Project as Ngawang Gilak's replacement in 1996. He was taken to Leh for one year, where he received basic training in Tibetan medicine but also in the detection of major biomedically defined diseases, their treatment with basic biomedical drugs, and the process of hospital referral (see Kuhn 1994, 64). This kind of training was unprecedented in Ladakh and very different from the familiar regimes of kinship-linked gyudpa, master-disciple apprenticeship, or college-based training. The aim was for Karma Targais to return to Samad with a small amount of money to purchase both biomedicines and Tibetan medicines and to practice what he had learned, instituting his own system of payment with the people.

However, he was inexperienced and insufficiently trained, and the Rupshupa did not come to trust his skills as a healer: "He was not a real amchi.... He was not able to tell us our problems or give good medicine" (Karma Otser). He was also a young man, unmarried, with few ties to keep him in Samad. Having lived in Leh for a year and returned to find an unwelcoming community who did not accept him or believe him to be competent, Karma Targais stayed for less than six months before leaving to live permanently in Choglamsar. Many suggested that his departure resulted from his unwillingness to return to the nomadic life, but some also mentioned that their lack of acceptance may have contributed to his decision to leave. A few referred to the animosity they felt when he demanded payment for medicines, given that he was receiving NGO support. As with Ngawang Gilak, the morally questionable act of asking for payment while receiving external financial assistance appears to have significantly damaged the relationship between amchi and community. Having said that, none of the Rupshupa I encountered were aware that the Leh Nutrition Project had stopped financial support for their amchi program in 1997, which actually played a large part in Karma Targais's decision to leave. Finding that life suited him better in the town, he, too, departed from Samad and ceased all medical relationships with the community.

Understanding Amchi Migration

Although necessarily brief, the preceding accounts illustrate how amchi migration was determined by the full range of push and pull factors that affected non-amchi, as well as a set of specific sociomedical issues. Old age, endogenous marriage, family commitments, serious illness, business interests both inside and outside the medical field, differential risk assessments, educational aspirations for children, and exposure to sedentary living all influenced the migration decisions of the Samad amchi. Interacting with these general factors were a set of practice-related issues situated in the negotiated space between amchi and community, including the rupture of hereditary lineage, new forms of training and legitimacy, the problematic transition from embedded therapeutic relations to cash-based transactions, and the vagueness surrounding the amount and purpose of external financial support. The interaction of these two sets of factors illustrates the limitations of simple or monocausal models in explaining the migration behavior of Ladakhi amchi. The Samad case therefore does not support Kuhn's (1994, 71) argument that freely accessible biomedical treatment undermined support for amchi in Ladakhi villages, while the possibility of higher incomes in Leh drew them to the town.[24] The severely limited access to biomedical services and the continued demand for Tibetan medicine in Samad limit the validity of the first of these suggestions, while the second is relevant only in certain cases. Of the five amchi included in this study, only Tenzin Sherab and Sherab Singe continued to practice after leaving Samad. Both found sedentarization easier owing to their ability to continue practicing Tibetan medicine and charging fees for their services, but this was not the major factor influencing their migration decisions.

Tibetan medicine formed an integral part of the livelihoods of amchi drongpa and certainly played a part in their decisions to migrate, but it cannot be taken as a primary factor without detailed knowledge of their circumstances, livelihood strategies, and decision-making processes. There is much here that calls into question the commonly deployed separation of domestic, medical, and other socioeconomic realms, demanding that attention be paid to a whole complex of nonmarket and nonmedical relationships, institutions, and processes, which are often misrepresented or simply ignored in social science literature, particularly that influenced by neoliberalism (Harriss-White 2003, 2005; Rankin 2004; White 1992; Wolf 1992).

Seeking Treatment Where There Is No Amchi

I turn now to examine how the absence of a medically and socially accepted amchi, combined with increased access to biomedical services, shaped medical pluralism and treatment-seeking behavior in Samad. A mobile medical aid center (MAC) has been assigned to the Rupshupa for the past twenty-five years, staffed (at least on paper) by a medical assistant (MA) and a nurse orderly (NO). The MA had three months of training in the diagnosis of major diseases, the provision of first aid, the dispensing of painkillers and antibiotics, and the hospital referral process for life-threatening cases. The NO had no formal training but had picked up basic diagnostic and pharmaceutical knowledge through observation and informal lessons while on the job. In addition to these permanent staff, a general practitioner visited for one day each month to examine serious cases and monitor the drug supply. The Rupshupa estimated that the MA was present for ten days per month during summer and between three and seven days per month during winter, on average. For the rest of the time, it was the untrained NO who gave consultations and prescribed medicines. I witnessed patients visiting the NO and after the most cursory "consultation" being handed broad-spectrum antibiotics without any clear diagnosis or advice concerning dosage and length of course. I also spoke with a young man who had been suffering from a painful impacted wisdom tooth for over six weeks, yet was given only mild painkillers and no referral advice. Despite this extremely poor service, the MAC was generally the first resort when people fell ill, and every Rupshupa I spoke to felt it was of great benefit to the community.

It was much more difficult for the Rupshupa to gain amchi consultation and treatment:

> I can only see an amchi when I am in Leh, but I never go there only for this reason. If I am in Leh to trade, buy supplies, or visit relatives, then I can visit the amchi. (Rinchen Targais)

> We can only go to the amchi when we are close to death. Unless we are very sick, we must stay here and suffer. (Tsering Yangzum)

Consulting an amchi required at best a long, expensive journey and a stay in a distant town. At worst, during winter, poorer Rupshupa had to undertake a hard trek through the snow to the road, followed by an uncertain wait to hitchhike over the icy passes to the town. Wealthier people paid large sums of money to hire a taxi for the entire journey. Given these conditions, there is indeed "a need to question the commonly deployed paradigm of pluralism in medical anthropology that privileges the patient and support group as agents freely choosing options from among the available array" (Connor 2001, 4). Choice of treatment for the Rupshupa was highly restricted and reflects differing degrees of marginality rather than simply the preference of the patient.

It was under these restricted conditions that the Rupshupa formed their views of biomedicine and its relative strengths and weaknesses. A widely held view was that biomedicine is powerful and rapidly treats symptoms but does not address the root causes of disease as Tibetan medicine does: "If you take doctor medicine for *cham pa* [common cold, flu], in ten minutes you feel better, but the next day you are sick again. The medicine doesn't cure you, it only distracts the disease" (Tsering Angchuk). Many also believed that for some illnesses and some people, biomedicine was ineffective and only Tibetan medicine would work: "As every person is different, it depends on your body if doctor medicine will work for you. It works for my wife, but for me it does nothing. I need an amchi if I am ill" (Tsering Tashi).

Tibetan medicine was particularly sought after in cases of chronic disease such as arthritis or joint problems, illnesses that do not fit biomedical categories, and those regarded as untreatable by biomedical doctors. Tsering Putit, a sixty-year-old woman, suffered from constant headaches and dizziness for many months. After being given painkillers but finding only temporary relief, she was told by MAC staff that they could do nothing for her. After a full year of suffering, she visited the hospital in Leh, where a similarly unsatisfactory diagnosis was given and another course of painkillers prescribed. Finally, she went to an amchi in Leh who diagnosed her affliction and offered dietary advice, a course of medicine, and a mantra to be recited. While this treatment was only partially successful in terms of alleviating her symptoms and she did not feel fully cured, the amchi's explanation and her own involvement in the treatment were a marked improvement for her, enabling her to get on with her day-to-day life.

Along with other similar cases, this lends support to Craig Janes's observation that "people seek a meaningful idiom through which to express suffering and produce diagnostic discourses that can be followed and provide relief" (1999, 1807). Biomedicine cannot replace indigenous medicine entirely, because explanations of illness and ways of coping with it are deeply engrained and remain symbolically and practically valuable. Thus, therapeutic pragmatism—the pursuit of various courses of treatment in the hope of relief—coexisted among the Rupshupa with a desire to understand the causes of ill health and the pathways to well-being within a familiar explanatory framework. The case of Tsering Putit suggests that relief from symptoms is of paramount importance, but if a cure is not found, an explanation of the illness and a course of remedial action are experienced as a significant improvement. The lack of a local amchi thus severely reduced the opportunities for Changpa to benefit from appropriate diagnosis and to experience a cure or partial remedy.

Spatial, temporal, and financial constraints had a significant impact on the nature of amchi consultations and on the forms of treatment used by Rupshupa. The multiple visits ideally needed for the amchi to accurately diagnose the disorder and adjust the treatment regime, and for the patient to pick up additional medicines, simply were not an option. One outcome of this was the emergence of a distinct treatment modality that was unusual in Ladakh and entirely unreported in anthropological literature about Tibetan medicine elsewhere. This is the adoption of long-distance treatment practices in which amchi in Leh prescribed various forms of medicine that were either taken back to Samad and used immediately to treat patients who were not able to make the journey, or stored in case of future need.

The group of Tibetan medicines known as *thang* are relatively simple formulas, most with fewer than ten components, which are administered as decoctions. In the early stages of acute disorders, they "ripen" disease and collect the "morbid humour" in specific locations (Meyer [1988] 2007, 183). Ideally, their prescription is followed up with another consultation, when the progression of the disorder is established and the appropriate *zhi* (appeasing) or *sbyang* (evacuating) medicines are given. Further consultations then confirm whether the treatment has been successful or not, enabling further alteration of the therapeutic regime. The use of thang is thus an early step in a progression of therapeutic stages, but this was problematic for the Rupshupa as it required a number of visits to the amchi. Instead, the most popular forms of thang were frequently purchased in large quantities by the Rupshupa and taken back to Samad, where they were stored away and used to treat minor ailments whenever they arose, without further amchi consultation. While my research suggested that this practice was not unheard of elsewhere in Ladakh, it was unusual and limited to places where access to amchi was problematic.

Tenzin Sherab confirmed that he supplied Rupshupa with various forms of thang while they were in Leh. Occasionally he also gave people the appropriate zhi and sbyang medicines to take back with them, without actually meeting the patient for whom they were destined. In these cases, an initial diagnosis could not be carried out, the nature and stage of the disease could not be ascertained, and the treatment could not be altered according to development of the disease. This represents a much more unusual therapeutic form, which Tenzin Sherab explained thus: "Because there is no amchi in Samad, the Rupshupa feel that it is their responsibility to care for those who are seriously ill if they cannot come to see an amchi in Leh. The family members of the sick person come to me, and I ask them to describe the symptoms. . . . Sometimes they also bring urine for me to examine. If I know the patient and the problem, I can give the correct medicines and explain how they should be taken." In such cases he gave careful instructions regarding dosage, monitoring of the patient's symptoms, and the circumstances in which the thang should be discontinued and more powerful medicines used. Thus, the amchi treated patients without actually meeting them face-to-face, forgoing the usual diagnostic techniques of observation, interrogation, and pulse diagnosis. He effectively employed "surrogate amchi" to observe the progression of disease and administer the treatments. Sherab Singe confirmed that he engaged in this form of practice also but less frequently than Tenzin Sherab as he was mobile and paid more regular visits to Samad. Both amchi pointed out the limitations of this method, noting that it was far from ideal and less likely to prove successful than a series of face-to-face consultations. They described it as a last resort for people without any other options, which would never be used if amchi were readily accessible.

Several kinds of *rinchen rilbu* (*rin chen ril bu*: "precious pills," i.e., containing precious substances like gemstones) were also regularly bought in fairly large quantities by Rupshupa while in Leh. These are expensive, pharmacologically complex, and powerful medicines, which can be taken without amchi consultation either for specific complex problems, like seizures or poisoning, or as health tonics. While rinchen rilbu carried great cultural, political, and economic significance both in Dharamsala (Gerke 2017; Kloos 2012; Prost 2008) and in the Tibet Autonomous Region (Hofer 2008a; Saxer 2013), the Rupshupa regarded them primarily in terms of their medicinal properties. Thus, several Rupshupa told me that when serious illnesses occur, no amchi is available, and biomedicine is ineffective, rinchen rilbu offer the only chance of avoiding permanent damage or death. For this reason, a variety of precious pills were purchased in Leh and stored in Samad in case of future need. However, Tenzin Sherab emphasized that it is essential to know which rinchen rilbu to use in any given situation and that few people in Samad had this knowledge. To address this problem, he offered basic training to a number of Rupshupa, who could be called on to advise others on appropriate usage when urgent cases arose. However, he pointed out the limitations of this: "Using rinchen rilbu in this way is a desperate thing, a last chance. Nobody knows if it will work, and often it does not. If an amchi is there, the chances are much better." The existence of these forms of treatment suggested a continued belief in the efficacy of Tibetan medicine for preventing and addressing ill health, despite the presence of the MAC and the highly problematic access to amchi. However, the lack of a locally based amchi had severely disrupted the therapeutic space and forced reliance on preventative, preliminary, or extreme treatments.

As well as transforming amchi-patient relations and treatment modalities, the absence of amchi had notable impacts on identity, resilience, and confidence among the Rupshupa, as the following quotes illustrate:

This *yul* [village; in this case, an area inhabited by a defined group of people] is not whole without an amchi: it is like we are missing our heart. (Urgyen Dorje)

Every yul has an amchi, but here we have none. We are not complete and we do not feel strong or confident living like this.... Amchi provide examples for the young people—how can we keep the community alive when there is no amchi to assist us and people think only of themselves? (Sonam Namgyal)

Above and beyond their medical duties, amchi tended to play important symbolic roles as figures of respect and providers of moral and religious guidance. Idealized representations of amchi were arguably accentuated in Samad by the continued absence of anyone able to live up to them. Stephan Kloos (2004, this volume) has shown how amchi can become figures of fear or contempt if their behavior is seen as straying too far from these ideals. An amchi who primarily seeks social power yet continues to demand the high level of respect reserved, at least in theory, for those with *sems bzang po* (a "good heart") may contribute to rather than reduce social tensions. The story of Ngawang Gilak involves an antagonistic relationship developing between amchi and villagers, where the disjuncture between ideal and reality was so stark that relations broke down altogether. Several Rupshupa commented that a bad amchi such as Ngawang Gilak, who lacked compassion but sought money and power, was worse than no amchi at all.

The general feeling in Samad was that a socially accepted, compassionate, and skillful amchi is an essential indicator of a strong and cohesive community and that the absence of such a person both reflected and exacerbated weaknesses in the fabric of contemporary Changpa life. The return of a good amchi was seen as necessary to help the community meet the challenges they faced, but as I have shown, this was far from a straightforward process. Indeed, the idealized image of the amchi itself can be seen as a significant factor preventing the successful integration of a new practitioner.

Conclusion

The demand for Tibetan medicine remained high in Samad in the early 2000s, despite its disrupted recent history. The Rupshupa agreed unanimously that the return of a reliable, skillful amchi was of great importance to their health and well-being, both as individuals and as a group. Older people, particularly those who remembered Ngawang Namgyal, were often more acutely aware of the lack than the younger generation, suggesting a degree of intergenerational variation. However, many young people also placed a high value on Tibetan medicine, despite having had only occasional direct experiences of it.

Highly restricted access to Tibetan medicine in Samad since the early 1990s had contributed to the substantial reconfiguration of amchi-patient relations as well as diagnostic and therapeutic practices. Long-term relationships between amchi and patients were severely disrupted, making diagnosis, follow-up consultations, and the adjustment of treatment regimes problematic. Given the lack of these crucial elements of diagnosis and therapy, there is much that resonates with descriptions of narrower and more drug-based forms of Tibetan medicine in the Tibet Autonomous Region and surrounding parts of China (Adams 2002a; Craig and Adams 2008; Hofer 2008a, 2008b; Janes 1999). However, in Samad it was due mainly to problems of access rather than to state-controlled modernization or profit-oriented pharmaceutical industrialization. Long-distance treatment practices, characterized by simplified and incomplete techniques of diagnosis and therapy and the use of surrogates to perform functions otherwise firmly rooted in amchi practice, would simply not be necessary were an amchi present in the community.

Most Rupshupa considered traditional medicine and biomedicine to be complementary, each with its own "sphere of usefulness" (Samuel 2001, 252). In cases of minor illness, most tended toward pragmatism, going first to the MAC before seeking the services of distant amchi if biomedicine proved ineffective. In more serious cases, decisions were based on wealth, livelihood demands, and mobility as much as personal preference, much more so than in villages where biomedicine was available but amchi still practiced. The Samad situation corresponds in some ways to the pragmatism described by Geoffrey Samuel (2001) in Tibetan refugee camps in other parts of India, although further study is required to establish the extent to which the lack of an amchi is shifting people's conceptualization and categorization of disease toward the biomedical.

In 2002, it seemed highly unlikely that an established amchi from elsewhere in Ladakh would spontaneously move to Samad to live and practice there on a permanent basis. If planned reintroduction of an amchi by an NGO or the government were to be successful, it would have to overcome the many logistical, social, economic, moral, and interpersonal problems that had caused previous attempts to fail. Neither the barefoot doctor-style training given to Karma Targais nor the limited instruction received by Ngawang Gilak was sufficient to confer legitimacy or inspire confidence. Perhaps more significantly, neither amchi was able to establish a system of remuneration that was clear to all parties and morally acceptable and affordable for the people, while also yielding sufficient income to support the practitioners' livelihoods.

In the early 2000s, relationships between amchi and patients were being renegotiated all across Ladakh. Considerable uncertainty and tension arose as idealized images and established norms came up against contemporary financial and social realities. In places where amchi were well established, new economic arrangements could be negotiated and adopted gradually, whereas in Samad a series of disruptions and disappointments left little time for such adjustment. This situation further contributed to the idealization of the amchi, based on memories of Ngawang Namgyal and the two amchi of Tibetan origin, which encouraged rejection of those who did not conform to these ideals. Rural-urban migration therefore emerges as an important factor shaping the future for Tibetan medicine in areas such as Samad, as well as in farming communities where migration pressure is also very strong.

This chapter shows how broad socioeconomic change processes, state interventions, and NGO activities combine to shape the possibilities for seeking, providing, and receiving traditional health-care services in Himalayan India. It focuses on the role of rural-urban migration in the disrupted recent history of Tibetan medicine in one nomadic community and considers the part it has played in reconfiguring medical pluralism and transforming clinical practice. I do not propose that the lack of an amchi directly *caused* rural-urban migration to increase—the sustainable livelihoods framework, enriched by ethnography, shows such a claim to be simplistic and incomplete. I rather argue that the absence of an amchi had very real impacts on people's access to and use of health services. This contributed to feelings of vulnerability, marginality, and deprivation, reflecting declining group cohesion and the disintegration of an institution that had once helped the Rupshupa to see themselves as complete and strong. Combined with the mounting difficulties that these people experienced in other areas of life, the lack of an amchi certainly acted as a tributary to the migration stream that linked Samad ever more closely to the sedentary world of the Indus valley.

Notes

I offer my deepest thanks to the Rupshupa for their unfailing generosity and openness. The Research Unit of Nomad RSI and the staff of both the Ladakh Society for Traditional Medicines and Ladakh Amchi Sabha made the research possible financially and logistically. Special thanks go to Thupstan Choszang for his constant companionship and assistance, and to Laurent Pordié for his invaluable advice during the drafting phase. The RATIMED Project (European Research Council

Grant 336932) supported the finalization of this work for publication. This chapter is dedicated to the memory of Gonbo Dorje, a talented young Rupshupa amchi who died under tragic circumstances in 2004.

1   See Alter (2005); Baer, Singer, and Susser (2003); Connor and Samuel (2001); Ernst (2002); and Nichter and Lock (2002).

2   Literature on this topic is scarce. Joseph Uyanga (1983) compared treatment-seeking behavior among migrant and nonmigrant populations in eastern Nigeria, finding "marked differences in disease beliefs and related healthcare behaviour between non-migrant rural households and rural urban migrant households" (579). However, no detailed analysis of migration processes or the role of traditional medicine practitioners in these processes is offered.

3   Melvyn Goldstein and Cynthia Beall (1984) suggest that nomadic pastoralists first arrived in the Changthang area between nine thousand and three thousand years ago.

4   During winter, daytime temperatures rarely rise above freezing and frequently fall below −20 degrees Celsius.

5   See Agrawal (1999) and Vira (1993) on the need for further research on new forms of population movement (including rural-urban migration) among nomadic pastoralists. The significant contribution of Kenneth Bauer (2004) and the collection of works edited by Aparna Rao and Michael Casimir (2003) go some way to addressing this gap.

6   Forms of migration include distress, economic, and circular migration, but these are not bounded or mutually exclusive.

7   Some suggested as many as twenty drongpa had left Samad, which matches Ajit Chaudhuri's (1999) figure. Taking 1980 as a rough baseline, this suggests a maximum of 25 percent of drongpa have migrated away, but the proportion could be as high as 40 percent in simple population terms, owing to the large number of individuals who have left.

8   The terrible winters of 1962–63 and 1998–99 illustrate the very real danger posed by heavy, early snowfalls and extreme temperatures (−50 degrees Celsius), which block the passes and trap the Changpa before they can reach their winter pastures. Livestock losses were as high as 70 percent in 1963 for many households, and similar losses were averted in 1999 only by a large relief operation (ApTibet 1999).

9   The Ladakh Buddhist Association played a major role in changing marriage practices, effectively ending the previously widespread practice of polyandry in most of the region (Mills 1998).

10 In 2001 market prices were roughly INR 3,000 for a prime ram, INR 2,000 for a goat, and INR 16,000 for a yak. A medium-sized herd of 150 sheep, 150 goats, and 10 yaks would thus raise INR 910,000, which is a vast sum in a country with a gross domestic product per capita of INR 21,537 (World Bank 2021).

11 Sarah Goodall (2004) confirms that individuals, both old and young, are leaving the community for these reasons but finds that the proportion doing so is similar to the proportion of these age-groups living in the original communities. This suggests that the full cross section of Changpa society is migrating and that older and younger people are not statistically more likely to migrate than members of other age-groups.

12 See Fjeld and Hofer (2010) for an overview of the significant but underresearched role of women in Tibetan medicine.

13 Literally translated, this term means "medicine fee," but the word *yon* is honorific and is also used for gifts of money and food offered to visiting monks. It refers to gifts that the giver is both obliged and honored to offer and that generate merit for both giver and receiver if offered selflessly.

14 *Trims* are guidelines and rules that provide normative and institutional frameworks for village life; see Pirie (2007, 55–58).

15 See Blaikie (2013) and Kloos (2004, this volume) for detailed discussion of these phenomena.

16 See Adams (2002a, 2002b, 2007); Adams, Schrempf, and Craig (2011); Craig (2006, 2012); Craig and Adams (2008); Hofer (2012, 2018); and Janes (1995, 1999, 2001, 2002).

17 In total, a government amchi received INR 5,100 per year in 2003.

18 A local nongovernmental organization, the Ladakh Society for Traditional Medicines, launched a four-year training program in Tibetan medicine in 1999. This program aimed to overcome the restrictions of the CIBS course by offering free standardized training to students from remote areas, who need not have graduated from secondary school (Pordié and Blaikie 2014).

19 Medico-spiritual lineages have long been the main channel of knowledge transmission, as well as cornerstones of amchi identity and legitimacy. However, as several chapters in this volume note, the meaning of *brgyud pa* is complex, and its role is changing. In the Changthang and throughout Ladakh, brgyud pa came to be idealized as a marker of patrilineal descent, in which senior amchi passed on their knowledge to their sons, nephews, or grandsons in an unbroken line. Although such patterns were important historically and retain a central place in idealized constructions of Tibetan medicine, they are by no means the only channel of transmission and are quite variable in practice. Many Ladakhis consider themselves lineage amchi despite studying under unrelated masters, showing that blood relations are not a necessary condition for the passing on or holding of a lineage. At the same time, some people from well-known amchi families refer to themselves as lineage amchi despite having received little or no training and not being actively engaged in medical practice, apparently in order to assume the social status attached to such lineages. While most amchi accept that lineages flow both within and outside of kinship groups, this understanding is less widespread among the lay community, who largely retain an idealized view. The patrilineal underpinnings of brgyud pa are further weakening as institutional instruction becomes increasingly common and widespread (Pordié and Blaikie 2014). For further discussion of brgyud pa, see Fjeld and Hofer (2010) and Hofer (2012, 2018).

20 These responsibilities include drongpa taking turns to care for all the yaks and horses of the community and for the livestock of the monastery.

21 Many Buddhist monks learn Tibetan medicine while living in their *gompa* (*dgon pa*: monastery), although this modality was never institutionalized in Ladakh as it was in Tibet (Pordié 2007).

22 Large numbers of Tibetan pastoralists took refuge in Ladakh during the 1960s. Following initial tension between Ladakhi Changpa and the refugees over pasture

rights and transhumance routes, the relationship settled down toward the end of the 1960s. Today the Tibetans live alongside the Ladakhis, in separate encampments but sharing migratory routes and pastures, with only occasional tension.

23 Choglamsar is a town near Leh where many Tibetan refugees and migrants from other parts of Ladakh, India, and Nepal have settled. The area known as Kharnak ling has received the majority of Changpa migrants from Rupshu-Kharnak.

24 Nor is this suggestion supported by other research (Pordié 2000), which finds only a small number of amchi hailing from remote areas practicing in Leh. Factors of institutional training, family background, and government postings appear more salient than biomedical dominance in causing amchi to leave their places of origin.

References

Adams, Vincanne. 1988. "Modes of Production and Medicine: An Examination of the Theory in Light of Sherpa Medical Traditionalism." *Social Science and Medicine* 27 (5): 505–13.

Adams, Vincanne. 2002a. "Establishing Proof: Translating 'Science' and the State in Tibetan Medicine." In *New Horizons in Medical Anthropology*, edited by Mark Nichter and Margaret Lock, 200–220. New York: Routledge.

Adams, Vincanne. 2002b. "Randomized Controlled Crime: Postcolonial Sciences in Alternative Medicine Research." *Social Studies of Science* 32 (5): 659–90.

Adams, Vincanne. 2007. "Integrating Abstraction: Modernising Medicine at Lhasa's Mensikhang." In *Soundings in Tibetan Medicine: Anthropological and Historical Perspectives*, edited by Mona Schrempf, 29–44. Leiden: Brill.

Adams, Vincanne, Mona Schrempf, and Sienna R. Craig, eds. 2011. *Medicine between Science and Religion: Explorations on Tibetan Grounds*. New York: Berghahn.

Agrawal, Arjun. 1999. *Greener Pastures: Politics, Markets, and Community among a Migrant Pastoral People*. Durham, NC: Duke University Press.

Ahmed, Monisha. 1999. "The Salt Trade: Rupshu's Annual Trek to Tso Kar." In *Ladakh: Culture, History, and Development between Himalaya and Karakoram*, edited by Martijn van Beek, Kristoffer Brix Bertelsen, and Poul Pedersen, 32–48. Aarhus: Aarhus University Press.

Ahmed, Monisha. 2003. *Living Fabric: Weaving among the Nomads of Ladakh Himalaya*. New York: Weatherhill.

Alter, Joseph, ed. 2005. *Asian Medicine and Globalization*. Philadelphia: University of Pennsylvania Press.

ApTibet (Appropriate Technology for Tibetans). 1999. *Newsletter No. 14.*

Ashley, Caroline, and Diana Carney. 1999. *Sustainable Livelihoods: Lessons from Early Experiences*. London: Department for International Development.

Baer, Hans A., Merrill Singer, and Ida Susser. 2003. *Medical Anthropology and the World System*. Westport, CT: Praeger.

Bauer, Kenneth. 2004. *High Frontiers: Dolpo and the Changing World of Himalayan Pastoralists*. New York: Columbia University Press.

Besch, Florian. 2006. "Tibetan Medicine off the Roads: Modernizing the Work of the *Amchi* in Spiti." PhD diss., University of Heidelberg.

Besch, Florian. 2007. "Making a Medical Living: On the Monetisation of Tibetan Medicine in Spiti." In *Soundings in Tibetan Medicine: Anthropological and Historical Perspectives*, edited by Mona Schrempf, 155–70. Leiden: Brill.

Blaikie, Calum. 2001. "Why Do the Nomads Settle? Livelihoods, Sustainability and Rural-Urban Migration among the Kharnak Community of the Changpa of Ladakh." Master's thesis, School of Oriental and African Studies, University of London.

Blaikie, Calum. 2011. "Critically Endangered? Medicinal Plant Cultivation and the Re-configuration of Sowa Rigpa in Ladakh." *Asian Medicine* 5 (2): 243–72.

Blaikie, Calum. 2013. "Currents of Tradition in Sowa Rigpa Pharmacy." *East Asian Science, Technology and Society* 7:425–51.

Blaikie, Calum. 2014. "Making Medicine: Materia Medica, Pharmacy and the Production of Sowa Rigpa in Ladakh." PhD diss., University of Kent.

Blaikie, Calum. 2015. "Wish-Fulfilling Jewel Pills: Tibetan Medicines from Exclusivity to Ubiquity." *Anthropology and Medicine* 22 (1): 7–22.

Chaudhuri, Ajit. 1999. *The Changpas of Rupshu-Kharnak: An Enquiry into the Survival Strategies of an Amazing People*. New Delhi: ACTIONAID.

Connor, Linda H. 2001. "Healing Powers in Contemporary Asia." In *Healing Powers and Modernity: Traditional Medicine, Shamanism, and Science in Asian Societies*, edited by Linda H. Connor and Geoffrey Samuel, 3–24. Westport, CT: Bergin and Garvey.

Connor, Linda H., and Geoffrey Samuel, eds. 2001. *Healing Powers and Modernity: Traditional Medicine, Shamanism, and Science in Asian Societies*. Westport, CT: Bergin and Garvey.

Craig, Sienna R. 2006. "On the 'Science of Healing': Efficacy and the Metamorphosis of Tibetan Medicine." PhD diss., Cornell University.

Craig, Sienna R. 2012. *Healing Elements: Efficacy and the Social Ecologies of Tibetan Medicine*. Berkeley: University of California Press.

Craig, Sienna R., and Vincanne Adams. 2008. "Global Pharma in the Land of Snows: Tibetan Medicines, SARS, and Identity Politics across Nations." *Asian Medicine* 4 (1): 1–28.

Darokhan, Mohammed D. 1999. "The Development of Ecological Agriculture in Ladakh and Strategies for Sustainable Development." In *Ladakh: Culture, History, and Development between Himalaya and Karakoram*, edited by Martijn van Beek, Kristoffer Brix Bertelsen, and Poul Pedersen, 78–91. Aarhus: Aarhus University Press.

de Haan, Arjan. 2000. *Migrants, Livelihoods and Rights: The Relevance of Migration in Development Policies*. Social Development Working Paper 4. Brighton: Institute of Development Studies.

Dignes, Martin, ed. 2014. *Medical Pluralism and Homeopathy in India and Germany (1810–2010): A Comparison of Practices*. Stuttgart: Franz Steiner.

Ellis, Frank. 2000. *Rural Livelihoods and Diversity in Developing Countries*. Oxford: Oxford University Press.

Ernst, Waltraud, ed. 2002. *Plural Medicine: Tradition and Modernity, 1800–2000*. London: Routledge.

Fjeld, Heidi, and Theresia Hofer. 2010–11. "Women and Gender in Tibetan Medicine." *Asian Medicine: Tradition and Modernity* 6 (2): 175–216.

Gerke, Barbara. 2017. "Tibetan Precious Pills as Therapeutics and Rejuvenating Longevity Tonics." *History of Science in South Asia* 5 (2): 204–33.

Goldstein, Melvyn, and Cynthia Beall. 1984. *The Nomads of Western Tibet: Survival of a Way of Life*. Oxford: Oxford University Press.

Goodall, Sarah. 2004. "Rural to Urban Migration and Urbanization in Leh, Ladakh: A Case Study of Three Nomadic Pastoral Communities." *Mountain Research and Development* 24 (3): 218–25.

Harriss-White, Barbara. 2003. "On Understanding Markets as Social and Political Institutions in Developing Economies." In *Rethinking Development Economics*, edited by Ha-Joon Chang, 481–98. London: Anthem.

Harriss-White, Barbara. 2005. "India's Socially Regulated Economy." Queen Elizabeth House Working Paper Series No. 133. Oxford: Queen Elizabeth House.

Hofer, Theresia. 2008a. "Socio-Economic Dimensions of Tibetan Medicine in the Tibet Autonomous Region, China: Part 1." *Asian Medicine: Tradition and Modernity* 4 (1): 174–200.

Hofer, Theresia. 2008b. "Socio-Economic Dimensions of Tibetan Medicine in the Tibet Autonomous Region, China: Part 2." *Asian Medicine: Tradition and Modernity* 4 (2): 492–514.

Hofer, Theresia. 2012. *The Inheritance of Change: Transmission and Practice of Tibetan Medicine in Ngamring*. Vienna: Wiener Studien zur Tibetologie und Buddhismuskunde.

Hofer, Theresia. 2018. *Medicine and Memory in Tibet:* Amchi *Physicians in an Age of Reform*. Seattle: University of Washington Press.

Janes, Craig R. 1995. "The Transformations of Tibetan Medicine." *Medical Anthropology Quarterly* 9:6–39.

Janes, Craig R. 1999. "The Health Transition, Global Modernity and the Crisis of Traditional Medicine: The Tibetan Case." *Social Science and Medicine* 48 (12): 1803–20.

Janes, Craig R. 2001. "Tibetan Medicine at the Crossroads: Radical Modernity and the Social Organization of Traditional Medicine in the Tibet Autonomous Region, China." In *Healing Powers and Modernity: Traditional Medicine, Shamanism, and Science in Asian Societies*, edited by Linda H. Connor and Geoffrey Samuel, 197–221. Westport, CT: Bergin and Garvey.

Janes, Craig R. 2002. "Buddhism, Science, and Market: The Globalization of Tibetan Medicine." *Anthropology and Medicine* 9 (3): 267–89.

Kloos, Stephan. 2004. *Tibetan Medicine amongst the Buddhist Dards of Ladakh*. Vienna: Wiener Studien zur Tibetologie und Buddhismuskunde.

Kloos, Stephan. 2012. "Die Alchemie exil-tibetischer Identität: Anmerkungen zur pharmazeutischen und politischen Wirksamkeit tibetischer Pillen." *Curare* 35 (3): 197–207.

Kuhn, Alice S. 1994. "Ladakh: A Pluralistic Medical System under Acculturation and Domination." In *Acculturation and Domination in Traditional Asian Medical Systems*, edited by Dorothea Sich and Waltraud Gottschalk, 61–73. Stuttgart: F. Steiner.

Last, Murray. 1986. "Introduction: The Professionalisation of African Medicine; Ambiguities and Definitions." In *The Professionalisation of African Medicine*, edited by Murray Last and Gordon L. Chavunduka, 1–28. Manchester: Manchester University Press.

Leslie, Charles. 1976. "Ambiguities of Revivalism in Modern India." In *Asian Medical Systems: A Comparative Study*, edited by Charles Leslie, 356–67. Berkeley: University of California Press.

Leslie, Charles. 1992. "Interpretations of Illness: Syncretism in Modern Ayurveda." In *Paths to Asian Medical Knowledge*, edited by Charles Leslie and Allan Young, 177–208. Berkeley: University of California Press.

McDowell, Chris, and Arjan de Haan. 1997. *Migration and Sustainable Livelihoods: A Critical Review of the Literature*. Working Paper 65. Brighton: Institute of Development Studies.

Meyer, Fernand. (1988) 2007. *La médecine tibétaine: Gso-ba Rig-pa*. Paris: Éditions du CNRS.

Miller, Daniel. 2000. "Tough Times for Tibetan Nomads in Western China: Snowstorms, Settling Down, Fences and the Demise of Traditional Nomadic Pastoralism." *Nomadic Peoples* 4 (1): 83–109.

Mills, Martin. 1998. "Belief and the Priest: Religious Reform and Ethical Self-Determination in Buddhist Ladakh." *Scottish Journal of Religious Studies* 19 (2): 167–85.

Nichter, Mark, and Margaret Lock, eds. 2002. *New Horizons in Medical Anthropology*. New York: Routledge.

Pirie, Fernanda. 2007. *Peace and Conflict in Ladakh: The Construction of a Fragile Web of Order*. Leiden: Brill.

Pordié, Laurent. 2000. "Tibetan Medicine: The Dynamic of a Biocultural Object in a Context of Social Change; A Case Study from Ladakh." Paper presented at the International Academic Conference on Tibetan Medicine, Tibetan Medical College, Lhasa, July 16.

Pordié, Laurent. 2002. "La pharmacopée comme expression de société; Une étude himalayenne." In *Des sources du savoir aux médicaments du futur*, edited by Jacques Fleurentin, Jean-Michel Pelt, and Guy Mazars, 183–94. Paris: Éditions IRD–SFE.

Pordié, Laurent. 2007. "Buddhism in the Everyday Medical Practice of the Amchi." *Indian Anthropologist* 37 (1): 93–116.

Pordié, Laurent, ed. 2008. *Tibetan Medicine in the Contemporary World: Global Politics of Medical Knowledge and Practice*. Abingdon: Routledge.

Pordié, Laurent, and Calum Blaikie. 2014. "Knowledge and Skills in Motion: Layers of Tibetan Medical Education in India." *Culture, Medicine and Psychiatry* 38 (3): 340–68.

Prost, Audrey. 2008. *Precious Pills: Medicine and Social Change among Tibetan Refugees in India*. Oxford: Berghahn.

Rankin, Katherine N. 2004. *The Cultural Politics of Markets: Economic Liberalisation and Social Change in Nepal*. London: Pluto.

Rao, Aparna, and Michael J. Casimir, eds. 2003. *Nomadism in South Asia*. New Delhi: Oxford University Press.

Rizvi, Janet. 1996. *Ladakh: Crossroads of High Asia*. Oxford: Oxford University Press.

Rizvi, Janet. 1999. *Trans-Himalayan Caravans: Merchant Princes and Peasant Traders in Ladakh*. Oxford: Oxford University Press.

Samuel, Geoffrey. 2001. "Tibetan Medicine in Contemporary India: Theory and Practice." In *Healing Powers and Modernity: Traditional Medicine, Shamanism, and Science in Asian Societies*, edited by Linda H. Connor and Geoffrey Samuel, 247–68. Westport, CT: Bergin and Garvey.

Saxer, Martin. 2013. *Manufacturing Tibetan Medicine: The Creation of an Industry and the Moral Economy of Tibetanness.* Oxford: Berghahn Books.

Scoones, Ian. 1998. *Sustainable Rural Livelihoods: A Framework for Analysis.* Working Paper 72. Brighton: Institute of Development Studies.

Sujatha, V., and Leena Abraham, eds. 2012. *Medical Pluralism in Contemporary India.* New Delhi: Orient Blackswan.

Uyanga, Joseph. 1983. "Rural-Urban Migration and Sickness/Health Care Behaviour: A Study of Eastern Nigeria." *Social Science and Medicine* 17 (9): 579–82.

Vira, S. 1993. *The Gujjars of Uttar Pradesh: Neglected Victims of "Progress."* Drylands Network Programme Pamphlet 41. London: International Institute for Environment and Development.

White, Jenny B. 1992. *Money Makes Us Relatives.* Austin: University of Texas Press.

Wolf, Diane L. 1992. *Factory Daughters: Gender, Household Dynamics, and Rural Industrialization in Java.* Berkeley: University of California Press.

World Bank. 2021. "GDP per Capita—India." Accessed March 17, 2021. https://data.worldbank.org/indicator/NY.GDP.PCAP.CN?locations=IN.

4. THE MONETIZATION OF TIBETAN MEDICINE

An Ethnography of Village-Based Development Activities in Lingshed

FLORIAN BESCH AND ISABELLE GUÉRIN

This chapter examines a development project implemented at the turn of the millennium in the remote Ladakhi village of Lingshed that aimed to revitalize Tibetan medicine and health care in the region. The project was solicited by the villagers and amchi themselves, who had already started to strengthen their medicine by establishing an amchi organization and a medical center. Unable to implement these projects on their own, they asked the international non-governmental organization (NGO) Nomad RSI to support them logistically and financially. The project eventually aimed to create a new health-care system that included a community fund to support the village amchi. As we show, this was a complete novelty that nevertheless needed to be incorporated within older values and norms regarding medical care and reciprocity.

In line with its experimental approach of accompanying and informing its applied interventions with nonapplied ethnographic research (Pordié 2001, 2005), Nomad RSI asked one of this chapter's authors, Florian Besch, to conduct a critical anthropological study of the project and its progress in real time. This allowed us as authors to analyze "the 'battlefields' of knowledge and power" (Arce and Long 2000, 8) that offered insights into the modes of cooperation and conflict among the actors involved (Gardner and Lewis 1996; Mosse 2001), which proved instrumental to the eventual success of the project. What initially began as a development failure was repeatedly reflected on; through the exchange of ideas and understandings within Nomad RSI and between the NGO and the villagers, this led to more satisfactory outcomes in the end. Throughout this process, the ethnographic observations and analysis presented in this chapter played an important role as a crucial resource for understanding both the social dynamics of Lingshed and Nomad RSI's place in them.

The formation of a new health-care system involved local processes of professionalization; we examine in particular the formalized and standardized introduction of money and its consequences.[1] How could money act as an agent of change as well as an agent of resistance? Monetary practices—a term we prefer to "money"—worked as prisms through which to observe the misunderstandings and the frictions raised by the project.[2] The analysis of monetary practices also sheds light on social interactions: investigating the way people do or do not use money reveals the nature of the village as a field—or microcosm—of social relations (Gallo 2015; Herzfeld 2015). Far from being a single functional instrument, as is widely assumed, money "talks" (Parry and Bloch 1989). Social relations, whether based on power or solidarity, hierarchy or equality, shape monetary practices as much as they are shaped by the use of the monetary instrument. In other words, the analysis of monetary practices is a good way to understand the continuously evolving articulation between the collective and the individual, and the village as a place of mediation between the universal and the particular (Shneiderman 2015).

This perspective calls for a consideration of money in all its complexity. John Commons ([1934] 1989) and Karl Polanyi (1968) were the first to suggest that money should be considered a social institution, that is, a range of regulations, norms, and conventions that shape personal practices while themselves being shaped by these very practices. Historically, the circulation of a large variety of monies was instrumental in the reproduction of social structures. "Single-purpose monies," whose applications were limited to specific social groups and specific exchanges, were explicitly used to reproduce power and relations of hierarchy or dependence, for instance, between master and servant, male and female, elder and younger, or indigenous and foreign. The monetization and homogenization of money—which took place during the seventeenth and eighteenth centuries in Western countries—aimed precisely to dissolve such personal ties. By allowing accountability and payment, the introduction of a general equivalent was supposed to free people from relations of dependence and subordination. Following the pioneering work of Commons and Polanyi, a number of empirical studies have shown to what extent the so-called intrinsic power of money is more ideological than effective. That money is an instrument of individual freedom cannot be denied—as we see in this chapter, the monetization of amchi services helped to reduce some relations of dependence. However, such a process is necessarily gradual, and money is only one part of this process. This chapter documents this by exploring the monetization and professionalization of rural Tibetan medical practice in the context of a community-based development project.

However, the development project examined here did not introduce money as such into the local society. The main objective was the financial participation of the villagers in the provision of amchi services, in order to ensure the sustainability of the care system. While money had already been partially used to compensate the amchi for their services, the project led to a reorganization, formalization, and standardization of this monetization. The resistance this process faced and the compromises it necessitated highlight the nature of the new relations between the amchi and their patients. The constant interplay among the villagers themselves and among all actors involved is analyzed as a part of the constitution of a new health-care system in the isolated village of Lingshed.

A Remote Village in a World of Donors: Development Projects as a New Market?

The changes that took place in the 1990s and 2000s in the Himalayan region of Ladakh were consequences of and reactions to increased social and economic interactions with metropolitan India and the world. The modernization of the region resulted primarily from the presence of the Indian Army, the establishment of a tourism industry, and the structural and political interventions of the central Indian government and the Jammu and Kashmir state government since the 1960s. Its carriers and visible expressions were and remain road construction, new technologies, and the increasing monetization of social relations. The matrix of social change has been explored especially in regard to politics and identity (van Beek 1999, 2000) and the ways it has influenced the practice of the amchi, the local practitioners of Tibetan medicine (Pordié 2000, 2002).

The Trans Singe-la area of Ladakh is located in a high desert landscape between the Zangskar valley to the west and the Indus valley to the east. The village of Lingshed lies at the center of this area, at approximately four thousand meters above sea level. It is the largest village in the area, with a population of approximately six hundred people in 2001. At that time, Lingshed was one of the remotest villages in Ladakh both geographically and in terms of its infrastructure. During the summer of 2001, the time of this research, the regional capital, Leh, was reachable only by a two-to-four-day trek followed by a ten-hour bus journey. The trek crossed a number of high passes, including the 5,160-meter Singe-la, which is usually blocked by snow from October to May. During this period, the only way to reach Leh is via the frozen Zangskar River, an extremely hazardous journey that is not always possible. This resulted in

Lingshed being almost entirely cut off from the outside world for six months of the year.

Despite this isolated location, Lingshed received up to twenty tourists per day during July and August by virtue of its location on one of the most frequented tourist trekking routes in Ladakh. The villagers were thus used to foreigners, and a fair number had some degree of interaction with them. Some, particularly the monks, tried to get individual sponsorships (*sbyin bdag*) from the tourists, benefiting from an idealized representation of Tibetan Buddhism in the West (Lopez 1998; Schell 2000). An increasing number of men from Lingshed became involved in the tourism industry during the summer months, mainly working as cooks, helpers, and "pony-men." Besides this, government jobs in the school or in the medical aid center offered new opportunities for educated villagers to gain income. Nevertheless, the fundamental basis of livelihoods in Lingshed remained subsistence agriculture, livestock rearing, and traditional crafts.

By the turn of the millennium, the cash economy had entered the village, and monetary payments for goods increasingly took the place of earlier forms of exchange. However, monetization and market exchange did not fully displace the underlying social relations but were rather embedded in existing social, cultural, and political institutions. For instance, on many occasions throughout the year, the Lingshedpa shared work of common importance by uniformly contributing the same amount of time or number of donkeys. For the construction of a public building, each family would send someone for the work, and, if needed, each household would offer one or two donkeys to carry loads. At the same time, new opportunities in terms of access to power, mainly through education and social capital, as well as new individual aspirations inspired by modern consumption and individual leisure, continually modified the balance of power relationships. There was an ongoing hybridization in which traditional ways of socialization evolved and were transformed by incorporating outside elements.

The social organization of Lingshed mirrored its geographic structure, with the monastery, or *gompa* (*dgon pa*), at the top and the village spreading out in the valley below. The monastic representatives had significant influence and power over the villagers' daily life. Decisions of common relevance were based on the recommendations of the monastery, despite the existence of males-only village meetings that also had decision-making power. The most influential Lingshedpa was Geshe Ngawang Jangchup, at the top of the religious, political, and social hierarchy, even though he did not have an official position in either the monastery or political life. Not only was he recognized as a Geshe (*dge bshes*: a high scholarly degree in Tibetan Buddhism), but he also had the ability to act as a "development broker" (Olivier de Sardan 1995). Thus, he acted as the key intermediary between the local population and the world of development funding, frequently traveling to Europe and the United States to give teachings, raise awareness of Buddhism, and gain support for his various projects. Based on his travels and contacts with Westerners, the Geshe had instigated most of the development activities and donor engagements in Lingshed, so much so that the village received considerable foreign help and financial assistance. He usually visited Lingshed for a few months each year, while his personal secretary managed his affairs in the village the rest of the year. The Geshe was considered Lingshed's "brain" owing to his superior knowledge and experience, and the villagers held his opinions in high regard.

Each year from the mid-1990s until 2001, Geshe Ngawang Jangchup organized a "General Seminar" that, although supposedly for the villagers, was regularly attended by a caravan of Western visitors and donors. In July 2001 nine private voluntary organizations (PVOs) consisting of about fifty foreigners in total were present, as were a fair number of tourists who were there by chance.[3] The Geshe gave Buddhist teachings to the Lingshedpa and to a lesser extent to the visitors and took the opportunity to secure the commitment of the assembled Westerners for the development of the village. The various PVOs and their projects and engagements were introduced to the Lingshedpa, while at the same time pleasing the foreign donors by thanking and honoring them warmly. Despite (or because of) its remoteness, Lingshed was supported by a total of fifteen nongovernmental and private organizations. Their projects displayed a wide variety of approaches. However, the majority of them reflected a donation-focused approach limited to Lingshed, with little or no coordination among their activities. Rather, the PVOs appeared to be in competition for a variety of reasons, which overall showed scant regard for the actual long-term future of the village.

While the situation was thus marked by redundancy, competitiveness, and inconsistency, it also resulted in much better medical and educational facilities than those available in the surrounding villages. Villagers thus came to regard the solutions to the problems of underdevelopment and life in a remote area as solvable through foreign financial support.[4] The involvement of the villagers in all projects remained central, however, and those (rare) organizations that sought genuine local participation had to be present in Lingshed for more than a few weeks per year in order to operate. Most important, they had to accept the high likelihood that the direction, form, and functioning of their project would end up differing significantly from initial plans or expectations.

Tibetan Medicine in Lingshed at the Turn of the Century

The initiative to improve traditional medicine in Lingshed came from both the amchi and the Geshe. It arose mainly as a consequence of a dramatic health-related event in the past and the dissatisfaction with the current state of amchi medicine. To understand the latter, we must examine the reciprocal system that previously ensured the amchi's livelihood. Before the appearance of biomedicine and its institutions, especially the medical aid center in Lingshed, people depended entirely on the amchi for health services. The amchi's responsibilities included obtaining medical training, collecting medicinal raw materials, making medicine, and visiting patients, which together consumed a significant amount of time.[5] Like other households, the amchi also had to secure their families' livelihood through livestock rearing and farming. While the amchi treated patients anytime it was necessary, in return villagers worked in the amchi's fields according to the requirements of the season (sowing, harvesting, threshing).[6] In addition, the amchi were freed from certain community tasks, and patients would sometimes reward them individually with gifts in kind, either immediately after the treatment or following successful healing (Pordié 2002). In this context, patients sometimes also gave small amounts of money, which, however, did not amount to an institutionalized form of remuneration. Neither the nature nor the value of the gift was fixed but depended on individual motivation. In other words, the amchi medical system used to be based on an *extended* reciprocal system, based on a set of rights and obligations that involved the whole community and included not only objects and services but also honor, prestige, humiliation, shame, and even disgrace (Mauss [1950] 1993).[7] To be indebted—or to receive (talking about debt or about gifts is largely a question of semantics)—is to manifest and express one's identity. However, the creditor, or donor, can turn against the debtor; they can at any time decide to "strangle" the borrower, who thus becomes irrevocably obliged to them. In this way, the most hierarchical relations can emerge: while the dominant party gives, the subordinate receives, their inferiority arising mainly from the inability to reciprocate. In other words, a gift can also be a "poison" (Mauss [1950] 1993), and a debt relationship may at once be a "bond of life" and a "deadly embrace" (Malamoud 1988). In the context of Tibetan medicine in Lingshed, this ambivalence became increasingly visible with the gradual erosion of the rights and obligations on which the reciprocal system relied.[8]

Any reciprocal system relies on a precarious equilibrium: at any moment, one of the two partners in the exchange may feel unfavorably treated. Like in Hanu (see Kloos, this volume), in Lingshed the amchi was seen by the villagers to have the opportunity to give them fewer or poorer-quality medicines. Patients' calculations of remuneration for the amchi thus always involved considerations about the potential future need for treatment. To an important extent, the amchi's social power—over and above their high social status—derived from such medical dependency. Besides this, of course, patients also felt moral obligations toward the amchi, especially after exceptional services rendered by the amchi, such as coming to the patient's house in winter, at night, or over a long distance; paying multiple visits; or supplying rare and expensive medicines. As our case shows (and also those by Kloos and Blaikie in this volume), any perceived imbalance in this equilibrium can quickly lead to social tensions and potentially the disruption of local health-care delivery.

The relationship between amchi and villagers underwent significant transformations a few decades ago when biomedicine was introduced into Lingshed in the form of a medical aid center. Offering a new opportunity to meet medical needs, the center marked the beginning of the end of the amchi's monopoly on local health care. Together with a generally rising level of individualism, it contributed to weakening the former reciprocal system, increasing the amchi's time constraints as the villagers reduced the amount of help they gave in the amchi's fields. Time that had previously been spent on the different aspects of medical work was now spent on agriculture and livestock. More than other villagers, the amchi felt the need to gain cash income, not only to be able to offer their children a school education, for example, but also to purchase the raw materials required for their drugs.[9] This economically difficult situation resulted in a decrease in the quantity of prepared medicines and a perceived decrease in their quality, as well as, according to the amchi, a stagnation of their knowledge.

This unsatisfactory situation had an important antecedent some sixty years ago—still very prominent in the memories of the villagers—when a smallpox epidemic seriously decimated Lingshed's population. Apparently the village amchi had tried hard but without success to deal with the epidemic, until he also died. This was the particular reason given by two of the three amchi active in Lingshed for why they had decided to learn Tibetan medicine.[10] Both of them, Sonam Dorje and Ngawang Tondup, had studied with different practitioners in the nearby Singe-la and Zangskar areas for several years; they were the only two fully practicing amchi in Lingshed in 2001 who had received complete training.[11] Despite their precarious economic situation, in which they saw their abilities and possibilities to heal gradually decreasing, they provided a large part of the health coverage of the village, especially during the winter months.

First Initiatives

In the early 1990s, the Lingshed amchi had first begun to notice a deterioration of their situation. They felt that they were not always able to treat patients satisfactorily, owing to the absence of medicinal resources and the time constraints that affected their production of medicines. At this time, the professionalization of Tibetan medicine in Leh and the emergence of targeted development projects had been underway for over ten years (Kuhn 1994), with the involvement of the Leh Nutrition Project, an association funded by Save the Children Fund, UK, and a governmental Amchi Research Unit. Geshe Ngawang Jangchup had also witnessed the state of the medical infrastructure in the Tibetan communities in Dharamsala and South India and the foreign support they were benefiting from, leading him and the amchi to consider initiating some form of activities related to amchi medicine in Lingshed.

In 1991 the amchi of the Trans Singe-la area founded the Trans Singe-la Local Doctors' Association (TSLDA), with the stated main objectives to raise community awareness on health, provide health care, and preserve the amchi medical tradition (TSLDA 1996). However, the association, mainly operated by the Geshe and amchi Sonam Dorje, remained structurally and functionally weak.[12] After years of little progress, the TSLDA requested the engagement of the France-based NGO Nomad RSI, which was just starting its work on amchi medicine in Ladakh.[13] The organization first evaluated the situation through months of qualitative research and interactions with the TSLDA and villagers. Its activities started in 1998 with a "drug-banks project" that supplied raw materials for the production of medicines to four (in 1998) or five (in 1999) amchi of the Trans Singe-la area. These drug banks were the first attempts to monetize amchi services: the medicine, instead of being part of the free service provided by the amchi, had to be paid for by the patients. They were expected to pay a certain amount of money (about one Indian rupee per teaspoon of medicines; one US dollar was equivalent to 48 rupees at the time), so that the amchi could replace the stock of raw materials on their own when needed.

The drug-banks project lasted only two years in Lingshed. Although the importance of the patients' financial contribution had been explained to the villagers and amchi and agreed to by them, none of them acted accordingly. The amchi argued that asking for money would be contrary to their ethical codes of practice (Pordié 2002, 190). According to Tibetan medicine's standard treatise, the Gyüshi (the Four Treatises), the amchi is supposed to be devoted to his work and his patients: his role consists in serving others and "treating all alike" (Rechung Rinpoche 1973, 91) with an altruistic mindset (Clark 1995).

These textual ideals strongly correspond to the amchi's personal aspirations, as the qualities most often mentioned in relation to amchi (by themselves and others) are "compassion, respect for living beings, honesty and generosity" (Pordié 2003, 18). More generally, the amchi stated that having a "good heart" (*sems bzang*) and demonstrating spiritual realization and moral perfection were important for any good medical practitioner (Pordié 2003, 18), determining at least partly the efficacy and quality of medicines and care. Although not all amchi showed such behaviors or interests, this ideal continued to influence social practices and especially patients' expectations (Kloos, this volume).[14] In Lingshed an amchi therefore could not charge money without risking being perceived by his own community as having lost his sense of care and devotion and—equally important—as having given up on the mutual social agreement concerning the way amchi medicine was practiced.

The amchi's reluctance to ask for money was combined with a silent agreement by most people in the village, who refused to pay money for medicines. Although the first social studies supported by the Nomad Research Unit had shown the complexity of the previous reciprocal system and its recent changes, the NGO took for granted that any work can be rewarded by money and that monetary exchange is a simple and sufficient guarantee of social balance. Nomad RSI assumed that the drug-banks project would reestablish reciprocity in the amchi-patient relationship. In a context where relationships between amchi and their patients took place within an extended reciprocal system involving the whole community, marked by rights and obligations, the introduction of a new system that directly benefited only the amchi was destined for failure.

Any development project can be considered a "political arena" where specific interests confront each other (Olivier de Sardan 1995). Some individuals try to preserve or reinforce their power, while others attempt to gain it. Everyone acts according to the perceived risks or opportunities that the project presents. When a development project deliberately modifies the nature of a specific sphere of exchange, as in Ladakh, the political dimension is further reinforced. The acceptance of the project by all the parties involved is contingent on a gradual process of redefinition, legitimation, and appropriation. In Lingshed this process had to take into account the new aspirations of the villagers (their capacity to combine different types of medicine, their desire to get out of relations of dependency) and the new aspirations of the amchi (their wish to relegitimate their role as healers, their increasing economic difficulties). This legitimation process also involved the introduction of a new actor, the NGO. At least initially, however, Nomad RSI considered itself as an external actor, focusing its efforts on helping the villagers and the amchi to find a new type of relationship, without fully realizing the extent to which it was a part of the new exchange system that formed around the project.

After the failure of the drug-banks project, Nomad RSI stopped the program because it showed no sustainable future. This worried the amchi because they thought the end of international support would not only directly affect their ability to treat patients in an acceptable way but also threaten their existence as practitioners. Via the Geshe and the TSLDA, the amchi asked Nomad RSI to return and rethink their support of amchi medicine. Seeing no easy or obvious solution other than formally monetizing the practice, as the amchi already had to buy most of their medicines, the NGO thus resumed discussions with the villagers about the concept of self-sufficiency, its reasons and consequences, and its actual financial framework and personal burdens.

Permanent Misunderstanding

In 1999 the amchi built a community health center (later to be named the Lingshed Amchi Health Centre [LAHC]) in their village with some funds from the West channeled through Geshe Ngawang Jangchup. The construction of the LAHC aimed to provide a permanent venue for the amchi's meetings, a place for the production and stocking of medicines, and a medical library. However, as the TSLDA was in no economic position to carry out these activities by itself, it requested Nomad RSI's assistance. Considering the LAHC as a new sign of local participation and commitment, the NGO proceeded to analyze the failure of the drug-banks project, with the aim of developing a new strategy that would involve the entire community in an effort to achieve what they called "local autonomy." In July 2000 Nomad RSI sent a team to Lingshed, led by a Japanese development worker, to evaluate and discuss the possibilities for a new project with the amchi and villagers. Based on their previous experiences, the team insisted on the aim of financial self-sufficiency. In Lingshed the development worker outlined a scheme that was also strongly favored by the Geshe, involving regular financial contributions by the village households to gradually ensure the financial autonomy of the center. Although sent only to carry out an initial evaluation, the NGO's representative introduced this scheme as if it was already sanctioned by the organization. Using fairly advanced economic calculations, his complex plan failed, however, to take into account the local social context of healer-patient relations and did not question what autonomy might actually mean for the villagers. By mostly consulting the men gathered in village meetings, the project also neglected input from the wider community, as a way to understand better the decision-making of men and women. Consequently, this plan could not be followed by the villagers nor the amchi and led to a loss of confidence about the future engagement of Nomad RSI. The amchi remarked later that the development worker spoke about the NGO lowering and stopping its financial support at an unspecified point in the future. It was not made clear to them why the organization wanted to reduce its financial input. They had the impression that Nomad RSI wanted to leave the village in the near future, and their faith in the NGO was further eroded.

In fact, Nomad RSI considered the community's financial participation as central to its plans. The NGO conducted a major meeting in Leh in November 2000, including one French and several Ladakhi representatives of the NGO and at least one representative from almost every household in Lingshed.[15] The project was discussed again at length, and the villagers agreed on a particular concept, which was proposed as a new health system for Lingshed. The LAHC would employ two amchi on a full-time basis, and they would earn 850 rupees per month. They would receive sufficient raw material for medicines and use their free time to study the medical texts, discuss clinical cases, and exchange knowledge. Each household of the village would pay a yearly contribution, for which they would get free access to all services and medicines at the center. Contrary to the previous drug-banks project, in which the medicine had to be paid for, the new system relied on a mutualization principle similar to the old reciprocal system still partially in place in Lingshed. Accordingly, the contribution was fixed as a uniform amount for all, regardless of status or health needs. The villagers committed to the amount of 100 rupees per family per year (Nomad RSI 2000).[16] The only exception was for the poorest, who were exempted from payment as a sign of village solidarity. The collected money would be laid down in a community health fund, which would be available to fulfill medicinal raw material requirements in the future.[17] Because of the community's financial commitment, the NGO considered the agreement on this system as a key step toward financial autonomy.

Nomad RSI planned to pay the major part of the project costs during the initial period and then gradually reduce its share and enlarge the community's share.[18] However, the formalization of the community's financial involvement in health care was a radical innovation in the context of Ladakh, leaving the Lingshed amchi and the villagers insecure. They did not immediately adopt the new system, either because its concepts were still unclear or simply because they were not convinced of its relevance. The villagers could be persuaded only by tangible facts. Words and promises—even their own promise to contribute—were not enough for them to assume ownership of the new project. The threat of the NGO's withdrawal likely also played a role in raising their suspicions. Whatever the reason, the NGO's numerous discussions and meetings did not succeed in putting the villagers at ease about the proposed project, and they returned with great uncertainty to their village for the winter season.

What Do We Pay For?

The remaining operational and functional decisions concerning the LAHC project were scheduled to be finalized during a week of discussions in July 2001 between two Nomad RSI members (the Ladakhi team leader and a British counterpart), the two Lingshed amchi, and a monastic representative of the TSLDA in Lingshed. It became clear to the NGO team at the first meeting, however, that the program could not be implemented as planned and discussed with the community in November. Instead, careful steps first had to be taken to regain the locals' confidence. The NGO had brought along medicinal raw materials and made these available for immediate use. When they further provided contracts for full-time employment for the two amchi working in the LAHC and explained their definite support for the center, the insecurities among the amchi were largely dispelled. Beyond mere offers and promises, the materiality of commodities and a contractual financial commitment pushed away fears and reassured the local people of the potential success of the program. Also, the project had reached a tangible stage—donations and contracts "lay on the table"—which is generally seen as a turning point in development worker–target population interactions in Ladakh (Pirie 2002).

The monastic representative of the TSLDA, Lama Samdrup, held a key role in the whole concept of the LAHC. Given his position as the right-hand man of Geshe Ngawang Jangchup, he became responsible for the center's finances, accountancy, administrative support, and monitoring. His first job was to collect the yearly community contribution, which was to be carried out mainly during the 2001 General Seminar, as most of the village was expected to be present. At the General Seminar, the two NGO workers formally launched the new amchi health system, with the Geshe explicitly asking for the villagers' participation. Within two days, Lama Samdrup received sixty-five contributions of 100 rupees from the villagers, which was perceived by all actors involved in the project as evidence of the success of the campaign and a sign of approval by the Lingshedpa. It seemed to confirm the agreement by all the men of the village the year before.

In reality, our interview data revealed that many of the villagers did not actually know what they were doing. Almost half of the informants pointed out that they did not know what the contribution was for, and of these, 75 percent were women. The ignorance among the women was striking, and it can be concluded that they had not been sufficiently involved in the design and implementation of the project. By not considering gender issues, a common failure of development projects was repeated here (Cracknell 2000; Gardner and Lewis 1996). Because a request from the Geshe counted as an order in Lingshed, almost every household paid the first yearly contribution to the community health fund immediately. The majority of villagers stated that they paid the contribution because the Geshe had requested it or because the whole village seemed to have agreed on it. But the relation between the health center and the contribution was not clear to all, and, more important, these people did not even know that they had paid for free access to all amchi services for a year.

In the course of project implementation in Lingshed, Nomad RSI put a special emphasis on Geshe Ngawang Jangchup, first, because of his social status and power in the village and, second, because it was seen as very difficult to proceed otherwise. The NGO made use of the Geshe's influence on the population, thereby reproducing the existing relations of power. However, this reliance on local hierarchical communication lines meant that the community was not successfully reached as a whole, nor was the local participation required for the project established. The Lingshedpa supported the new health system not because they understood or approved of its principal idea but simply because they respected the Geshe's request. The concept of self-sufficiency and the corresponding new health system had still not become part of the villagers' understanding. Moreover, a series of events during the establishment of the LAHC had created further problems in the local perception of the NGO's intentions, at least for a time.

The Amchi-Policeman

Just before the two village amchi were supposed to sign their contracts for the LAHC, it came to the attention of the Nomad RSI team that amchi Ngawang Tondup had already worked for a month as an apprentice home guard in the village and planned to join the Indian Police Force after his training was completed.[19] They felt the two positions (amchi and home guard) to be mutually exclusive and were disappointed because the amchi had not told them about his employment (Nomad RSI 2001). The NGO team had taken it for granted that he only had his farming occupation in addition to his role as an amchi, and this revelation appeared to undermine any constructive work because the basis of cooperation was not clear. Without asking why the amchi had accepted the police job, they gave him a stark choice: to decide within one day between his job with the police and the amchi position at the LAHC. In turn, the amchi gave very little explanation of his actions and did not really try to justify himself, although his motive was rather simple: his livelihood was at stake. While the NGO job did not offer him any long-term security, the police job was likely to become a government job with a lifelong salary. The amchi restrained himself from going further into an open argument, following the Ladakhi social norm of avoiding conflict (Pirie 2001), and left the LAHC job the next day. The Nomad RSI team, Lama Samdrup, and amchi Sonam Dorje noted the decision with great disappointment and regret. They were aware that it would be difficult for a single amchi to fulfill the needs of the whole community and to ensure permanent services. However, failing to find an alternative solution, they signed the contracts assigning Sonam Dorje as the only amchi in the LAHC.

After the Nomad RSI team had left, community interactions and some pressure on amchi Ngawang Tondup came into play in Lingshed. People who became aware of the incident began calling for him to be reinstated at the LAHC. Neither his nor the NGO's decision made sense to the people, and the outcome was not considered to be satisfactory. Even the police officers shared this opinion, although they were not Lingshedpa. The members of the LAHC were also convinced that having both amchi serve in the center would be the best solution and that the meeting with the NGO had involved some kind of miscommunication. As for amchi Ngawang Tondup, he himself was extremely unhappy with the situation and wanted to straighten it out as quickly as possible. Ngawang Tondup thus wrote a letter to Nomad RSI in Leh, in which he expressed his regret about the situation. The NGO quickly sent another team back to the village in September, two months after the first team had returned to Leh, to find a solution with the two amchi and the lama. Since the winter was close, a quick decision had to be made to avoid its postponement until the next spring, six to eight months later; based on a shared wish to reach a positive outcome, a common agreement was easily found. As it became clear that the police job demanded little in terms of working hours and was therefore fully compatible with the amchi's commitments to the LAHC, the solution was simple: in case of necessity, the two amchi would keep the LAHC open by mutually backing up one another's absences. Immediately after all the details were cleared up, amchi Ngawang Tondup was reintegrated into the program.

The Flavor of Success

After this incident and its resolution, the amchi themselves seemed to have a clearer appreciation of the NGO's aims and position. A major conflict and its subsequent resolution had generated a better reciprocal understanding (see Arce and Long 2000; Novellino 2003). The amchi now deployed their energies in explaining the new health system to each patient, thus making the whole community feel involved. They took a firmer and more determined view of the project and became fully dedicated to its success. In this way, individual contacts and meetings served to spread the news about the project to an extent that the NGO had not been able to achieve before. Based on the events surrounding amchi Ngawang Tondup, the new efforts of the amchi cemented the relation of the entire community to the LAHC and facilitated the first steps in the collective reappropriation of the project. Two months after the launch of the LAHC, most people knew that both amchi were now posted in the health center. The villagers were also aware that their contribution entitled them to free medical treatment from the center for a full year. Furthermore, the villagers stated that the money requested was not a large amount and was easily affordable for most households, contradicting assumptions about Lingshed's limited economic environment (see Lee 2001). This change in the perception of the LAHC can be traced back to the engagement of the amchi and to the rising number of patients coming to the LAHC. The actual benefit became apparent to the visitors, who in turn spread the word among their relatives and neighbors.

The villagers viewed the availability of amchi services and treatment through the LAHC as a great benefit. The knowledge that medicine for (hypothetically) any disease could be produced offered a new sense of security, for both the villagers and the amchi. The first and second annual evaluations by the Ladakh Society for Traditional Medicines (LSTM) showed that the two amchi had a total of six hundred patients during the first year (2001) and nearly eight hundred the following year.[20] These are high figures considering the total number of villagers, which suggests that the center was increasingly accepted. The LAHC had a total of 97 (2002) and 107 (2003) different kinds of medicines, of which about 90 had been manufactured by the amchi at the LAHC (Chodon 2002; Choszang 2003). According to the amchi, the variety and the quantity of medicines was a great improvement compared to their previous situation. They had a full supply of medicinal raw materials, giving them the ability to devote unprecedented time and energy to their profession. The frustration of not being able to cure patients owing to a lack of raw materials was now a thing of the past. The center gave the amchi more confidence, and through this they appeared to have reached a better level of understanding with the foreign organization. As far as the villagers were concerned, this amchi medicine development project had a direct and beneficial outcome, which they had not perceived before. The villagers' financial engagement in the form of the community health fund showed immediate results, which made them willing to pay the contribution in subsequent years. In 2003 the contribution was raised to 150 rupees, following a decision made by the villagers themselves (Choszang 2003). They said that the center was clearly benefiting the village as a whole and that they were opposed to the previous drug-banks project because it benefited only the amchi. During that project the NGO support was interpreted by the community as individual help rather than collective assistance. As soon as the LAHC project was regarded as supporting the community, it was perceived as a collective issue, and the ethical and social issues that had undermined the drug-banks project disappeared. After the miscommunication and difficulties in the early stages of the project, a form of mutual understanding was eventually reached.

A New Health-Care System

Let us now consider the impacts of the project itself by first recalling the initial situation that led to its emergence. The medical legitimacy of the amchi had been degraded to a large extent by the erosion of the reciprocal system on which the remuneration of amchi services was based. The project's ability to solve this problem was fundamental to its success. To start with, the amchi pointed out one main advantage of the center: the increased capacity to follow up on the cases of particular patients, thanks to the "patient record book":[21]

> In the Trans Singe-la area there are five, six villages . . . and in searching the patient books the amchi can extract what kind of disease is more common in a particular region. Then he can think about why this disease is more common than the other diseases. . . . Is it because the food is not so nutritious? Or is this place especially cold? Then, what types of precautions should we take? . . . According to this, the amchi can advise the patients in explaining that the region is very cold, and so he gives advice: "You should not eat uncooked food early in the morning. Do not eat in a hurry, and protect your body from the wind, you have to wear warm clothes." . . . Or the amchi can find unusual diseases. At that time they can keep control over the patients; they can make people aware that this disease

spreads. He can tell them that they have to prevent, pay attention, and take care. . . . In this way they can provide very good treatment. (Amchi Sonam Dorje)

In former times amchi kept their patients' data in their heads. Through the introduction of the record books, they now saw the benefits of recording these data on paper, leading them to readily adopt the new system and fill out the record books meticulously. The record book was seen as a tool for prevention and gave the amchi some security with regard to epidemics. The sense of insecurity created by the smallpox epidemic was at least partially healed, in that the chances of such a disaster occurring again were seen to be reduced. The amchi also mentioned the benefits offered by the change in the location of their practice and stated that the impact of the shift in workplace on the whole household was significant. As Sonam Dorje described, whereas before they had practiced at home with all the distractions of family life, the LAHC provided them a dedicated workplace. Finally, the amchi also felt a revalorization of their role, expressed in the fact that they now saw their medical practice as a job: "That job means to work under a center and to get a salary. Now . . . I have a job, and I am getting a salary. I am happy . . . to help other people, to help the public, the villagers. Because this job doesn't mean to help an individual person, it means to help the public, to help the villagers . . . I am working for others, that means 'I am an amchi,' I am working for the others through this job" (amchi Sonam Dorje).

The amchi thus found themselves playing a relevant role in modern Ladakh. Their practice entered an official dimension that reflected social demands and contemporary individual aspirations. Yet Sonam Dorje was also a *gyudpa* (lineage) amchi with eight generations behind him, and this was a major element of both his medical and social legitimacy in the village. His new situation, rather than undermining this heritage, seemed to further complete and reinforce his status while participating in Ladakhi modernity. This amchi considered that his job allowed him to perform the amchi's work as it was philosophically and ethically conceptualized, something he had always wanted. The 2003 evaluation by the LSTM reaches the same conclusion: "The [amchi] feel that they are working as real amchi now" (Choszang 2003, n.p.).

The villagers saw the center as a positive development in medical care for a variety of reasons, such as the availability of the amchi at any time, since the medical service was seen as something that was due to them. The introduction of monetary compensation for the amchi service, after many misunderstandings, was finally accepted and even fully appropriated, since it responded to the uncertainties, ambiguities, and risks of unbalanced relations in the former system of reciprocity. As we have seen, the gradual erosion of the former system had confronted the patients with difficult questions regarding how often they should consult the amchi or what to do in case of minor illnesses. The villagers said they used to hesitate to see the amchi or would call him only for very serious cases. The LAHC made the two amchi independent from direct individual donations and in this sense freed not only the amchi but also their patients. The former system, in its eroded form, was actually seen as a burden to both parties. The center gave them confidence and absolved them from hesitation, disappointment, and shame.

After many reevaluations and changes, the new health system offered a way out of the social tensions that had arisen from both the project and the economic difficulties of the amchi. The community fund can be considered a hybrid arrangement, formally *monetizing* the health system without commodifying it as such, which would imply a direct financial exchange between the amchi and the patient. Here there was no price for services or medicines but only a compensation system based on a mutualization principle. The community fund reinforced a form of solidarity that still prevailed in Lingshed. However, the LAHC depersonalized medical practice to some extent by introducing financial compensation and the attendant shift from the private (the amchi household) to the public sphere. This situation therefore contrasts with other issues of depersonalization of care, which are often connected to the use of ready-made medicines (Pordié 2014, 73).

Conclusion: Constructing Projects and Money

The development project examined in this chapter was rooted in the initiative of the amchi, who wanted to improve both their lives and the conditions of their medical practice. As we have seen, the villagers' inputs gave important boosts at different stages of the process, but they were not independent from other actors and power structures. Geshe Ngawang Jangchup, along with state institutions, contributed strongly to the establishment of an ideology of modernization in Lingshed, where local principles and external ideas were combined. The course of the project showed how these elements combined in a local version of a modern health-care system and the professionalization of traditional medicine, neither of which, it is important to add, implied the biomedicalization shown in other contexts (Janes 1995, 1999; Pigg 1995). The final configuration involved a peculiar, adapted version of professionalization characterized by a certain flexibility allowing an amchi to also work as a farmer or as a police officer.

The NGO followed multiple routes, changed direction, and encountered resistance and failure. Solutions came into being not as the result of planned community participation but through mistakes, exchanges, and interactions that together opened new spaces for reorienting the project. Conflicts provided opportunities for the NGO to rethink the project and for the local population to increase their involvement. The project was also subject to conjectural factors (human resources, events of many kinds), which happened to be predominant and fundamental. Although the project activities roughly followed the original plan, there were simultaneous and continuous microdeconstructions and reconstructions. The dynamic of the project surpassed the course planned by the NGO and revealed an unusual trajectory that refuses any theoretical labeling. The organization ended up following the project more than leading it. The project therefore had a number of inconsistencies that can be located between the organization's deep knowledge of the field and the way the project actually faced the local reality. The conversion of such knowledge into practical development activities remained a major challenge.

At the village level, we have witnessed a repeated negotiation and reconfiguration of the individual and collective spheres, which were in a state of flux. The articulation between individuality and community was reflected and consolidated by visible elements (buildings) and the depersonalization of the amchi practice, while the individual case of the amchi-policeman was transformed from a personal to a collective issue. This very issue became, unintentionally, the turning point of the project. The spatial change in the amchi's practice had an instantly visible effect on the healer-patient relationship, therefore making it one of the most important elements of the new health-care system and a significant factor in ensuring its sustainability. The monetization of healer-patient relations, in contrast, had to undergo a longer process of clarification before it was considered socially acceptable. The NGO's initial argument for autonomy was not sufficient, and change was accepted only when a compromise respecting the relations between the amchi and the villagers was reached. This compromise revealed new kinds of exchange relations between the amchi and the villagers, the introduction of money being but one part of this process.

After a prolonged period of crisis and difficult transformations, Tibetan medicine in Lingshed emerged in a structurally stronger position than anywhere else in rural Ladakh. In the end, Lingshed's amchi health center—seen as an instance of "local modernity" (Appadurai 1996)—thus validated the NGO's approach of developing traditional medicines through institutionalization, structural changes, and the integration of modern elements, while refraining from any attempt to integrate them with biomedicine. Since the official recognition of Sowa Rigpa by the government of India in 2010 and the introduction of the National Rural Health Mission program in Ladakh, including a government-funded Sowa Rigpa Center in Lingshed, these foundations—laid during a difficult time of transition—have been further strengthened, and amchi medicine's future today looks brighter than ever.

Notes

1 Although the term "professionalization" is used in several different ways in Asian learned medicines and in the context of state-organized involvement of indigenous healers in Africa and Asia (e.g., Green 1987; Last and Chavunduka 1986; Leslie 1974, 1976), these examinations are closely linked to the concept of Western professions (Last 1996).

2 Money does not exist per se: it exists only in the diverse forms attributed to it by individuals, hence the term "monetary *practices*," which designates the various methods of perception and utilization of the monetary tool (Blanc 2000; Guérin 2002; Guérin and Servet 2003).

3 Some of the PVOs came to Lingshed almost every year, on a very regular basis, many for health-related humanitarian purposes. They supported the government medical aid center with (bio)medicines, vitamins, and goods; set up health camps; and/or worked on health prevention, women's health, and birth control.

4. All aspects of health resources and school education in the village were, or had been, supported by foreign donors or NGOs. This included the school, the village amchi, and some of the medical aid center provisions, as well as the nunnery and the monks' school.

5 While medical training was concentrated in the winter months, the collection of plants, minerals, and so on was carried out only in summer. Time was scarce in summer because sufficient food had to be produced during the short summer season to secure the household for the next winter.

6 One person from each household would work one full day in the amchi's fields.

7 This system was also prevalent in earlier times under different arrangements; Laurent Pordié (2002, 190) notes that "when Ladakh was a kingdom amchi were granted lands as payment. . . . Later on, villages were provided with a 'field of medicines' in which the inhabitants used to work alternately and thus enabled the amchi to spend most of his/her time gathering raw materials, making drugs and visiting patients."

8 The act of donating is a complex process in Tibetan societies that goes beyond the classical works presented here; while these works are relevant to our situation, they do not offer an understanding of donation at large. For a detailed presentation on donation in the case of Tibetan medicine in Ladakh, see Pordié (2008, 160–63).

9 As mentioned earlier, small amounts of money were sometimes given in return for the amchi's service but it was generally so little that it could not be considered as income.

See Pordié (2002) for an analysis of the causes and consequences of the change in supply modalities of medicinal raw materials and their impacts on the amchi's economic situation.

10 Although one of them was a lineage amchi (*gyudpa*), he specified that the epidemic was the main factor in his decision to become an amchi.

11 The third amchi, Tsering Tondup, had worked for ten years as a government-supported amchi and was assigned to the village of Yulchung, a day's walk from Lingshed. Also, a lama-amchi resided at the monastery but had not yet completed his medical education and was therefore only occasionally asked for treatment by the monks.

12 Although the TSLDA theoretically gathered all amchi of the Trans Singe-la area, its human resources were very limited. The two Lingshed amchi largely embodied the opinion of the TSLDA; for the purposes of this case study, we do not distinguish between the TSLDA's and the amchi's opinions.

13 The organization set up its first projects in the late 1990s in close collaboration with existing local structures. Its programs had, over time, become increasingly self-managed, leading to the creation of an independent Indian body. In 2001 it was a fully established Ladakhi NGO, the Ladakh Society for Traditional Medicines (LSTM), although Nomad RSI still provided some funds, technical assistance, and administrative and capacity-building training. Academic fellows and postgraduate students from abroad were regularly taken onboard by Nomad RSI to conduct research on diverse contextual and practical aspects of the programs. We use the name of the international NGO for clarity; also, at the time of the research, the Ladakh program had not yet become fully autonomous. However, because autonomy was reached shortly after the research period, the LSTM's reports and documents are referenced as such.

14 A comparison of young rural and urban amchi who benefited from institutional medical education is quite revealing. Pordié's work shows that, of forty-seven rural amchi interviewed, forty (i.e., 85 percent) "responded foremostly that they entered this path out of compassion." In towns, the amchi first mentioned the "social advantages" (status, recognition, possible employment, etc.) that their education conferred (2003, 44–45).

15 The schedule of the project was spread out over quite a long period, mainly owing to the difficulties of transportation and communication, but also to make sure the villagers were not invited during harvesting periods or other times of intense activity.

16 This financial solution was chosen from among various other ideas discussed earlier with the villagers: exchange of food and materials, an income-generating cooperative for the health center, and so on. All these other plans were subsequently abandoned.

17 Nomad RSI agreed to provide the initial medicines and raw materials for the center. It was calculated that in subsequent years an annual amount of approximately 8,800 rupees would be collected, which would be sufficient to cover the cost of future raw materials (Nomad RSI 2000). This figure was reached based on eighty-eight households each paying 100 rupees—our own research revealed a total of only seventy-five households.

18 Besides the increasing share of the costs to be borne by the community, further income was expected from the Indian government and, to a lesser extent, from tourism.

19 The police was a new institution in the village at that time, and the Indian Police Force had recruited some villagers for training as home guards.

20 By this time the Ladakhi organization LSTM had become independent from Nomad RSI and conducted the evaluations itself (see note 17).

21 The patient record book in this medical system was initially introduced in Ladakh for the government amchi and was extended by Nomad RSI first to the drug-banks project and then to the LAHC.

References

Appadurai, Arjun. 1996. *Modernity at Large: Cultural Dimensions of Globalization.* Minneapolis: University of Minnesota Press.

Arce, Alberto, and Norman Long. 2000. "Reconfiguring Modernity and Development from an Anthropological Perspective." In *Anthropology, Development and Modernities: Exploring Discourses, Counter-tendencies and Violence,* edited by Alberto Arce and Norman Long, 1–31. London: Routledge.

Blanc, Jérôme. 2000. *Les monnaies parallèles: Diversité et unité du fait monétaire.* Paris: L'Harmattan.

Chodon, Karma. 2002. "Lingshed Amchi Health Center (LAHC): Evaluation Results." Unpublished report, Ladakh Society for Traditional Medicines.

Choszang, T. 2003. "Lingshed Amchi Health Center (LAHC): Evaluation Result." Unpublished report, Ladakh Society for Traditional Medicines.

Clark, Barry. 1995. *The Quintessence Tantras of Tibetan Medicine.* Ithaca, NY: Snow Lion.

Commons, John R. (1934) 1989. *Institutional Economics: Its Place in Political Economy.* New Brunswick, NJ: Transaction.

Cracknell, Basil E. 2000. *Evaluating Development Aid: Issues, Problems and Solutions.* New Delhi: Sage.

Demenge, Jonathan P. 2013. "The Road to Lingshed: Manufactured Isolation and Experienced Mobility in Ladakh." *Himalaya* 32 (1): 51–60.

Gallo, Ester. 2015. "Village Ethnography and Kinship Studies: Perspectives from India and Beyond." *Critique of Anthropology* 35 (3): 248–62.

Gardner, Katie, and David Lewis. 1996. *Anthropology, Development and the Post-modern Challenge.* London: Pluto.

Green, Edward C. 1987. "The Integration of Modern and Traditional Health Sectors in Swaziland." In *Anthropological Praxis: Translating Knowledge into Action,* edited by Robert Wulff and Shirley Fiske, 87–97. Boulder, CO: Westview.

Guérin, Isabelle. 2002. "Le sexe de la monnaie." *Le Journal des Anthropologues* 90–91 (December): 88–103.

Guérin, Isabelle, and Jean-Michel Servet. 2003. *Microfinance: From Daily Survival to Social Change.* Pondy Papers in Social Sciences 30. Pondicherry: French Institute of Pondicherry.

Herzfeld, Michael. 2015. "The Village in the World and the World in the Village: Reflections on Ethnographic Epistemology." *Critique of Anthropology* 35 (3): 338–43.

Janes, Craig R. 1995. "The Transformations of Tibetan Medicine." *Medical Anthropology Quarterly* 9 (1): 6–39.

Janes, Craig R. 1999. "The Health Transition, Global Modernity and the Crisis of Traditional Medicine: The Tibetan Case." *Social Science and Medicine* 48 (12): 1803–20.

Kuhn, Alice S. 1994. "Ladakh: A Pluralistic Medical System under Acculturation and Domination." In *Acculturation and Domination in Traditional Asian Medical Systems*, edited by Dorothea Sich and Waltraud Gottschalk, 61–74. Stuttgart: F. Steiner.

Last, Murray. 1996. "The Professionalization of Indigenous Healers." In *Medical Anthropology: Contemporary Theory and Method*, edited by Carolyn F. Sargent and Thomas M. Johnson, 374–95. Westport, CT: Praeger.

Last, Murray, and Gordon L. Chavunduka. 1986. *The Professionalisation of African Medicine*. Manchester: Manchester University Press.

Lee, Richard V. 2001. "Doing Good Badly." *Ladakh Studies* 16:26–28.

Leslie, Charles. 1974. "The Modernization of Asian Medical Systems." In *Rethinking Modernization: Anthropological Perspectives*, edited by John J. Poggie and Robert N. Lynch, 69–108. Westport, CT: Greenwood.

Leslie, Charles, ed. 1976. *Asian Medical Systems: A Comparative Study*. Berkeley: University of California Press.

Lopez, Donald. 1998. *Prisoners of Shangri-La: Tibetan Buddhism and the West*. Chicago: University of Chicago Press.

Malamoud, Charles. 1988. *Lien de vie, nœud mortel: Les représentations de la dette en Chine, au Japon et dans le monde indien*. Paris: Éditions de l'École des hautes études en sciences sociales.

Mauss, Marcel. (1950) 1993. *Sociologie et anthropologie*. Paris: Presses Universitaires de France.

Mosse, David. 2001. "Social Research in Rural Development Projects." In *Inside Organisations: Anthropologists at Work*, edited by David N. Gellner and Eric Hirsch, 157–82. Oxford: Berg.

Nomad RSI. 2000. "Report of the Meeting about the Medicinal Plant Center with Trans Senge La Villagers." Unpublished report, Nomad RSI, November 7.

Nomad RSI. 2001. "Report of Nomad Visit to Lingshed: Lingshed Amchi Health Center." Unpublished report, Nomad RSI, August 7.

Novellino, Dario. 2003. "From Seduction to Miscommunication: The Confession and Presentation of Local Knowledge in 'Participatory Development.'" In *Negotiating Local Knowledge: Power and Identity in Development*, edited by Johan Pottier, Alan Bicker, and Paul Sillitoe, 273–97. London: Pluto.

Olivier de Sardan, Jean-Pierre. 1995. *Anthropologie et développement: Essai en socio-anthropologie du changement social*. Paris: Karthala; Marseille: APAD.

Parry, Jonathan, and Maurice Bloch. 1989. *Money and the Morality of Exchange*. Cambridge: Cambridge University Press.

Pigg, Stacy L. 1995. "Acronyms and Effacement: Traditional Medical Practitioners (TMP) in International Health Development." *Social Science and Medicine* 41 (1): 47–68.

Pirie, Fernanda. 2001. "The Impermanence of Power: Village Politics in Ladakh, Nepal and Tibet." Paper presented at the 10th Colloquium of the International Association for Ladakh Studies, Mansfield College, Oxford, September 7–10.

Pirie, Fernanda. 2002. "Doing Good Badly or at All?" *Ladakh Studies* 17:29–32.

Polanyi, Karl. 1968. *Primitive, Archaic, and Modern Economies*. Boston: Beacon.

Pordié, Laurent. 2000. "Tibetan Medicine: The Dynamic of a Biocultural Object in a Context of Social Change." In *Anthology of the International Academic Conference on Tibetan Medicine*, 935–36. Beijing: Chinese Medical Association of Minorities.

Pordié, Laurent. 2001. "Research and International Aid: A Possible Meeting." *Ladakh Studies* 15:33–45.

Pordié, Laurent. 2002. "La pharmacopée comme expression de société: Une étude himalayenne." In *Des sources du savoir aux médicaments du future*, edited by Jacques Fleurentin, Jean-Marie Pelt, and Guy Mazars, 183–94. Paris: Éditions IRD–SFE.

Pordié, Laurent. 2003. *The Expression of Religion in Tibetan Medicine: Ideal Concepts, Contemporary Practices and Political Use*. Pondy Papers in Social Sciences 29. Pondicherry: French Institute of Pondicherry.

Pordié, Laurent. 2005. "L'inéluctable rencontre: Traditions de soins et développement sanitaire." In *Panser le monde, penser les médecines: Traditions médicales et développement sanitaire*, edited by Laurent Pordié, 5–29. Paris: Karthala.

Pordié, Laurent. 2008. "Reformulating Ingredients: Outlines of a Contemporary Ritual for the Consecration of Medicines in Ladakh." In *Modern Ladakh: Anthropological Perspectives on Continuity and Change*, edited by Martijn van Beek and Fernanda Pirie, 153–74. Leiden: Brill.

Pordié, Laurent. 2014. "Pervious Drugs: Making the Pharmaceutical Object in Techno-Ayurveda." *Asian Medicine* 9 (1–2): 49–76.

Rechung Rinpoche. 1973. *Tibetan Medicine: Illustrated in Original Texts*. London: Wellcome Institute of the History of Medicine.

Schell, Orville. 2000. *Virtual Tibet: Searching for Shangri-La from the Himalayas to Hollywood*. New York: Henry Holt.

Shneiderman, Sara. 2015. "Regionalism, Mobility, and 'the Village' as a Set of Social Relations: Himalayan Reflections on a South Asian Theme." *Critique of Anthropology* 35 (3): 318–37.

TSLDA (Trans Singe-la Local Doctors' Association). 1996. *Local Doctors' Programme*. Unpublished paper, TSLDA, September.

van Beek, Martijn. 1999. "Hill Councils, Development, and Democracy: Assumptions and Experiences from Ladakh." *Alternatives* 24 (4): 435–59.

van Beek, Martijn. 2000. "Lessons from Ladakh? Local Responses to Globalization and Social Change." In *Globalization and Social Change*, edited by Johannes Dragsbaek Schmidt and Jacques Hersh, 250–66. London: Routledge.

5. THE AMCHI AT THE MARGINS

Notes on Childbirth Practices in Ladakh

LAURENT PORDIÉ AND PASCALE HANCART PETITET

The social study of birth opens up a range of questions on maternity along an axis that runs from private life to the state. The event of birth appears as an experience of the body and the construction of the person and helps to understand maternity in its social, familial, medical, and technological environment. Obstetric practices are therefore embedded in a broad contextual sphere, for which the anthropology of reproduction offers some useful approaches. Reproduction touches on the relationship between nature and culture, production and reproduction, the individual body and body politics, and the examination of how power works and is thus a vibrant category for an anthropological understanding of the world (Ginsburg and Rapp 1995). Traditional birth practices have been studied extensively and are the subject of a vast literature that could be, perhaps schematically, organized into two clusters (McClain 1989). The first explores social organizations, theories of procreation, precautions and prohibitions around pregnancy, and representations of childbirth, the pregnant body, and the supernatural world. This sociocultural take on birth contrasts with the second cluster, issuing from a "biomedical approach" (McClain 1989) that considers traditional childbirth practices as an ultimate form of recourse in a context of unsuitable biomedical health care and inaccessible obstetric services. In this vacuum, traditional birth attendants are often integrated into the framework of development programs and agencies for a variety of trainings inspired by biomedical practices and conceptions surrounding childbirth (Pigg 1997). While families and traditional birth specialists may still have important social and symbolic functions, they have thus been displaced and downgraded by the biomedicalization of birth, coupled with the rise of technology (Casper 1998; Cominsky 2016; Morgan 2009). Birth has become largely, if not exclusively, a biomedical affair where the biological body finds itself embedded within increasing regimes of surveillance (Foucault 1994). This has direct implications for alternative childbirth practices and nonbiomedical conceptions of the body, as shown in Tibet by poststructuralist approaches to the production of knowledge claims and their effects in the world (Adams 2001).

This chapter takes all that into account by considering the role of the practitioner of Tibetan medicine (amchi) in childbirth in two distinct settings of Ladakh, in northwestern India. We examine how birth occurred and how it was managed in the very isolated area of Shun-Shade at the turn of the millennium and contrast this with material from the urban milieu in Leh, the capital city of the region. This comparison allows us to explore the amchi's position on the margins in both territorial/political and medical terms. Shun-Shade is a salient case of a territorial periphery where the practice of Tibetan medicine has been central while biomedical coverage remains poor or nonexistent. The case of Leh stands in stark opposition. This town is the political center of the region, marked by rapid urban and biomedical developments. But it is also a place where, in the early 2000s, the practice of the amchi was increasingly being marginalized. Both cases show the amchi as a peripheral agent on the margins, either territorial (where he was the only medical recourse) or medical (when he was at the heart of the urban/biomedical world), and their comparison can provide important insights into social and therapeutic transformation, medical power, control over bodies, and authority in childbirth.

We pay particular attention to a set of emergency practices among the amchi, including a treatment based on blessed butter (*sngags mar*) fashioned in the form of a fish and prescribed in the case of complicated childbirths. These undocumented practices were present in both of our research contexts, and their analysis helps to unpack the positionality, transformation, and aspiration of Tibetan medical practice in a plural medical society. With the advent of Indian biomedical infrastructures and hegemony, the role of the amchi in childbirth was increasingly limited to exceptional events, especially in the urban milieu. While the biomedical provision of care for pregnancy and childbirth in the maternity hospital in Leh was a valued recourse (Wiley 2002), we will see how the unexpected occurrence of a complication during labor at the hospital redirected the therapeutic trajectory of the patient toward the amchi. Our rural-urban comparison thus illustrates and adds complexity to the concept of "authoritative knowledge" in obstetrics (Jordan 1993). Indeed, the authority of knowledge in our study field is not necessarily the authority of medical power. Finally, by introducing the question of amchi obstetrics into contemporary issues of Tibetan medicine in Ladakh, this chapter is also situated in a more political approach to reproduction.[1]

Giving Birth in Shun-Shade

The region of Ladakh comprises two administrative districts: Leh and Kargil. The Shun-Shade area, to the east of Zangskar and under the administrative control of the Kargil district, is one of the remotest places of the region. The two biomedical health facilities closest to Shun-Shade are located in Ladakh's capital, Leh, reachable in three days (a two-day trek to the nearest road and a one-day bus ride), and in Zangskar's main town, Padum, reachable in four or five days of trekking over inhospitable high-altitude terrain. This makes Shun-Shade a particularly important example of what may be called the "territorial periphery." The zone under study included four Buddhist villages—Sattak, Yarshun, Mashun, and Shade—home to a total of 250 people in 2001.

A widespread perception that we encountered in Shun-Shade was that a child about to be born was the reincarnation of a deceased person. During their pregnancy, several of the women in Sattak speculated about whose reincarnation their unborn child would be.[2] It was not uncommon for parents to be attentive to the words and behavior of their child so as to understand some elements of its past life. Yangchen Lhamo remarked, "When my son was a baby, he was saying that he had four cars and that he must go and get them. . . . He was certainly very rich before." Dawa Drolma later added that she was convinced her daughter was the reincarnation of the deceased grandmother from the house next door: "When she was two, she used to go to the neighboring house screaming, 'I am the grandmother.' She used to take the grandmother's personal objects and bring them back home." People in Shun-Shade thus had clear ideas on what happens before childbirth.

The amchi we spoke with understood the phenomena preceding birth in a very similar—although generally much less elaborate—manner to that found in the classical texts. "When a person dies, there are forty-nine days before she is reincarnated. The consciousness can then choose any womb to take life. If the person made wrong choices in a past life, she will take a dark womb. If the person performed good actions, she will take a nice and pleasant place," said amchi Sonam Thundup.[3] That the consciousness enters the womb because it is directed by the effects of earlier acts and their "stains" underscores the role of karma in reincarnation. Karma conditions the reincarnation as a human being, as well as dictating who the parents will be, for conception also depends on compatibility between the karma of the reincarnating being and that of its future parents. The amchi referred to the explanatory treatise devoted to embryology (*chags tshul*) in their most influential (and often sole) classical book, the Gyüshi (*rgyud bzhi*), and gave less or more detail on the original causes of conception, fetal development, and the signs of childbirth.[4] Their knowledge of embryology largely depended on their knowledge of this canonical text. They identified the three zoomorphic phases, which correspond to the development of the embryo in three phases, linked to the three terms of pregnancy. These phases are known to the amchi as "fish," "tortoise," and "pig," which provides an image of the body of the fetus at different moments of its evolution. The amchi also explained the various aspects of physiological development and the way the body and organs are formed. They used two diagnostic methods to determine the sex of the fetus: the pulse was taken at the beginning of pregnancy, and the position of the fetus in the womb was examined. If the fetus was positioned on the right, the Zangskari amchi would affirm that it was a boy, and if it was on the left, a girl.[5]

In the villages of Sattak and Yarshun, pregnant women received no special care during their pregnancy. Their way of life, behavior, and diet remained more or less the same. The women had a poor diet in general and continued to work in the fields as long as their physical state permitted (see also Craig 2009). Their hard and impoverished lives left women with little time to be weak, including during labor and delivery. The amchi affirmed they had no particular role vis-à-vis these women, apart from recommending appropriate behavior and diet.

All the amchi we worked with in Zangskar were male, a gender that represented 93 percent of the total amchi population of Ladakh at the time of our research. The entire region then had between 110 and 140 practicing amchi (including Tibetan amchi residing in Ladakh) and thus about 7 to 10 female amchi overall (Pordié 2003, 16). In Shun-Shade the parturient women did not mind being consulted and treated by male healers, but they rarely managed to follow their instructions. It was not easy for them to improve their diet and reduce their workload during pregnancy insofar as this advice ran counter to the other demands of life.[6] Aside from problems related to the availability and economic accessibility of certain products (meat, eggs, fruit, and vegetables), it was not common for a young wife who had newly moved in with her in-laws to demand special treatment. Such a request would be seen by other members of the household as putting one's pregnant state to the fore and would thus be inappropriate and shameful (Wiley 2002). In addition, women avoided discussing their pregnancy publicly so as not to attract the wrath of the spirits or cause jealousy among their fellow villagers, because such occurrences were thought to be potentially harmful to the baby.[7]

The women in the Shun-Shade area give birth at home in the presence of family and neighbors. According to the amchi, the fetus, who is responsible for the onset of labor, also decides when to enter the world.[8] Childbirth takes place in one of the rooms of the house, where the woman stays throughout her entire period of labor. The key recommendation during the hours between the first labor pains and birth is to keep the body warm. Thus, the woman in parturition should be wrapped in blankets, the warmth of which is said to "improve the vitality" and "relax the muscles" (amchi Sonam Thundup). Women take turns caring for the future mother, which mainly involves preparing hot soup and massaging her skin with butter.[9] Local techniques to alleviate labor pains include applying a heated powder made of sheep excrement as a poultice to the kidneys and massaging the kidneys with salt. Delivery usually happens in a vertical position on the knees, wrapped up in the warmth of the covers.[10] Women told us that they would not look at, or check, the vulva when assisting in a birth; similarly, they would not provide manual assistance to control the rotation of the head of the fetus or the elasticity of the perineum.

Newborn babies are wrapped in clean linen, and the placenta is placed in a piece of cloth or linen. If present, the father of the child or, in the case of a polyandrous marriage, the eldest brother cuts the umbilical cord. This practice does not follow the instructions of the Gyüshi, which states that the cord should be cut by a woman who has already experienced childbirth. Nor does our research support Sarah Pinto's (1999) assertion regarding the absence of male involvement in childbirth in Tibetan culture, because of impurity or dirtiness associated with birth.[11] The practice of having a man cut the cord—or involving a male amchi in case of complications—was common in Shun-Shade, although the placenta (along with blood, urine, feces, and amniotic liquid) was indeed considered an excretion of childbirth and thus impure. It was associated with *drib* (*grib*), a concept of pollution.[12] So as not to offend the tutelary deities, the *lha*, and specific categories of "masters of the ground," the placenta should be seen by neither men nor dogs, nor should it be exposed to the outdoors.[13] Instead, it is buried at a prescribed place by the amchi, who, in Yarshun, was also an *onpo* (*dbon po*), a ritual astrologer. Otherwise, the deities' wrath could lead to illnesses among newborn children.[14] As Geoffrey Samuel (2006, 124) remarks, the interventions around childbirth and the personal and cultural environment of birth affect the way the parturient deals with the process of childbirth. The rituals undertaken for the placenta cast light on the social management of childbirth (R. Jeffery and P. Jeffery 1993), on forms of social belonging and societal bonds (Santoro 2011), and on the logics underlying the representation of the body, the person, and the role of cultural "symbols" (Samuel 2006).[15]

In the births we could observe, the women in parturition were separated from the rest of the community, their bodies wrapped in blankets and concealed. For a period after giving birth, they remained in a phase of marginality—secluded in their houses and expected to follow defined prescriptions (see also Gutschow 2004, 209–10)—which, according to the classic schema of *rites de passage*, is associated with pollution by the products excreted at childbirth. Even after gradually being reintroduced to the rest of the group, they remained in a state of impurity for some time, although the duration varied from case to case. They had to avoid transgressing taboos such as collecting water or stepping over an irrigation rivulet, for this could bring misfortune to the baby, the household, or even the entire hamlet or village. The husband was also considered to be polluted and had to follow certain rules, although generally for a shorter period than his wife. Indeed, the state of impurity also applied to the house itself, which, as shown by Kim Gutschow (2004, 210), could be rid of pollution through varying complex purification and propitiation rites (*bsangs*) performed by monks. Hence, besides the treatment of the placenta and the prescriptions followed by both parents, a series of important rituals also addressed the purification of the house and the propitiation of local and monastic deities.

Abnormality and the Role of the Amchi

In Shun-Shade the amchi remained the only medical recourse in cases of complicated deliveries. The complications we noted were obstruction, placental retention, and hemorrhage at the expulsion of the afterbirth, which, in the absence of effective medical care, inevitably led to the death of the woman in childbirth.[16] The most frequent sign of abnormality in childbirth was an extended period of labor lasting more than twelve hours. This would lead to a referral to the amchi, a decision that could be made by anyone attending the woman in parturition.

This practice was primarily due to structural elements that effectively limited the options available to the people of Shun-Shade. Health service facilities were located at a considerable distance from the area. No biomedical services were available in this zone at the time of our research in 2001.[17] Moreover, there were no formalized birth attendants in Ladakh at all.[18] This can be explained by the taboos imposed by the *pha spun*, village groups formed by a few families or houses, based on the worship of the same tutelary deity (lha) (Dollfus 1989, 181), who maintain reciprocal privileges and duties among themselves. Traditionally, a woman could only manage the childbirth of another person from her own pha spun. Social equality united the people of the same pha spun, and this could explain the absence of candidates to assume the role of birth attendant and deal with impurities. This explanation echoes what some authors have shown in India and Nepal, countries in which the local birth attendants, or *dais*, were poor women who, for a little money, were willing to handle the impurities of childbirth (P. Jeffery, R. Jeffery, and Lyon 1989; R. Jeffery and P. Jeffery 1993; Pigg 1997). In Ladakh, although they generally held a high social status in their community, the amchi sometimes considered themselves immune to the impurities and negative effects connected with childbirth on account of the protection bestowed by Sangye Smanla (*sangs rgyas sman bla*), the Buddha Master of Remedies (Pordié 2007, 105).

The major reason cited by the amchi to explain complications in childbirth was the responsibility of the woman herself: "She was not able to keep her body warm." For them, the consequence of this was an augmentation of the *rlung* (wind), some causes of which were "desire," "jealousy," "excessive exercise on an empty stomach," and "speaking much to say nothing."[19] From conception onward, the pregnant woman was held completely responsible for the well-being of the fetus and for all incidents arising during pregnancy and childbirth. The woman's responsibility extended to the level of physical, social, and moral propriety.[20] The amchi also stated that the act of labor in childbirth results in the action of the "wind that blows downward" (*thur sel rlung*, an abridged form of *thur du sel-ba'i rlung*), which is responsible for pushing the fetus out.[21] The amchi observed that the thur sel rlung is seated in the genital center and circulates as far as the intestines, the bladder, the sexual organs, and the thighs. It controls the functions of respiration, expectoration, muscular activity, speech, menstruation, micturition, defecation, the ejaculation of sperm, the discharge of menstrual blood, the opening and closing of the uterus, and childbirth.

The concept of rlung is central to the Tibetan medical system and links the body to the mental faculties.[22] The mind and rlung are inseparable as the consciousness needs the physical support provided by rlung. The amchi understood the aggravation of rlung to be a factor responsible for the obstruction of the birth canal, and directed their interventions to the various dietary and behavioral causes of such disturbances.[23] These practices cast light on the different explanatory registers of the disorder signified by complications in delivery. But under what conditions did the amchi intervene during childbirth, if at all?

Although the Gyüshi makes no mention of childbirth practices among the amchi (Parfionovitch, Meyer, and Dorje 1992), our ethnographies in Zangskar show that the amchi indeed played a role; this may be very limited, but it nevertheless existed. When a labor was prolonged for many hours without any indication of an imminent birth, the amchi prepared a mixture of butter, pepper (*pha ri lu*: *Piper* sp.), *Myristica fragans* (*dza ti*), and seeds from another unidentified plant (*chega*). This mixture was used to massage, successively, the kidneys, the thighs, and the legs. The preparation was thought to increase the efficacy of the hand massage. Performed at length, this had the effect, according to the amchi from Yarshun, of "causing poisons and tensions to leave the body." The application, when carried out in a circular fashion, was said to focus the action on the massaged area. Should this first practice not succeed, the amchi prescribed the *agar so-nga* (*a ga ru so nga*) medicine, a composition of thirty-five (*so nga*) medicinal substances, of which *a ga ru* (*Aquilaria agallocha*) is the main ingredient. This treatment was indicated for illnesses related to an aggravation of the rlung. According to the amchi, it made it possible "to make the rlung go out." When delivery was still late in coming, despite these two interventions, the amchi would fashion a fish from yak butter and give it to the woman in parturition, as described in the next section. If this practice in turn failed, the last recourse consisted of the manual extraction of the fetus. Failure here would result in the death of the fetus and, in the following few hours, that of the woman.

The Butter Fish

The butter fish remained a major element in the amchi's treatment of complications experienced in childbirth. An effigy in the form of a fish was prepared from yak butter. Amchi Sonam Thundup from Yarshun stated that it was a matter of "what the women prefer; otherwise, they would spit it out." The preparation entered a ritualized framework during which the amchi recited specific mantras (*sngags*) and imbued them into the butter. The fish (*nya*) was thus made of blessed butter (*sngags mar*) and was generally called as such, *nag mar* or *nags mar*. While most amchi had no idea how the mantra consecrated the butter—an *acte de parole* efficacious in itself—amchi Dorje from Sumdo claimed that "the mantra carries an invisible and imperceptible 'wind' (rlung), which comes from Sangye Smanla (*sangs rgyas sman bla*)." Once fashioned and consecrated, the fish was given to the woman, who had to ingest it at once, head first. The practice of the butter fish also appears to have existed among the Tibetans. Thubten Sangay (1984, 8) wrote that "a small piece of butter is moulded into the shape of a fish with two eyes. The mantra '*Om ka-ka-mahi-lam-phye ki-ki-mahi-lam-phye shon-shon-mahi-lam-phye ma-mo-hbyung bzhihi-lam-phye*' (Ladakhi phonetics) is recited a thousand times and blown onto the butter which is given to the mother to swallow head first, without biting into it."[24] It is possible that the practice of the butter fish in Ladakh is related to the dried fish from Lake Mapam-yumtso (or Manosarowar) in Tibet, which is one of the commonly mentioned medicines given to women with difficult childbirths, but we lack evidence to confirm this hypothesis.

Among the different products derived from cows and yaks, the fatty substances include clarified butter (*shun mar*), the cream and cheese from an animal that has just given birth, and the cream deposited on the walls of the milk container (*jo mar*). Butter is used in a variety of medicinal compounds, including for newborn babies (Van Vleet 2010–11, 363–65). In contrast to butter from goat's milk, which has cold qualities, yak butter, similar to sheep butter, has warm qualities (Meyer 1983). In Zangskar the fish was made from clarified butter, which, according to chapter 16 of the Gyüshi in its description of the different fatty substances and their therapeutic action, is "the best fatty substance. It sharpens the intellect, clarifies the memory, increases body warmth, strength and longevity" (Meyer 1983, 300). Tibetan medical theory associates pregnancy with a "hot" state. It is recommended that the woman should not consume "cold" food during the period of gestation (see also Wiley 2002) and that she should keep her body warm. According to the amchi, the absorption of the fish follows this logic, as its basic matter is characterized by a warm potential.[25] It enables a reduction in excess rlung, in this case cold in nature, which represents one of the causal explanations for complications in childbirth.

The effigy in the form of a fish does not appear to have any particular symbolic relation to the amchi's descriptions of the three phases of pregnancy. Although it belongs—as do the otter, the crane, and the stork—to the aquatic animal group in the classification of meat given in the Gyüshi (Meyer 1983, 229), fish was not generally eaten by the Buddhist population of Ladakh.[26] Ladakhi Buddhists often claimed that one needs to kill a lot of fish, and thus take many lives, to feed a family. They therefore preferred to eat yak meat, for "a single yak feeds the entire family." Some also said that fish should not be killed because they are shy animals. However, not eating fish also relates to the explanation of the Zangskari supernatural world, in which animals living in water or those in close contact with the earth are related to the deities/spirits of the subterranean and aquatic worlds, the *klu*. The worship of the klu has developed under the influence of the Indian mythology of the *nāga* (snake divinities). The klu are mainly described as zoomorphic and may thus appear in the form of fish (nya) (see, for elsewhere in Ladakh, Dollfus 2003; Kaplanian 1987). In general, people also did not eat fish because they considered them to be pure, a quality that mirrored the inherent purity of the klu (Dollfus 2003, 11). In contrast to men, who are associated with the lha and with social institutions, women are thought to be closer to the klu owing to their daily tasks of hoeing, irrigation, water collection, and milking and thus more vulnerable (Dollfus 1996; Kaplanian 1987). In order to please the klu, women wear the *perak* (*be rag*), a headdress sewn with turquoise thread in the shape of a cobra, and conch-shell bracelets (*dung lag*) (Karmay and Sagant 1987). The klu are thought to be sensitive to their habitat and could react violently to any kind of human pollution, such as excrement and blood, as well as to any contact with iron.[27] A complication during a birth could express the discontent of the klu, assaulted by the pollution of the blood and excrement of childbirth. However, in "responding to an aggression even if the culprit meant no harm . . . , the *klu* bestow kindness on whomever worships them devoutly" (Dollfus 1996, 33). In keeping with this necessity, as in other rituals for spatial purification and for the elimination of stains owing to impure acts, fashioning a fish out of butter is similar to making an offering.[28]

The actions of the amchi during childbirth link the gestures and the prescription of substances with the recitation of mantras. Ideally, treatments in Sowa Rigpa are administered on the basis of a principle of progressiveness according to the severity of the disease (Meyer 2006). They include an initial behavioral and dietetic stage, then the provision of powders and pills, followed by external therapies and, finally, rituals.[29] In an extreme situation that endangers the life of both of the woman and the unborn child, if no other remedy is able to bring about birth, the practice of the butter fish appears to combine different phases in medical treatment (medication and ritual). The amchi thus gives meaning to an illness, assigning to it organic, emotional, and supernatural origins. The corresponding therapeutic schema conceives the failure of a therapy not necessarily as the failure of its efficacy but as a reason to conduct a more thorough investigation into the moral nature of the two beings present: that is, the mother and the child. That is why, according to amchi Tsering Phuntsog, the failure of treatments used for complicated deliveries indicates the karmic character of the problem, which cannot be healed through ordinary remedies.

Parallel Views in the Urban Milieu

Whereas the amchi in the remote area of Shun-Shade should not be overlooked as a key actor in the case of complications during childbirth, in the city of Leh, where birth was already increasingly seen as a medical event, the vast majority of women gave birth in the hospital in the presence of biomedical personnel.[30] The amchi stood at the margins of the medical world, his role secondary or even nonexistent. Especially—but not only—in the case of complicated births, the presence of an obstetrics department in the Sonam Norbu Memorial Hospital in Leh, which was free of charge and judged to be of good quality, appears to be the major factor in the transfer of responsibility for childbirth from the woman's family or the amchi to the medical personnel of the maternity ward. This transformation had much to do with the social image of biomedicine and its clinical performance but also with the distribution of wealth and power in the family and community in rural Ladakh, since they influenced the move to the hospital (Gutschow 2010; Hancart Petitet 2005). In addition, local state policies favored the development of biomedicine, in particular with regard to maternity and childbirth. The role of the state in the provision of care at birth is a fundamental structural factor in contemporary changes in the health field (Ginsburg and Rapp 1995).[31]

The amchi in Leh noted that their patients did not expect them to attend their pregnancies and deliveries. However, when biomedical care proved to be unsuccessful, they were often asked to intervene at the last stage of long therapeutic itineraries in cases of infertility or complications experienced in childbirth. All the amchi we talked to in Leh knew of the butter fish, and some of them used it in particular circumstances, regularly but not frequently. The modalities of such a practice are illustrated in the following case. When a complication occurred during labor in a hospital and a cesarean was advised, the family of the woman about to give birth requested time to consider the matter. During this period, one of the family members went to Amchi K., to whom the situation in the hospital was described in detail. The relative explicitly asked him to provide the "fish that induces delivery" in the shortest possible time. The amchi swiftly made the preparation, and the relative returned to the hospital with the carefully packed fish. This he gave secretly to the woman, who gulped it down as soon as the situation allowed, concealing her act from the hospital staff. No perceptible mantra recitation was involved. This could be argued to be a case of reritualizing the butter fish through forms of secret practice in the biomedical milieu.

The fact that the amchi's practice was not recognized as such in India was also a matter of concern for many amchi in urban Ladakh. They hoped to have their medicine recognized by the central government of India, in order to receive stronger economic and structural support, but also to prevent any legal complications. "We could get imprisoned if we have a problem with a patient, because today we need to be legal. Although we have practiced for over a thousand years here, we are not legal," said amchi Tsering Phuntsog in 2001. He was the chief amchi for the government and took charge of the "Amchi Clinic" at the same hospital in Leh in 2004. He was aware of the butter fish practice but was not involved in the cases we witnessed. His remarks, however, shed light on a great paradox: the amchi considered his practice illegal and feared jail, despite working as a government officer in a biomedical environment. His medicine was, at the time, not recognized as an Indian system of medicine, but he received a salary and project grants from central Indian institutions. Some said that the medicine of the amchi was simply tolerated. In fact, it was considered as belonging to the category of tribal medicine and received minor support for this reason.[32] In the domain of childbirth, however, there was no room for the amchi, and their medications, such as the butter fish, were considered inappropriate. The chief gynecologist at the hospital in Leh strictly proscribed any recourse to the amchi in matters of childbirth, which included the butter fish. According to her, their involvement during a complicated birth was characterized by inefficacious practices and by a late referral of the woman in parturition to the hospital, often with fatal consequences.

In this context, the practice of the butter fish remained secret, and the ritual surrounding it had to be altered by concealing the mantra recitation. This reconfiguration facilitated the integration of this practice into the biomedical milieu. This transformation involved, on the one hand, the patient's requirement for a rapid therapeutic solution in an emergency in an unfavorable medical environment and, on the other hand, the expertise of the biomedical staff, which did not answer to the need experienced by the patient.

In hospitals, this recourse to the amchi took place only in an extreme circumstance (cesarean). This reversal of the therapeutic recourse was the decision of the patient and her family. Its purpose was pragmatic and aimed to avoid surgery and its consequences. As described in many studies of health-seeking behavior, the patient explored the array of available therapeutic possibilities when her distress was greatest. It also expressed a swing in the perception of the reason for the disorder from a biomedical explanation toward that of amchi medicine, which is more familiar to the woman in parturition, although distinct from her own representations. For example, in biomedicine, dynamic dystocia (absence of dilation of the cervix, insufficient uterine activity) or mechanical dystocia (feto-pelvic disproportion, malposition of the fetus, and so on) is the factor responsible for the presentation in the genital channel. The amchi perceive this problem as the disturbance of the nyes pa, a result of the machinations of angry deities, and/or a consequence of karmic law. In the case presented above, the amchi saw the complication in his own physiological terms (rlung), and the woman and her family believed in what the amchi said and in the efficacy of his medicine. They did not ask the amchi for detailed explanations but did mention their fear of the wrath of village deities. Although rejected by the biomedical institution, the practice of the amchi in childbirth was still legitimated by the patients because it held meaning for them.[33] This offered a signifier to the patient, in contrast to the biomedical explanation, which uses a system of interpretation and care for illness that places the-body-as-object at its center as the almost-exclusive place of action. The amchi intervened when the need arose for a treatment of the-body-as-subject.

The secrecy of the practice of the butter fish in hospitals illustrates the significance of biomedicine as the reference point in obstetrics. Biomedicine is a form of authoritative knowledge that is reproduced within a "community of practices" in a specific social situation such as childbirth. Brigitte Jordan (1993) thus showed how biomedical authority ultimately came to dominate childbirth and how the distribution of power among medical practitioners is linked to their ability to make use of technology. This dominance results in the exclusivity of the proposed treatments, the impossibility for people accompanying the woman to enter the labor ward, and the obligation to assume a certain physical position at childbirth. Thus, whereas in Zangskar the women in labor were traditionally surrounded by members of their family or people from the immediate neighborhood and adopted a semivertical position, in the hospital in Leh, anyone not part of the hospital staff was left outside, and the woman had to adopt a dorsal decubitus with the knees pulled back for childbirth. However, the intrusion of the butter fish into the hospital milieu and the patients' therapeutic itineraries in such a context challenged biomedical authoritative knowledge. For these patients, amchi knowledge also had authority in the case of complications experienced in childbirth in a place where medical authority is typically assigned to biomedicine. The amchi was sought beyond his usual context, when the biomedical staff offered the family a practice (the cesarean) that involved a higher degree of technology. Beyond the medical institutional framework, the construction of authoritative knowledge rested on what the parturient woman believed was good for her, both in a pragmatic sense and in her search for meaning.

Conclusions

Although there is no mention of the amchi taking a therapeutic role in childbirth in the classic medical treatises, the practitioners in rural Zangskar did in fact intervene in this domain. This function has not received much attention in the research on childbirth in the areas of Tibetan culture. In Ladakh, Andrea Wiley notably observed an "absence of involvement [in prenatal care and birth] of traditional institutions such as Tibetan medicine" (2002, 1089). Wiley, however, cited earlier works in which the intervention of the amchi in cases of complications in pregnancies or deliveries was observed, such as those of M. I. Nazki (1986) and Helena Norberg-Hodge and Hazel Russell (1994). But in no case were the social or symbolic dimensions of the practice the subject of detailed investigations. Indeed, the functions of the amchi were primarily of this order and were only to a much lesser extent directly medical or technical. This chapter does not aim to exaggerate the limited role of the amchi or to extol the effectiveness of their practices in relation to childbirth. Our aim was to bring these practices to light. To conclude this chapter, we would like to raise some issues that may be helpful to understand the emergence of an amchi practice in childbirth in Ladakh.

Matters pertaining to childcare were seriously considered in the Tibetan medical milieu in 1916 Lhasa, when the Thirteenth Dalai Lama implemented a program for the newborn. This was based on a medical manual on childcare (*byis pa nyer spyod 'gro phan snying nor*; *On Childcare: Treasure of the Heart Benefiting Beings*) written in the same year by his most senior personal physician, Jampa Tupwang (Van Vleet 2010–11). At the time of our research, this kind of manual was unknown to the amchi we worked with. In Ladakh the harshness of the rural environment in the region and the isolation of the populations during several months of the year could have played a role in the appearance of an emergency practice in cases of complications experienced in childbirth. The social and political events that determined the changes in amchi medicine in contemporary Ladakh also contributed to transforming the amchi's knowledge and practice relating to birth. The case of development projects is here exemplary, since institutions, both governmental and nongovernmental, have played an important role in the transformation of Tibetan medicine in the region. In Tibet, for example, Jennifer Chertow (2003) found that nongovernmental projects, alongside those of the state, had a certain impact on childbirth practices. Similarly, the amchi's assumption of obstetric responsibility could be a possible consequence of training sessions organized in Ladakh. Since 1989 the Department of Health of the Ladakh Autonomous Hill Development Council had conducted regular training workshops for rural amchi, in which matters of childbirth were repeatedly addressed. Concomitantly, since the mid-1980s, the organization Leh Nutrition Project (funded by Save the Children Fund, UK) ran a multiyear project on issues surrounding mother and child health in which amchi—some of them from Zangskar—were included. Similarly, for a period of about ten years from the late 1990s, the French organization Nomad

RSI organized regular training seminars for the amchi. The role of biomedicine in local and international health organizations' interventions with the amchi varied depending on the approach but remained largely dominant, apart from a few exceptions. Generally, the presence of Ladakhi biomedical doctors at seminars intended for amchi was particularly pronounced in the domain of pregnancy and childbirth. This domain represented, on the one hand, a major issue for public health in Ladakh, where biomedicine showed real technical mastery and superiority, while, on the other hand, neither Tibetan medical texts nor the amchi were able to describe an obstetrics practice that would possibly be satisfactory in the eyes of development agents. The amchi were well aware that their knowledge on birth was scant and their practice limited to behavioral and dietary recommendations and to a small set of practices. This explains why there was an explicit demand among the rural and urban amchi for training in this domain from biomedical doctors. The technical aspects pertaining to childbirth thus appear to be more heavily influenced by biomedicine than other areas of the amchi's practice. It remains to be seen, however, how the representations of conception, pregnancy, and birth and the associated taboos are also modified in the process.

The biomedical doctors never intervene solely as technicians. They also convey a whole set of medical ideologies that aim to eliminate "superstitions" in particular. The chief gynecologist at the hospital in Leh spoke in this manner to the amchi at training seminars or other official encounters. She benefited from a status recognized by the medical communities in Ladakh, and her position was influential. Her paper at the Forum on Amchi Medicine: Training and Healing Material Exchange, held in Leh, October 19–29, 1998, covered the broad subject of "pregnancy and delivery cases" and presented her arguments in an exemplary fashion. She told the amchi that some of their practices and superstitions should be banned, while introducing new ideas and denigrating some of the conceptions in Tibetan medicine. She touched both on the legitimacy of their medical practices and on their beliefs in regard to childbirth. She sparked a debate among the amchi, who discussed her comments later in the evening. Amchi Tsewang Norbu exemplified the position of the majority: "Dr. Ladhol knows many things. . . . We also have ideas and knowledge, but we should learn, we must learn from her."

As shown by the variations in the practice of the butter fish in the urban area, biomedical science refuses both the amchi's thought world and their practices because the consequences are deemed problematic. While this is justified from the point of view of public health, the social dimension of the role of the amchi in childbirth is dismissed. Biomedicine largely dominates the medical arena of childbirth and tends to gain ideological credit in the social world. The amchi are subordinate health actors in a global medical system. They remain peripheral agents on the margins, whether they are the only available medical resources in the deep rural setting of Shun-Shade or a last-resort alternative to biomedicine in urban Leh. Biomedicine occupies an increasingly central role in the amchi's practice concerning birth. The negation or the recognition of their practice by different forms of power (biomedical, local, or international organizations) places the problem of reproduction at the very center of contemporary issues in Tibetan medicine in Ladakh. These issues also concern gender politics, understood as the place of gender in broader configurations of meaning, interaction, and power.

As noted earlier, in the late 1990s and early 2000s, the Tibetan medical milieu was demographically dominated by male practitioners (Pordié 2003, 16). The period of research, however, was a crucial turning point regarding Ladakh's general modernization and Tibetan medicine's gender reconfiguration. The medical department of the Central Institute of Buddhist Studies in Choglamsar, located in the outskirts of Leh, had eleven students in 1999, among whom female students were in the majority. Similarly, the Dusrapa school (named after the diploma it conferred, *sdus ra ba*) set up by Nomad RSI in 1999 had twenty-two students who graduated in the mid-2000s, of whom 50 percent were women. Since 2010 these graduates have constituted more than half of the Tibetan medical practitioners officially posted in National Rural Health Mission clinics throughout Ladakh (Blaikie 2019). The feminization of Tibetan medicine is increasing, as it is in other areas of Tibetan culture (Craig 2009; Fjeld and Hofer 2010–11). A question remains as to how this feminization could change the amchi position toward birth and childcare, along with their practices. An alternative route could thus be taken in which more women could involve themselves in rethinking the role of Tibetan medicine in birth and childcare. One of the leading female amchi figures of Ladakh took such a route in the 2000s and led a nongovernmental organization's local project on the matter for several years. Her actions had a lot to do with gender politics. In a male-dominated environment, her efforts came up against many hurdles that both her competencies and her determination helped to cross (Pordié 2016). Feminist studies would see here a dynamic of resistance (Collier and Yanagisako 1989), informed by the way this female amchi behaved and subsequently gained credit in the real world (Conkey and Gero 1997). Would the transformation of Tibetan medicine's gender open up new avenues for such dynamics and undertakings? Further investigation is needed to answer this question.

Notes

We would like to thank Stephan Kloos and the three anonymous reviewers for their useful comments on this chapter. The research has been conducted in the framework of the Nomad Research Unit, to which we extend our gratitude.

1 Research was conducted within the framework of Nomad RSI, an organization that contracted anthropologists to gather relevant information with the aim of translating it into sensitive development programs (see the chapter by Besch and Guérin, this volume). This chapter presents part of the results obtained between 1998 and 2003, especially in 2001. Both authors have done ethnographic work alone or in tandem, both in Leh and in rural Zangskar. The work in Shun-Shade presented in this chapter was conducted by Pascale, while Laurent mostly covered other isolated areas and the capital, Leh. The authors had regular and intensive exchange during the fieldwork and after.

2 This situation shows a significant difference from Hindu India, where the concepts of karma and reincarnation are known to a fraction of the society only (priests, some members of the upper castes, scholars) and generally ignored by the common laypeople, especially those belonging to the lower castes (see Deliège 2001).

3 These ideas are found in the *Bardo Thödol* (*bar do thos grol*), a mortuary text read over a dead or dying person to help him or her escape from rebirth or have a good rebirth in the next life. The book describes the states that separate the moment of death from that of birth. *Bardo* designates the intermediary state in which the individual finds himself or herself after death and before rebirth. At the time of death, the five fundamental elements constituting the physical body dissolve, and the consciousness is set free in space. The spirit of the deceased is then directed according to his or her karma to agreeable or disagreeable experiences. He or she must follow the teachings of the lama (*bla ma*), the spiritual master, to attain liberation from the cycle of rebirth (*saṃsāra*). The chapter entitled "The Closing of the Door of the Womb" explains how the deceased must proceed in order not to be attracted by the womb and, in the case of failure, how to choose a good womb (see Govinda 1980).

4 The primary causes of conception, for example, are said to be the union in the mother's womb of a psychic individuality in search of a new incarnation with the nonvitiated sperm and menstrual blood of the parents. The secondary causes are the gathering of the five fundamental elements. This is also found in medical theory. See Meyer ([1981] 2002, 1987) and Parfionovitch, Meyer, and Dorje (1992). For a specific study on embryology in Tibetan medicine, see Garrett (2008).

5 This diagnostic aspect is mentioned in the *Exegetical Tantra*, chaps. 1 and 2, p. 181, lines 70 and 71 (Parfionovitch, Meyer, and Dorje 1992).

6 In the Tibet Autonomous Region, some villagers, both men and women, may recommend that women be active during pregnancy. The women often "work right up until the onset of labor" (Adams et al. 2005, 832–33).

7 See also Adams et al. (2005, 829–30) on the Tibet Autonomous Region.

8 The explanatory treatise of the Gyüshi gives reasons for this, however, without the amchi having mentioned them: "In the course of the thirty-seventh week, the consciousness of the fetus, afflicted by the state of dirtiness, foul odors, obscurity, and imprisonment, conceives of the idea of escaping" (Meyer [1981] 2002, 112).

9   Massaging with warm butter several parts of the body (e.g., temples, palms, feet) of women in labor was also practiced in most rural societies with Tibetan cultural origins across the Himalayan region.

10 Amchi Yeshi Dhonden states that the advantage of the kneeling position is that "the baby's weight works for the childbirth, whereas 'on back' the weight works against it" (1980, 36). According to Jacques Gelis (1984), the squatting position, as in having a bowel movement, is the most instinctive posture.

11 Pinto explores the concept of impurity, dirtiness, and messiness with regard to childbirth in Tibetan culture. She states, "Keeping birth within the realm of women only is felt to be entirely logical behavior, as birth is believed to be something that concerns women alone, something 'naturally' female. To include men in this process, it seems, would be entirely illogical and unnecessary" (1999, 164). Kim Gutschow (2004, 209), in contrast, also noticed the involvement of men in the cutting of the cord in Zangskar, as did Santi Rozario and Geoffrey Samuel (2002) elsewhere in the Indian Himalayas.

12 See Gutschow (2004, esp. 199–215) for an account of impurity and drib (*grib*) in childbirth in Zangskar and more generally in Tibetan culture. Also see Rozario and Samuel (2002) for a comparative study among Tibetans and Indians in Dalhousie, India.

13 Isabelle Riaboff (1997) notes that the Zangskarpa have relationships with three main categories of originally non-Buddhist deities: the lha (gods), the *klu* (spirits of the underworld and aquatic milieu), and the *'dre* (demons). The wheel of life is conceived of as a vertical cosmic space in which living beings are ordered. One finds, from bottom to top, the beings of the underworld, the starving spirits, animals, humans, the titans, and then the lha. The latter are, according to the same arrangement, the lha of the domain of form and, above them, the lha of the domain of the absence of form. The klu are associated with the subterranean world ("lower world," *og' la*) and the lha with the zenith ("upper world," *steng la*); humans are between the two ("median world," *bar la*). The 'dre lack a specific topographic location. In her research elsewhere in Ladakh, however, Pascale Dollfus (1996) observed that a specific class of demon, the *bstan*, are associated with the median world. In addition, despite the liturgical context in which the "Master of the Ground," *sa bdag*, is distinguished from the klu (aquatic and subterranean deities), the villagers seem to also classify the klu as specific categories of "Masters of the Ground."

14 In her study in the Ladakhi village of Photoksar, Fernanda Pirie (2006, 183) suggests that drib (*grib*) is a cosmological concept that has pragmatic significance for the villagers and is not morally imbued. Babies and mothers are particularly vulnerable to spirit attack and must "avoid proximity to, and even sight of, shrines of powerful protector deities lest they be struck by illness." Such pragmatic behaviors were also found in Tibet by Vincanne Adams and colleagues (2005, 828–29). In this case, however, the occurrence of pollution is also presented as the conflation of moral and spiritual significations.

15 The precautions vary in degree and can reach the point of lending the placenta an anthropomorphic character, as among the Malaysians, where it is described as

the youngest brother of the newborn child (Laderman 1987). See also Bonnemère (2000) for comparative materials in Oceania.

16   For a study of maternal mortality in Ladakh, see Hancart Petitet (2005). For a critical analysis of the establishment of facts on, and quantification of, maternal mortality in Tibet, see Adams (2005).

17   The situation seems to have since changed, as a nurse midwife was reported to be practicing in Shade in 2006 (Kim Gutschow, personal communication). See Gutschow (2004, chap. 2) for a description of the health services in Zangskar.

18   Like other Himalayan places of Tibetan culture (Craig 2009), Ladakh has no specialized attendants for birth events. We do not use the term "traditional birth attendant" because it is a category with political connotations that was invented to satisfy a bureaucratic function in international development and public health administrations (Pigg 2001).

19   According to the Gyüshi, the disorders of wind (*rlung gi nad*) may be classified into sixty-three types, forty-eight of which are general and fifteen specific. See Meyer ([1981] 2002) and Adams (1998) for more details.

20   This is also found in classical texts. The relationship between the mother and the intra-uterine child appears in the work entitled *The Jewel Ornament of Liberation*, by Gampopa (Sgam-po-pa), a Tibetan doctor, philosopher, and saint from the eleventh century, who described the misery experienced by a being in the womb (Gampopa 1959). The way pregnancy and childbirth are conceived in theories of procreation also sheds light on the hierarchy of genders (Héritier 1996). The Gyüshi indicates, for example, that the spirits "of little merit are thereby born as womankind endowed with breasts and womb and red menstrual blood" (*Instructional Tantra*, chaps. 74–82, in Parfionovitch, Meyer, and Dorje 1992, 107). On the subject of women in Zangskar in general, their status, and local conceptions and meanings pertaining to the impure nature of the woman's body, see Gutschow (2004). For other accounts from South Asia, see Samuel (2006).

21   There are five types of rlung, each responsible for a variety of bodily, physiological, or mental actions, described in detail in Tibetan medical theory: (1) *srog 'dzin rlung*: "life-grasping" rlung, seated in the heart; (2) *gyen rgyu*: "upward-moving" rlung, seated in the chest but circulating in the nose and throat; (3) *khyab byed*: "all-pervading" rlung, seated in the head but circulating in all parts of the body; (4) *me mnyam*: "fire-accompanying" rlung, seated in the abdomen but circulating in all parts of the intestines and stomach; and (5) *thur sel rlung*.

22   These considerations were expressed only by the amchi. None of the villagers whom we met in Ladakh had any detailed understanding about even the most basic concepts of Tibetan medicine (e.g., *nyes pa*, the humoral physiological principles). This shows a very different picture from the situation that Adams and colleagues (2005, 830) describe in their study of childbirth among villagers in Tibet.

23   This is also found in the Gyüshi, which states that the birth canal can be blocked by a malfunction or stagnation of rlung to explain the prolongation of the term of labor (Parfionovitch, Meyer, and Dorje 1992). According to Lobsang Dolma Khangkar (1986), prolongation of a pregnancy could also result from a malfunctioning of the

thogs me rkyen, resulting in a bad position and presentation of the fetus in the birth canal—this she presented as the rlung of the thirty-eighth week, which is responsible for the fetal position with cephalic presentation at childbirth. However, none of the amchi referred to this specific rlung, nor did they say, as found in the Gyüshi, that the term may be prolonged when the mother has lost blood during gestation or when she has eaten to excess.

24 The text also gives information about another ritual in which the mantra is identical but the practice differs. This practice does not exist in Zangskar today and seems to have fallen from favor among Tibetans. It involves a preparation made with a peacock feather and eight hairs from a bear; these are burned, and the ashes are mixed in a glass of water. The mother then drinks this preparation, which is supposed to induce delivery immediately (Sangay 1984).

25 Tibetan medical theory pertaining to pharmacology is highly complex (see Meyer 2006, 20–23). Five levels of action are mentioned in the classical texts (cosmophysical elements, tastes, postdigestive tastes, potentialities, and the synergy issuing from various combinations). However, in practice, the potentialities of the drugs (*nus pa*), together with their various combinations, play a significant role over and above the other levels of action.

26 There were, however, exceptions, as some Buddhist Ladakhis in rural and urban areas ate fish to complement or vary their diet. An urban minority had also taken up freshwater fishing and ate, often in situ, the fish they caught.

27 See Gutschow (2004, 111, 203) on Zangskar, and Kaplanian (1987) and Dollfus (1996) on elsewhere in Ladakh.

28 By the same token, some women in Stok, in the Indus valley, also spoke of various practices involving fish, such as eating a dried fish from Lake Manosarovar in Tibet when labor is difficult. The Tibetan astrologer Jhampa Kalsang Tsipa Kachupa advised Tibetans to save the life of an animal, usually including a fish, about to be slaughtered when the birth chart made by the astrologer showed any threat to the child's life (Kalsang 1992).

29 Modifications should, however, be noted in which the amchi depart from the rules of progressiveness given in the medical texts. This results from the socioeconomic changes in Ladakh and the patients' desire for a rapid recovery. The amchi immediately prescribed treatments based on plants, which thereby acquired a new temporal positioning in the therapy (Pordié 2002).

30 According to Andrea Wiley (2002), the penetration of biomedical maternity care in Ladakh has been facilitated by the lack of involvement of traditional institutions and the high rate of miscarriage and neonatal mortality, among wider ecological and cultural factors. See Wiley (2002, 2004) for an analysis of the reasons for the increase in the use of prenatal services and hospitals in Ladakh. Similarly, see Rozario and Samuel (2002) for elsewhere in the Indian Himalayas.

31 In Tibet, government health policies also encourage women to visit hospitals or biomedical clinics, which has led to the compilation of a census register of rural populations and helps to monitor people's attitudes toward central policies, especially those aiming to control births (Chertow 2003). Jennifer Chertow sees in

these processes an expression of the new modes of governance in rural Tibet and of women thus becoming part of China's nation-building project.

32 The recognition of Sowa Rigpa by the government of India occurred in 2010, after many years of efforts partly conducted by Ladakhis (Blaikie 2016; Kloos 2016), thus significantly changing the landscape of the practice.

33 This point has been illustrated in Ladakh by the manner in which the amchi mobilized certain cultural and religious elements in the practice of their medicine, notably in the case of behavioral recommendations (Pordié 2007).

References

Adams, Vincanne. 1998. "Suffering the Winds of Lhasa: Politicized Bodies, Human Rights, Cultural Difference, and Humanism in Tibet." *Medical Anthropology Quarterly* 12 (1): 74–102.

Adams, Vincanne. 2001. "Particularizing Modernity: Tibetan Medical Theorizing of Women's Health in Lhasa, Tibet." In *Healing Powers and Modernity: Traditional Medicine, Shamanism, and Science in Asian Societies*, edited by Linda Connor and Geoffrey Samuel, 197–246. Westport, CT: Bergin and Garvey.

Adams, Vincanne. 2005. "Saving Tibet? An Enquiry into Modernity, Lies, Truths, and Beliefs." *Medical Anthropology* 24:71–110.

Adams, Vincanne, Suellen Miller, Jennifer Chertow, Sienna Craig, Arlene Samen, and Michael Varner. 2005. "Having a 'Safe Delivery': Conflicting Views from Tibet." *Health Care for Women International* 26 (9): 821–51.

Blaikie, Calum. 2016. "Positioning Sowa Rigpa in India: Coalition and Antagonism in the Quest for Recognition." *Medicine, Anthropology, Theory* 3 (2): 50–86.

Blaikie, Calum. 2019. "Mainstreaming Marginality: Traditional Medicine and Primary Healthcare in Himalayan India." *Asian Medicine* 14 (1): 145–72.

Bonnemère, Pascale. 2000. "Le traitement du placenta en Océanie: Des sens différents pour une même pratique." *Sciences Sociales et Santé* 18:29–36.

Casper, Monica. 1998. *The Making of the Unborn Patient: A Social Anatomy of Fetal Surgery*. New Brunswick, NJ: Rutgers University Press.

Chertow, Jennifer. 2003. "Gender, Medicine, and Modernity: Childbirth in Tibet Today." *Harvard Asia Quarterly* 7 (4): 17–28.

Collier, Jane, and Sylvia Yanagisako. 1989. "Theory in Anthropology since Feminist Practice." *Critique of Anthropology* 9 (2): 27–37.

Cominsky, Sheila. 2016. *Midwives and Mothers: The Medicalization of Childbirth on a Guatemalan Plantation*. Austin: University of Texas Press.

Conkey, Margaret, and Joan Gero. 1997. "Programme to Practice: Gender and Feminism in Archaeology." *Annual Review of Anthropology* 26:411–37.

Craig, Sienna. 2009. "Pregnancy and Childbirth in Tibet: Knowledge, Perspectives, and Practices." In *Childbirth across Cultures: Ideas and Practices of Pregnancy, Childbirth and the Postpartum*, edited by Helaine Selin and Pamela Stone, 145–60. London: Springer.

Deliège, Robert. 2001. "L'ethnographie contre l'idéologie: Le cas de l'hindouisme." *L'Homme* 120:163–76.

Dhonden, Yeshi. 1980. "Childbirth in Tibetan Medicine." *Tibetan Medicine Series* 1:36–40.

Dollfus, Pascale. 1989. *Lieu de neige et de genévriers: Organisation sociale et religieuse des communautés bouddhistes au Ladakh*. Paris: Éditions du CNRS.

Dollfus, Pascale. 1996. "Maîtres du sol et dieux du territoire au Ladakh." *Etudes Rurales* 143–44:27–44.

Dollfus, Pascale. 2003. "De quelques histoires de *klu* et de *btsan*." *Revue d'Etudes Tibétaines* 2:4–39.

Fjeld, Heidi, and Theresia Hofer. 2010–11. "Women and Gender in Tibetan Medicine." *Asian Medicine* 6 (2): 175–216.

Foucault, Michel. 1994. *Histoire de la sexualité*. Vol. 1, *La volonté de savoir*. Paris: Gallimard.

Gampopa [Sgam-po-pa]. 1959. *The Jewel Ornament of Liberation*. Translated by Herbert Guenther. London: Rider Books.

Garrett, Frances. 2008. *Religion, Buddhism and the Human Embryo in Tibet*. London: Routledge.

Gelis, Jacques. 1984. *L'arbre et le fruit: La naissance dans l'Occident moderne XVI–XIXe siècle*. Paris: Fayard.

Ginsburg, Faye, and Rayna Rapp. 1995. *Conceiving the New World Order: The Global Politics of Reproduction*. Berkeley: University of California Press.

Govinda, Anagarinka, presenter. 1980. *Bardho-Thödol: Le livre tibétain des morts*. Paris: Albin Michel.

Gutschow, Kim. 2004. *Being a Buddhist Nun: The Struggle for Enlightenment in the Himalayas*. Cambridge, MA: Harvard University Press.

Gutschow, Kim. 2010. "From Home to Hospitals: The Extension of Obstetrics in Ladakh." In *Medicine between Science and Religion*, edited by Vincanne Adams, Mona Schrempf, and Sienna Craig, 185–214. Oxford: Berghahn Books.

Hancart Petitet, Pascale. 2005. "Mortalité maternelle au Ladakh: De la santé publique à l'anthropologie." In *Panser le monde, penser les médecines: Traditions médicales et développement sanitaire*, edited by Laurent Pordié, 123–43. Paris: Karthala.

Héritier, Françoise. 1996. *Masculin/Féminin: La pensée de la différence*. Paris: Odile Jacob.

Jeffery, Patricia, Roger Jeffery, and Andrew Lyon. 1989. *Labour Pains and Labour Power: Women and Childbearing in India*. London: Zed Books.

Jeffery, Roger, and Patricia Jeffery. 1993. "Traditional Birth Attendants in Rural North India: The Social Organization of Childbearing." In *Knowledge, Power, and Practice: The Anthropology of Medicine and Everyday Life*, edited by Shirley Lindenbaum and Margaret Lock, 7–31. Berkeley: University of California Press.

Jordan, Brigitte. 1993. *Birth in Four Cultures: A Crosscultural Investigation of Childbirth in Yucatan, Holland, Sweden, and the United States*. Prospect Heights, IL: Waveland Press.

Kalsang, Jhampa. 1992. "Traditional Community Role of the Tibetan Astro-Practitioner." *Tibet Journal* 17 (3): 47–50.

Kaplanian, Patrick. 1987. "Entre *lha* et *lhu*: Conception de la maladie chez les Ladakhi." In *Etiologie et perception de la maladie dans les sociétés modernes et traditionnelles*, edited by Anne Retel-Laurentin, 145–56. Paris: L'Harmattan.

Karmay, Samten, and Philippe Sagant. 1987. "La place du rang dans la maison sharwa (Amdo ancien)." In *Architecture, milieu et société en Himalaya*, edited by Denis Blamont and Gérard Toffin, 229–60. Paris: Éditions du CNRS.

Khangkar, Lobsang Dolma. 1986. *Lectures on Tibetan Medicine*. Dharamsala: Library of Tibetan Work and Archives.

Kloos, Stephan. 2016. "The Recognition of Sowa Rigpa in India: How Tibetan Medicine Became an Indian Medical System." *Medicine, Anthropology, Theory* 3 (2): 19–49.

Laderman, Carol. 1987. *Wives and Midwives: Childbirth and Nutrition in Rural Malaysia*. Berkeley: University of California Press.

McClain, Carol Shepherd, ed. 1989. *Women as Healers: Cross-Cultural Perspectives*. New Brunswick, NJ: Rutgers University Press.

Meyer, Fernand. (1981) 2002. *Gso-Ba Rig-Pa: Le système médical tibétain*. Paris: Éditions du CNRS.

Meyer, Fernand. 1983. "Pratiques alimentaires et diététiques médicales en milieu tibétain." *Informations sur les Sciences Sociales* 22 (2): 283–309.

Meyer, Fernand. 1987. "Essai d'analyse schématique d'un système médical: La médecine savante du Tibet." In *Etiologie et perception de la maladie dans les sociétés modernes et traditionnelles*, edited by Anne Retel-Laurentin, 227–49. Paris: L'Harmattan.

Meyer, Fernand. 2006. "La rationalité théorique de la médecine tibétaine au prisme de son traité de référence: De la physiologie à la pharmacopée." In *La médecine tibétaine: Sources, concepts et pratique actuelle*, edited by Jacques Fleurentin and Jean-Pierre Nicolas, 13–23. Metz: Société Française d'Ethnopharmacologie—Institut Européen d'Ecologie.

Morgan, Lynn. 2009. *Icons of Life: A Cultural History of Human Embryos*. Berkeley: University of California Press.

Nazki, M. I. 1986. "Childbirth and Child-Rearing in Ladakh." In *Ladakh: Life and Culture*, edited by K. N. Pandit, 54–72. Srinagar, Kashmir: Centre for Central Asian Studies.

Norberg-Hodge, Helena, and Hazel Russell. 1994. "Birth and Child-Rearing in Zangskar." In *Himalayan Buddhist Villages*, edited by John Crook and Henry Osmaston, 519–31. Bristol: University of Bristol.

Parfionovitch, Yuri, Fernand Meyer, and Gyurme Dorje, eds. 1992. *Tibetan Medical Paintings: Illustrations to the Blue Beryl Treatise of Sangye Gyamtso, 1653–1705*. 2 vols. New York: Harry N. Abrams.

Pigg, Stacy Leigh. 1997. "Authority in Translation: Finding, Knowing, Naming, and Training 'Traditional Birth Attendants' in Nepal." In *Childbirth and Authoritative Knowledge: Cross-Cultural Perspectives*, edited by Robbie David-Floyd and Carolyn Sargent, 233–62. Berkeley: University of California Press.

Pigg, Stacy Leigh. 2001. "Les politiques de développement et les politiques de la santé: Les contradictions de la prévention du sida au Népal." *Anthropologie et Sociétés* 25 (1): 43–62.

Pinto, Sarah. 1999. "Pregnancy and Childbirth in Tibetan Culture." In *Buddhist Women across Cultures: Realizations*, edited by Karma Lekshe Tsomo, 159–68. New York: State University of New York Press.

Pirie, Fernanda. 2006. "Secular Morality, Village Law, and Buddhism in Tibetan Societies." *Journal of the Royal Anthropological Institute* 12:173–90.

Pordié, Laurent. 2002. "La pharmacopée comme expression de société: Une étude himalayenne." In *Des sources du savoir aux médicaments du futur*, edited by Jacques Fleurentin, Guy Mazars, and Jean-Marie Pelt, 183–94. Paris: Éditions IRD–SFE.

Pordié, Laurent. 2003. *The Expression of Religion in Tibetan Medicine: Ideal Conceptions, Contemporary Practices and Political Use*. Pondy Papers in Social Sciences 29. Pondicherry: French Institute of Pondicherry.

Pordié, Laurent. 2007. "Buddhism in the Everyday Medical Practice of the Amchi." *Indian Anthropologist* 37 (1): 93–116.

Pordié, Laurent. 2016. "The Vagaries of Therapeutic Globalization: Fame, Money and Social Relations in Tibetan Medicine." *International Journal of Social Science Studies* 4 (2): 38–52.

Riaboff, Isabelle. 1997. "Les *lha*, une catégorie zangskarie à géométrie variable: Ou, que sont les dieux devenus?" In *Recent Research on Ladakh 7: Proceedings of the 7th Colloquium of the International Association for Ladakh Studies Held in Bonn/Sankt Augustin, 12–15 June 1995*, edited by Thierry Dodin and Heinz Räther, 335–78. Ulm: Ulmer Kulturanthropologische Schriften.

Rozario, Santi, and Geoffrey Samuel. 2002. "Tibetan and Indian Ideas of Birth Pollution: Similarities and Contrasts." In *The Daughters of Hariti: Childbirth and Female Healers in South and Southeast Asia*, edited by Santi Rozario and Geoffrey Samuel, 182–208. London: Routledge.

Samuel, Geoffrey. 2006. "Healing and the Mind-Body Complex: Childbirth and Medical Pluralism in South Asia." In *Multiple Medical Realities: Patients and Healers in Biomedical, Alternative, and Traditional Medicine*, edited by Helle Johannessen and Imre Lázár, 121–35. New York: Berghahn Books.

Sangay, Thubten. 1984. *Tibetan Tradition of Childbirth and Childcare: A Stairway to the Heaven of the Compassionate One*. Tibetan Medicine 7. Dharamsala: Library of Tibetan Work and Archives.

Santoro, Pablo. 2011. "Liminal Biopolitics: Towards a Political Anthropology of the Umbilical Cord and the Placenta." *Body and Society* 17 (1): 73–93.

van Beek, Martijn. 2000. "Lessons from Ladakh? Local Responses to Globalization and Social Change." In *Globalization and Social Change*, edited by Johannes Schmidt and Jacques Hersh, 250–66. London: Routledge.

Van Vleet, Stacey. 2010–11. "Children's Healthcare and Astrology in the Nurturing of a Central Tibetan Nation-State, 1916–24." *Asian Medicine* 6 (2): 348–86.

Wiley, Andrea. 2002. "Increasing Use of Prenatal Care in Ladakh (India): The Roles of Ecological and Cultural Factors." *Social Science and Medicine* 55 (7): 1089–102.

Wiley, Andrea. 2004. *An Ecology of High-Altitude Infancy: A Biocultural Perspective*. Cambridge: Cambridge University Press.

6. A CASE OF WIND DISORDER
The Interplay of Amchi Medicine and
Ritual Treatments in Zangskar

KIM GUTSCHOW

This chapter analyzes the idiom of "wind disorders" (*rlung*) in the Zangskar region of the Western Himalayas to illustrate how an illness episode—from disease through diagnosis and healing—produces local meaning while seeking to restore individual and social well-being. I argue that the idiom of wind in amchi medicine (as Sowa Rigpa, or Tibetan medicine, is known in Zangskar) refracts individual dis-ease or disorder by (1) identifying its probable causes, (2) seeking to disarm the causal factors with medical or ritual means, and (3) restoring individuals and their communities to a state of health or harmony. I am also interested in how patients and healers—in medical and ritual realms—negotiate illness by pursuing a common goal through different but intersecting therapeutic paths. Every illness episode offers a series of moments in which patients and providers choose to make meaning out of ambiguous circumstances according to uniquely crafted but culturally shaped scripts (Kleinman 1980, 1988, 1995, 2006). This search for healing by patient and provider elucidates overlapping and contested paths, including the dialogic search for diagnosis, treatment, and potential cure. In our case, the path of healing illustrates fluid boundaries between medicine and ritual, as well as between private and public discourses around healing. Although the socioeconomic context has shifted considerably since my research was conducted in the 1990s, the general patterns of healing I describe—disease, disorder, diagnosis, treatment, and resolution—can still be found in Zangskar today.

The practice of amchi medicine in Zangskar was never secularized forcibly by the state as happened in the Tibet Autonomous Region (TAR) or Mongolia (Adams 2001; Craig 2012), yet it has modernized slowly in recent decades in response to the global rise of Tibetan medicine as a multimillion-dollar industry by the turn of the millennium and the official recognition of Tibetan medicine by the Indian state in 2010 (Blaikie 2016; Kloos 2016).[1] While the Tibetan medicines produced in the TAR and Dharamsala have become global commodities that rely on international markets and consumers, Zangskari medicines then and now are still produced mostly for local consumption. In Zangskar, as in the Ladakh Union Territory that it is part of, the increasing profitability of Tibetan medicine in India and abroad has meant sharp rises in the costs of materia medica and local plant-based ingredients (Blaikie 2009, 2018; Pordié 2008). By the early years of the new millennium, many Zangskari amchi had adapted to the rising costs of medicinal raw materials in India by limiting the ingredients they used in their medicinal formularies or reselling Tibetan medicines to patients rather than mixing their own medicines. Zangskari amchi who began selling their medicines rather than handing them out for free or in exchange for a bartered meal faced initial criticism from their clients. Yet in recent years, especially among younger amchi, it has become customary to charge a nominal fee for medicines in Zangskar.

Rural training in Ladakh has also undergone shifts as the paradigm of hereditary knowledge, or *gyudpa* (*brgyud pa*), that involves a master-disciple paradigm has adapted to a more hybrid model. Besides the multiyear apprenticeship with a chosen master that continues to be the heart and soul of amchi training in Ladakh, students may undertake more formal study of Tibetan medicine at the Central Institute of Buddhist Studies, which was founded in 1989, and the Men-Tsee-Khang in Dharamsala, which was established in 1961 and remains the premier institute of Tibetan medicine in Asia (Craig 2007; Kloos 2017b; Pordié and Blaikie 2014). In Ladakh, amchi have modernized their practices not by rejecting Buddhist rites but rather by incorporating Tibetan medical and biomedical knowledges and speaking in a language that is more widely accessible to a range of clients, local and foreign (Adams, Schrempf, and Craig 2010; Pordié 2008). In Zangskar, as in Ladakh, amchi still interact and coexist with a wide range of healers including monks, nuns, oracles, exorcists, and astrologers, who have thrived because of a growing rather than shrinking need for their services in increasingly complicated times (Gutschow 2004a, 2004b, 2010; Pordié 2007, 2008).[2] Health concerns faced by amchi and other local Buddhist healers include a range of psychosocial stressors such as rising economic scarcity, socioeconomic uncertainty, political instability, communal violence, and climate change across the Himalayas. Further, households must juggle increasingly fragmented livelihoods as many have at least one or more members engaged in wage labor, tourism, or temporary out-migration to the Indian plains for education or employment, besides the subsistence agriculture that continues to dominate the local Ladakhi economy. Individual health mirrors wider societal well-being, which has been disrupted by rising inequality, scarcity, and other forms of structural violence.

In Zangskar as in both the TAR and elsewhere in India, rlung relates to modernization, frustrated social mobility, and the gaps between aspirations and socioeconomic realities that reflect the endemic social hierarchy and corruption of the Indian state. Both Ladakh and the TAR are remote regions subject to state manipulation and development schemes that benefit only a small sector of elites. Studies of wind disorders among the Tibetans link the phenomenon to modernization, lack of social mobility, and the oppressions that Tibetans face within the TAR and in India (Adams 1998; Deane 2014; Jacobson 2000, 2002, 2007; Janes 1999a, 1999b). Yet Craig Janes (1999b) cautions against reading rlung disorders merely as a "medical weapon of the weak" that is manifested by those with the least socioeconomic power, because he finds that rlung disorders are common among middle-class individuals whose attempts at upward mobility are denied. I agree that for Ladakhis as for Tibetans, rlung disorders are a multivalent phenomenon that relates to thwarted socioeconomic mobility and a lack of social justice. They also relate to the promotion of Buddhist identity within political contexts where religion and ethnicity are contested and communal categories are used to promote and consolidate political or social power. For Zangskari Buddhists, this can mean promoting and asserting their Buddhist identity within Kargil district, where Muslims are the majority and hold more political and social power (Gutschow 2004a; Gutschow 2006).

Ethnographic Methods

The ethnographic research for this essay was conducted in the Zangskar and Ladakh regions of the Indian Himalayas for forty-seven months between 1990 and 2003, including a concentrated period of PhD research between 1990 and 1998, three winter residences (1994, 1995, and 1996), and annual trips lasting several months between 1998 and 2003. I studied classical Tibetan at Harvard and became fluent in Zangskari between 1990 and 1992; all of my interviews were conducted in the local Tibetan dialects of Zangskari and Ladakhi. The winters in Zangskar were especially isolated in the 1990s, as there was no reliable phone or internet and the only means of communication with Ladakh was a police radio, which failed even in medical emergencies, resulting in several deaths, during my fieldwork period. Straddling the greater and lesser Himalayan ranges with less than 1 percent of their regions arable or cultivatable, Kargil and Leh districts together compose the newly established Union Territory of Ladakh that was created on October 31, 2019, alongside the Union Territory of Jammu and Kashmir. Demographically, Ladakh Union Territory had a population of roughly 275,000 in 2011—46 percent Muslims, 40 percent Buddhists, and 12 percent Hindus.[3] This essay focusses on Buddhists, who make up over 90 percent of Zangskar's population.

During my fieldwork, I mostly lived at a Buddhist nunnery in Karsha and studied directly under one of the most renowned Zangskari amchi, Lonpo Sonam Angchug, who was not only an amchi but also an astrologer, a teacher of Tibetan at the local public schools, a historian, the author of several short books about Zangskari history and medicine, and the founder of a medical and astrology institute (Men-Tsee-Khang) in Karsha village in 2005. I traveled to most of Zangskar's 100 hamlets, interviewed and spent time visiting patients with many of the region's renowned amchi, and studied the central text of Tibetan medicine, the Gyüshi (*rgyud bzhi*), with local amchi as my guides. In terms of the case study I describe, I was present when Ngawang had his psychotic break, observed one of several rites conducted on his behalf, and spent several weeks afterward interviewing family members, amchi, and ritual healers familiar with his case. I also followed up in subsequent years to confirm Ngawang's condition and his ongoing relationship with Dragom Rinpoche, who had first conducted the healing ceremonies I observed. I have changed the names of Ngawang and his family but not those of the healers, who consented for their names be used in this account.

A Case Study of Wind Disorder in Zangskar

Ngawang was the youngest of three brothers from a remote village in Zangskar. His eldest brother had inherited the family estate, and his second brother had become a monk, yet Ngawang's prospects were uncertain. Unmarried and mostly unschooled, he wondered how he could secure enough income to move out of his brother's house and establish a family of his own. In his early twenties, he began to work as a horseman, ferrying tourists and their supplies along a popular north-south trekking route between Darcha (which lies just beyond the border of Zangskar and the neighboring state of Himachal Pradesh) and Lamayuru (which lies in northern Ladakh Union Territory). Because of its remoteness from the neighboring but guerrilla-ridden Kashmir valley, Ladakh has seen a steady influx of visitors since the region was opened to foreign tourists in 1976, and in 2019 it was estimated that over 300,000 foreign and Indian tourists visited. While working as a trekking guide in 1991, Ngawang earned 150 Indian rupees per day for every horse he hired to tourists or larger trekking companies. This was a modest income in Zangskar, where government servants like teachers earned less than five thousand rupees a month at that time. By the end of the summer in 1991, he had saved nearly six thousand rupees, which was subsequently stolen from his hotel room in Manali. Unlike in the villages of Zangskar, where a network of friends, relatives, or acquaintances might have led him to the thief, the midsized hill town of Manali—which teemed with merchants, government contractors, and investors from the Indian plains; Tibetan refugees; and foreign tourists and residents—provided no easy means for finding the thief.

The loss of an entire summer's earnings precipitated Ngawang's deep depression during the coming winter. After Ngawang became very listless and socially withdrawn, his family called two local amchi from nearby villages who offered similar diagnoses of a wind disorder (*rlung gi nad pa*), which they treated with the standard array of herbal medicines they had prepared themselves. The second amchi also applied moxibustion—placing burning herbs on Ngawang's skull and upper vertebrae—on astrologically auspicious days. When Ngawang showed no sign of improvement, his family summoned a more senior amchi from the more distant village of Bya, who diagnosed a wind disorder complicated by phlegm (*bad kan*) and treated him with different medicines and two more courses of moxibustion. By May, Ngawang's condition had improved somewhat, but he was still withdrawn.

Most of the villagers agreed that his condition worsened during the summer of 1992 after a series of unfortunate events. During his work as a horseman on the three-week trek from Darcha to Lamayuru, Ngawang began to commit a series of mysterious thefts along his route, to everyone's surprise. In what was considered highly unusual behavior for a Zangskari, Ngawang began to filch small items from each of the local homes where he had stayed, and it was rumored that he had stolen over a thousand rupees from a home in Lamayuru. In most cases, the thefts were discovered only after Ngawang had moved on, but then his luck worsened. After he lost two horses on a subsequent trek out of Padum, villagers reported that he became deranged and suffered what seemed to be a more severe form of wind disorder or a psychotic break. His eccentric behaviors included overt hostility toward close friends as well as delusions of grandeur. He shouted epithets and threw stones at friends while alternately blessing strangers with his rosary as if he were a high monk.

When Ngawang returned home at the end of the summer, he was suffering from increasingly violent and irrational behavior. One night he broke most of the windows in his village—windows that had been shipped at considerable expense by truck from Srinagar to Padum and then by horse to his distant village.

The amchi from Bya now interpreted his illness as madness (*smyo ba*) caused by demonic attack (*gdon*).[4] In response, the local headman called a village-wide meeting to discuss what should be done before Ngawang caused any more harm to fellow villagers or their property. After a lengthy democratic decision-making process, Ngawang's family agreed to lock Ngawang in their household storeroom for a few weeks, where they kept him as comfortable as possible. By offering Ngawang just enough food and Tibetan medicine during this period of solitary confinement, the family tried to sap the strength of the demons that had precipitated his mental breakdown. Not surprisingly, Ngawang became manic soon after being released from his month-long confinement, so his family decided to invite a renowned Tibetan Rinpoche (reincarnate monk) to perform an exorcism.

When Dragom Rinpoche arrived in Ngawang's village in late September, he was riding a white horse and accompanied by roughly a dozen monks from Phugthal monastery, where he had been giving a teaching. As Rinpoche dismounted directly in front of Ngawang's house, the assembled villagers bowed in greeting, but Ngawang usurped this reception by dodging in front of the faithful and blessing them himself. Rinpoche simply ignored him and strode purposefully into the house wearing a blue motorcycle helmet—a protection against falls from his horse as much as the low Zangskari doorways, I was told by his assistants. Once inside, Rinpoche climbed onto a low throne covered with the finest rugs, where he was served a feast of delicacies generally reserved for festivals or weddings, including fresh fruit, stewed apricots in clarified butter, fried noodles, and meat momos. Rinpoche began a set of tantric meditations (*sadhana*) to invoke the tantric protectors he would call on during the exorcism. After performing a brief divination ceremony (*mo*) and consulting his astrological texts, he announced that the spirits possessing Ngawang were a pair of male and female demons (*dri pho* and *dri mo*) and explained the nature of the exorcism rite that was to follow.

Following this ritual diagnosis, the crew of monks began to prepare a small universe of effigies (*glud*) for the rest of the day. After mixing barley flour and water into dough, the monks molded a set of grimacing figures, one black and one white, that depicted the male and female demons currently occupying Ngawang's consciousness (*rnam shes*). Further sets of effigies representing the demonic entourage (*'khor lo*) included 120 tiny figurines placed on four boards arranged facing the four cardinal directions. Each board contained thirty figures set in three rows—ten dogs, then ten yaks, and finally ten humans—all dusted with a colored powder according to the direction in which the figures would be tossed.[5] Ngawang observed the preparations, at times intervening to lift the effigies to his chest or jumping erratically. His motions were jerky, and his voice changed to a high-pitched and strangled whine, while his eyes rolled wildly during these episodes. All day, he appeared to be rapidly alternating between dissociation and ordinary consciousness, while the monks watched with awe and amusement.

After the effigies were brought into Rinpoche's chambers late in the day, Ngawang was called into the room. Rinpoche summoned the tantric protectors once more, commanding the demons to leave Ngawang's body and enter the central effigies.[6] The efficacy of the ritual depended on the Rinpoche's prowess in calling on his tantric protectors to coerce the demons into leaving Ngawang's body. Ngawang showed a surprising deference at this moment, as he prostrated himself fervently and eagerly accepted a protective amulet from Rinpoche. The audience of villagers took Ngawang's subordination as proof that the demons possessing him were subject to the power of the tantric protectors.[7] At dusk—when demons are believed to prowl—four volunteers each took a board of the tiny effigies roughly a hundred paces from the house in the four directions. The smaller effigies were cast into the wild grasses beyond the edges of the village fields, as it is inauspicious and polluting to toss effigies into cultivated land. The larger effigies were tossed into the streambed far below the junction of the stream with any irrigation channels that fed the village fields.

After completing the exorcism, Rinpoche blessed each village house by tossing barley seeds and distributing blessed medicinal balls (*sbyin rlabs*) to all present. While the monks readied their horses for departure, Ngawang grabbed Rinpoche's horse and rode headlong out of the village with the monks in full flight. After the monks gave chase and managed to wrestle Ngawang off the horse, Ngawang continued his antics by blessing the villagers as if he were a Rinpoche. When Rinpoche rode off down the valley with a procession of monks, Ngawang ran alongside and tried, without success, to grab the horse's bit from a villager assigned to deflect him. After chasing the procession to the last chorten at the far edge of the village, Ngawang walked slowly back to his home, alone. Now that the energy of the ritual pomp had dissipated, Ngawang wandered moodily about in the eerie silence. He jumped and shouted mantras while circumambulating his house, before adopting even stranger behavior. I saw that he had tied a rope around his waist and was dragging a cushion behind him while braying like a donkey.

His condition seemed to have gone from bad to worse. Earlier that day, an oracle from Lingshed who was part of the Rinpoche's entourage had been briefly possessed by two spirits, Kha che dmar po and rDo rje Shug ldan. He prophesied that Ngawang's situation would improve only after the winter. The villagers did not view the Rinpoche's treatment as a failure but rather as a first step toward a cure that would require merit making and further ritual interventions before the negative karma could be fully expiated. In other words, the villagers suspected that Ngawang's demonic attack was the result of deeper karmic causality that could be undone only through a lengthy healing process of merit making, ritual, and other healing actions.

When Ngawang's condition did not improve despite a month of merit making, including reading religious texts and reciting prayers (*mani*), he was taken to Leh town for further treatment by Ladakhi and Tibetan doctors who were living in the Tibetan refugee settlement of Choglamsar. During an audience with Dragom Rinpoche in Leh, Ngawang suddenly stated a wish to become a monk. Rinpoche advised him to wait and spend the winter studying religious texts and taking Tibetan medicines, so he began to train as an oracle, seeking out a teacher in Leh; many oracles began their apprenticeship with similar possession experiences.[8] His initial tutelage involved lengthy séances in which his teacher and other senior oracles interrogated Ngawang so they could identify the spirits haunting him, while banishing the remaining demonic influences. His initiation as an oracle concluded with the critical "separation rite" (*lha 'dre phye byes*) in which the spirits inhabiting his consciousness were named and bound by oath to work for broader Mahayana aims, including the welfare of all sentient beings.[9]

The following summer, Ngawang returned to Zangskar, where he was ordained as a monk by Dragom Rinpoche. Arriving far later than the time specified by Rinpoche—an insult had he not been an oracle—Ngawang was ordained as a monk by a slightly annoyed Rinpoche. He was possessed in the presence of Rinpoche and the senior officiating monks, all of whom verified the deities inhabiting Ngawang's consciousness. Ngawang's fame soon spread through Zangskar, and the next year he was named resident caretaker (*gnyer pa*) of Rinpoche's palace (*pho drang*) in Zangskar's central town of Padum. After working diligently as a caretaker for the Rinpoche who had helped cure him, Ngawang's thefts were later forgiven, and eventually he regained most of his former social status in Zangskar.

Diagnosis and Treatment of Wind Disorders in Zangskar

Let us consider how Ngawang's case reflects the more general ways that wind disorders are diagnosed and treated in Zangskar. The methods of diagnosis and treatment of wind disorders in Zangskar are based on the Gyüshi, the foundational text in Tibetan medicine and the single text that most amchi in Zangskar study and eventually memorize. In the Gyüshi, patient diagnosis involves pulse reading, urine analysis, and verbal or visual examination of the patient. In Zangskar both pulse and urine analysis are considered advanced and subjective techniques that reflect an amchi's experience and training with a particular teacher, and thus it is not uncommon to have slightly conflicting diagnoses between two amchi who trained with different teachers.

Most Zangskari amchi begin by reading a patient's pulse before moving to a verbal and visual examination of the patient. In pulse reading the amchi lays three middle fingers across each of the patient's wrists, taking up to several minutes to read each wrist. Each half of a finger reads a separate set of organs on each side, for a total of twelve organs as specified in the Gyüshi.[10] In Tibetan medical literature, the pulse is read or measured in highly figurative and metaphorical language to indicate a variety of physiological disorders. For instance, one kind of wind disorder is characterized by a pulse that is adrift, empty, and discontinuous, "like a melon floating on water, push it down and it pops up" (Clifford 1984, 101). In Ngawang's case, the pulse diagnosis was critical to the general diagnosis of wind disorder made by all the amchi who treated him, yet it was the third and more senior amchi from Bya who offered a more sophisticated diagnosis and treatment that led to Ngawang's improvement in the spring of 1992. Yet each of these amchi treatments would prove insufficient in the face of the psychotic breakdown that happened during the summer of 1992, which was later divined to be a demonic attack.

After taking a patient's pulse, most Zangskari amchi I observed would resort to visual and verbal examinations to complete their diagnosis. The visual examination covers the patient's tongue, complexion, and any other parts of the body as necessary. The verbal examination covers not only the patient but also their family members as it addresses diet, behavior, and all events that may have contributed to the illness. By talking to a patient's family, the amchi can elicit and cross-check significant details within the patient's illness narrative. In rural Zangskar, where many villagers know each other, the contextual richness of the amchi's diagnosis is supplemented by his knowledge of the patient's relatives, village, or family circumstances. Because most amchi are called locally to the villages nearest to where they live, there is a good chance they have interacted with members of the household or village to which they are called or even consulted with other amchi on the case. Most amchi that I observed operated on a collegial basis, sharing their diagnoses and treatment plans with the families in question as well as with other amchi.

In Ngawang's case, it was considered perfectly acceptable to consult several amchi and even to treat Ngawang simultaneously with medicines from different amchi as long as all healers were informed of these arrangements. Further, the interview with family members and fellow villagers provided important details that Ngawang was unable or unwilling to provide, especially after his psychotic break. These details included the rumors about Ngawang's thefts, which Ngawang consistently denied, as well as descriptions of his delusionary behaviors, such as blessing villagers or treating close friends with arrogance or hostility. An amchi's knowledge of a patient's family or at least of other members of their village is premised on an abundance of amchi across Zangskar. This was the norm until 2000, when roughly three-fourths of Zangskar's 100 hamlets still had a resident amchi, who was almost always male. The most significant changes in recent decades have been a sharp decline in the number of amchi in remote Zangskari villages and a rise in the number of female amchi, especially in urban areas like Leh and its surroundings.

When I conducted my research in the 1990s, many Zangskari amchi still made daily or weekly visits on foot or horseback to their most serious patients to track the progress of their treatments and readjust their diagnosis and treatment as needed. This continual adjustment or fine-tuning of both diagnosis and treatment in response to how the patient's pulse and other symptoms shift daily in the course of disease is central to the success of Tibetan medicine and may be overlooked in the modern urban clinics in Leh, Kathmandu, Delhi, or abroad, where patients purchase Tibetan medicine over the web or the counter (Craig 2012; Jacobson 2000; Pordié 2008).

I observed that many Zangskari amchi diagnosed and treated simple cases using pulse, verbal, and visual examination without ever using urine analysis. Yet most of my informants could recite the proper way to conduct a urine analysis by measuring the color, cloudiness, odor, steam, sediments, and surface bubbles or scum of the urine.[11] The most knowledgeable amchi in Zangskar each stressed the importance of urinalysis for serious ailments that proved most impervious to diagnosis or treatment, such as severe wind disorders. For Meme Palchung from Bagartse, for instance, the proper analysis of a wind disorder caused by spirit attack (gdon) required divination, such as superimposing a virtual grid of nine squares (*me ba dgu*) onto the surface of the cup of urine in order to divine the source of illness by seeing the location where the bubbles arose and their relative duration.[12] Meme Palchung believed that Ngawang's illness could have been more properly diagnosed and treated had the first amchi conducted a urine analysis, for instance.

Most Zangskari amchi offer treatment in four stages, depending on the severity and course of the disease. The first stage of therapy involves diet and behavior modification that is adapted to the disorder, the patient's underlying constitution, the season, and the place in which the illness occurred. Tibetan medicine and Indian Ayurveda both classify people by identifying three basic humors—wind (rlung), bile (mkhris pa), and phlegm (bad kan)—that are the premise of both health and illness. Although people have a slight predominance of one or two of these humors, they are healthy when the humors are in homeostatic balance and unhealthy when they are unbalanced. The humors are known as "faults" (nyes pa in Tibetan, dosa in Sanskrit) because each is related to one of three mental poisons (dug gsum) that are the obstacles to enlightenment within Tibetan Buddhism. While wind arises from desire ('dod chags), hatred (zhe sdang) gives rise to bile, and ignorance (gti mug) to phlegm. Ultimately, all three faults are premised on basic ignorance, and only enlightenment, which implies the removal of all ignorance, can free the body from its faults, their attendant suffering, and the wheel of life or rebirth that they produce.

In Tibetan medicine, individuals, seasons, days, and times of the day are each described by a dominant humor, and treatment must take into account a person's underlying constitution; the place where the person lives; the season, month, day, and even time of day of the illness; and the diet that exacerbates the illness or most promotes healing.[13] Tibetan medicine includes an elaborate dietology that draws from Indian Ayurveda, in which foods are classified according to their climate, taste (rasa), and the bodily humor (dosa) they nourish.[14] Most Zangskari amchi prescribe or proscribe foods and behaviors according to this complex calculus, described at length in the Gyüshi and other texts. In general, wind disorders are fueled by the consumption of coarse, bitter, sour, spicy, or astringent foods and by plants or animals that grow in high or dry climates. Commonly avoided foods include chilies, onions, honey, ginger soup, goat's milk, soybeans, alcohol, and pork. By contrast, foods used to treat a wind disorder include meat stew, medicinal butters, clarified butter, and barley or pea flour gruel (thug pa) with meat or dried yak cheese.

Most amchi I observed and interviewed were quick to offer dietary and behavioral advice and some general suggestions about lifestyle or circumstantial events that may have contributed to the illness. Yet they rarely offered any forms of therapy or personal counseling directly in terms of suggestions for improving family dynamics or communication, for instance. As such, Ngawang's case was rather typical given that none of the amchi made explicit behavioral suggestions about how Ngawang might overcome his anxiety about his lost earnings or take remedial actions to compensate the households from which he had stolen items the previous summer. Ngawang's initial behavioral treatment—enforced confinement—was radical but not unheard of in Zangskar. Several amchi mentioned that they had either used or heard of forcible confinement being used in other cases when it seemed patients might harm themselves or others. One of these cases involved a young man who was believed to be suicidal after spiraling into depression following being involuntary discharged from the army and dropping out of school. Because amchi treatments had little effect over a period of months that stretched into years, the patient was flown to the distant city of Jammu one winter, where he received electroshock therapy, with limited success. It took years before he fully recovered, but he eventually married and lived in his older brother's house. This case also illustrates the growing use of allopathic treatments alongside amchi treatments, particularly in urban areas or among elites who can afford the expensive allopathic medicines or treatments outside Ladakh.

In Zangskar the second stage of amchi treatment, often concurrent with the first stage, involves medicinal pills or powders taken with hot water or decocted. In some cases, the amchi may prescribe an herbal mixture to strengthen or "draw out" the illness so as to sharpen his diagnosis in order to prescribe more specific medical treatments. In such cases, the prescribed herbs may exacerbate the illness until it peaks, at which point a new set of medications is prescribed. While amchi in Leh usually administer herbs in the form of hardened pills, produced locally or in Dharamsala by Tibetan doctors, most Zangskari amchi and patients are unable to afford these ready-made pills. During my research, most Zangskari amchi still produced their own medicinal mixtures from powdered herbs or materia medica that they bought locally, in Leh, or in neighboring Manali and other Indian hill towns where medical markets flourish. Owing to the rising cost of ingredients and the lack of standardized prices for medicines or amchi services, the locally produced medicines suffered from a limited range of local ingredients, as noted earlier.

A third stage of treatment is given if herbal treatments have little noticeable effect after a few weeks. This third stage includes massage, enemas, purgatives, or moxibustion—in which the amchi applies the burning tip of the rolled-up gerbera root, or a golden needle to specific points on the skull, vertebrae, or elsewhere on the body. The major points for moxa or acupuncture are charted in the Blue Beryl, a classic text composed by the seventeenth-century Desi Sangye Gyatso, who founded the Men-Tsee-Khang (School of Astrology and Medicine) in Tibet. Moxibustion may be given only on specific days of the month according to astrological calculations.[15] When a patient's illness stubbornly persists after the first three stages of therapy, the amchi may resort to a fourth stage, namely, ritual diagnosis and treatment. In some cases, ritual and merit-making activities are prescribed alongside herbal treatments from the beginning to benefit the patient most quickly if a spiritual or karmic cause is suspected. Ritual cures are considered the most effective in ailments caused by spirits or resulting from prior karma. The amchi and other healers may use a range of methods including divination, astrology, and oracular consultation to help interpret the spiritual or karmic forces causing the ailment. Many amchi are trained to do basic divinations and astrological calculations so that they can recommend appropriate rituals or merit-making practices for their patients.

If a succession of medical diagnoses and treatments fail, the patient or their family may call in further healers or even consult allopathic providers. These latter are scarce across much of rural Zangskar, but patients can travel to the Community Health Center in Zangskar's central town of Padum or to Leh hospital; the more easily accessible Kargil hospital is notorious for having poor-quality care and corruption (Gutschow 2010, 2016). Given this contin-uum of healing, most Zangskari amchi may suggest a patient visit and even themselves consult with a range of other local healers—astrologers (*rtsis pa*), oracles (*lha pa*), exorcists (*dbon po*), and monks—during their diagnosis and treatment of the most stubborn cases.[16] These traditional healers all draw on shared idioms of karma and responsibility, although their emphases may differ. They recognize the primacy of the law of karma, yet each healer focuses on a slightly different paradigm of secondary or contributing causes (*rkyen*). In rough terms that do not do full justice to the complexity of possible diagnoses and treatments, I argue that the amchi discourses emphasize diet and behav-ior, oracle discourses emphasize spirit possession and attack, and astrological discourses seek planetary and other astrologically determined sources of dis-harmony. When amchi and other Ladakhi healers adopt a fluid and holistic view that incorporates a wide range of contextual phenomena, they sacrifice the sharp focus of biomedicine.[17]

Describing Wind as Mental Disturbances in Tibetan and Amchi Medicine

Zangskari amchi do not always separate mental disturbances from other so-matic disorders. But they tend to use several dominant idioms or terms for mental disorders, including "wind disorder" (rlung gi nad pa), "mind disor-der" (*sems nad*), and "madness" (smyo ba), which may or may not have a wind component. The Gyüshi does not have a separate category for mental disorders but subsumes them under three categories: wind disorder (rlung gi nad), de-monic attack (gdon), and "channel disorder" (*rtsa dkar*).[18] Tibetan medicine emphasizes wind because it is the vehicle for consciousness and the mind, which is central to Buddhist practice, ethics, and philosophy. The notion of wind as a vehicle is visualized using the metaphor of wind as a horse on which consciousness rides into the world. Without a stable wind, the mind literally will fly away. As one Tibetan doctor aptly stated, "It is like a tree supporting a bird. If there is no tree, where will the bird stay?" (Dr. Pema Dorje, quoted in Clifford 1984, 136).[19] As two famous doctors have stated, the mind "is the architect of all our suffering and happiness" (Dr. Yeshi Donden, the Dalai Lama's personal physician, and Mr. Gyatso Tshering, quoted in Dummer 1994, 36). The idiom of wind offers a unique insight into the ways that the mind both creates and responds to the suffering inherent in existence, according to the Buddha's first noble truth. The Gyüshi lists five different types of wind: life-sustaining, ascending, pervasive, metabolic, and descending, each of which sustains a wide variety of bodily functions.[20] As such, wind affects not only the beating of the heart but also the rate of digestion in the stomach and intestines and the way that the bladder and colon produce elimination. Wind exists on a different plane from the other two humors. While bile and phlegm are contraries that cancel each other out, wind is a pivotal humor that has the power to decrease or increase either bile or phlegm. This primacy and omnipresence of wind is central to Tibetan medicine, Indian Ayurveda, and traditional Chinese medicine.[21]

In amchi medicine, most cases of demonic attack or channel disorders exhibit some psychiatric symptoms, while some wind disorders do not manifest as psychiatric disturbances. In short, wind disorders can induce a wide range of somatic effects including restlessness, frequent sighing, vertigo, tremors, erratic or diffuse pain, lassitude, insomnia, fright on awakening, protruding eyes, frequent moaning, delirium, and anger. However, the category of wind disorders includes clearly mental and psychiatric ailments such as amnesia, mania, catatonia, depression, dysphasia, dyslalia, and hyperactivity.[22] The Gyüshi classifies wind disorders into sixty-three types: forty-eight general disorders and fifteen specific wind disorders otherwise known as mental disturbances (smyo ba). The forty-eight general types of wind disorder are subdivided into twenty-eight primary types grouped according to the bodily system they affect—the skin, muscular, adipose, vascular, or lymphatic system—and twenty secondary types grouped according to their bodily effects (muscular rigidity, muscle wasting, swelling, contraction, deformity, delirium, coma, and pain).[23]

Mark Epstein and Lobsang Rabgyay (1982) describe the Gyüshi classificatory schema of mental disturbances as consisting of seven categories, according to the underlying cause. The first three types involve a disturbance of mind caused by an underlying imbalance of one of the three bodily humors. For instance, patients suffering from a wind type of mental disturbance exhibit excitability, sadness, constant crying, abrupt anger, or an inability to concentrate and remember. The bile type of mental disorders might manifest as varying degrees of addiction, self-destructiveness, violence, or obsessive grudges. Finally, the phlegm type of mental disorders may manifest as a person being withdrawn, silent, introverted, depressed, or drowsy. The fourth type of mental disturbance involves all three humors simultaneously. The fifth, sixth, and seventh groups of mental disturbances arise from depression, toxins, and harmful spirits respectively. Epstein and Rabgyay add that excessive fasting, sex, sleep, or forceful retention of excreta can all exacerbate wind disturbances. By contrast, using a more psychoanalytic lens, Terry Clifford (1984) groups the major causes of mental disturbance as karma, humoral imbalance, grief-worry, toxins, and evil spirits. Clifford's category of grief-worry is similar to Epstein and Rabgyay's category of depression, although Clifford emphasizes compulsive thoughts over lost love, status, or possessions. In Epstein and Rabgyay's (1982, 80–91) account, depressive mental disturbances are caused not only by loss but also by excessive self-absorption, self-criticism, antipathy, or anger. Both Clifford and Epstein and Rabgyay define toxins as poisons administered by others or the accidental but toxic combination of certain foods. Clifford (1984, 138–39) clarifies the psychological factors that compound the three major types of humoral mental disorders by focusing on emotions. In her analysis, an excess of lust, mental strain, emotional attachment, or grief may cause a wind type of mental illness. Likewise, too much anger or aggression may lead to a bile type of mental disorder, and excess confusion, ignorance, sloth, or social withdrawal may cause the mental disorders associated with phlegm.

Clifford singles out karma as a specific cause, while Epstein and Rabgyay represent the Tibetan and Zangskari understanding that all illness is ultimately due to karma and secondarily due to a precipitating cause. In short, if karma is the major cause of an illness, then herbal treatments can provide only limited treatment, and ritual or merit making will be required.[24] Both Clifford and Epstein and Rabgyay describe the idiom of demonic attack (gdon) in varying fashion. They combine Buddhist and psychoanalytic approaches to describe demons as embodied emotional affect or projections.[25] Like Epstein and Rabgyay, Clifford describes demons as the projection of intense fear, anger, or grief. Clifford betrays her psychoanalytic leanings by depicting demons as unconscious or subconscious fantasies, yet she also cites the twelfth-century yogini Machig Labdron, who said that demons are anything that obstructs Buddhist practice.

While Zangskari amchi recognize that all ailments are ultimately due to karma, they focus on the secondary or conditioning causes that are more susceptible to treatment. However, when they encounter ailments that remain impervious to medical diagnosis or treatment, they tend to fall back on the idiom of karma. In Ngawang's case, the villagers understood Rinpoche's explanation that Ngawang's ailment was due to past karma (*ngan ma'i las*) and could be cured only through individual merit making. In this analytic schema, ritual is a necessary catalyst that begins the healing process by freeing Ngawang from the immediate danger of the demons, but it alone cannot produce a complete cure. For this, Ngawang would need to undertake extensive merit making and behavioral changes that might undo the effects of prior karma and further move Ngawang into a healthier state where he might generate positive karma and heal the familial and social disruptions that his illness and behavior had caused. So how does the demonic attack relate to this broader theory of karma?

In Zangskari idiom, past karma propels every individual through many rebirths within what is colloquially known as the wheel of life (*srid pa'i 'khor lo*). This wheel is divided into six realms: the three upper realms are human (*mi*), god (*lha*), and demigod (*lha ma yin*), and the three lower realms are animal (*sems can*), hungry ghosts (*yi dvags*), and hell beings (*dmyal ba*). Many of the demons (*'dre*) believed to attack people—like ghosts (*srin 'dre, ro langs*), king spirits (*rgyal po*), and rock spirits (*btsan*)—are classified together with hungry ghosts (yi dvags), all of which cause people harm if angered or not properly propitiated.[26] As coinhabitants of this multivalent realm of life where all actions have effects that influence or determine future events and relationships, demons and people are in mutual relationships and must negotiate their conflicts or interactions. In recommending or performing divinatory or propitiatory rites to appease these invisible beings that inhabit the other four realms besides the visible realms of human and animal life, the amchi accepts the provisional reality of these undesirable spirits. Both healer and patient understand demons as beings that can be offended and appeased through ritual negotiation.

One Zangskari amchi classified six types of madness (smyo ba) that arise from nonhumoral causes as follows: (1) excessive desire or ambition, (2) problematic family relations, (3) misfortune or disaster, (4) improper tantric study, (5) witchcraft, and (6) spirit attack. The first four kinds of mental disturbance in this Zangskari schema are related largely to the patient's inner social or psychic dynamic, while the latter two are considered external attacks. This Zangskari amchi explained that medicine alone can treat disorders arising from the first three causes, but disorders caused by tantric study, witchcraft, or spirit attack all require ritual intervention and/or merit making as part of the cure. In Ngawang's case, because both internal factors (excessive desire and misfortune) and external factors (spirit attack) were contributing causes, his cure could be effected only by ritual treatment.

Ritual Therapy and Therapeutic Resolution

The practices and discourse of wind disorders and mental disorders in Zangskar emphasizes the logic of appeasement, resolution, and social closure that is central to what Vincanne Adams, Mona Schrempf, and Sienna Craig (2010, 13) have termed the "morally charged cosmology" of Buddhist and shamanic rites (see Desjarlais 2016; Ortner 1978; Riaboff 1997; Samuel 1993). I want to single out how therapeutic rites for mental disorders focus on healing and reintegration rather than destruction or symbolic violence. Both spirit attack and witchcraft are instructive in this regard. In Zangskar the most common rites of appeasement for spirit attack—such as ransom offerings (be le), subdual of demons ('dul ba, sri gnon), or exorcisms (rgya bzhi)—are premised on negotiations between human and spirit realms and a recognition of their profound interdependence that draws on the deep Buddhist law of interdependent origination (Gutschow 2004a; Samuel 1993). Because it is assumed that human witches or demonic spirits are operating involuntarily or unintentionally, neither spirits nor witches are punished or destroyed in Zangskar. Instead, in a Buddhist strategy that emphasizes nonharming, integration, and negotiation, attempts are made to appease or defuse the tension with offended spirits in order to restore individual health or social harmony.

Many exorcisms, including the one described in this case study, feed the demons and with varying degrees of forcefulness request the demons to cease and desist rather than attempting a symbolic destruction. Like demonic attack, witchcraft is understood as a set of negative actions directed against a person that results in illness or other harm (Gutschow 2004a). To treat witchcraft, an amchi, an oracle, or an exorcist may be called to identify a witch by grabbing the patient's fourth finger and thereby channeling the voice of the witch. If the patient in that moment yields the name of the witch, rites are held to destroy the witch's negative influence by burning a piece of the witch's clothing or a piece of paper with their name on it. Unless witches are suspected to have administered poison—which is very hard to prove—the goal of the witchcraft rite is to defuse the negative energy directed at the patient rather than punishing or killing the witch as in Africa, for instance, where witches may be ostracized or subjected to horrific types of physical harm, including stoning (Ashforth 2005; Comaroff and Comaroff 1999; Moore and Sanders 2001).

In Zangskari idiom, attributing illness to external forces *outside the patient*, like local spirits, allows individuals to participate in their own cure through transactional rites. This healing logic of identifying external sources of suffering rather than internal ones, like the patient's karma or the three humors and mental poisons, allows patients to negotiate with the spiritual, social, or psychic obstacles that have been created in the course of the ailment. During rites of ablution and purification, when patients are purified with sacred water, the officiant and patient both call on the subterranean spirits known as *klu* and local protective divinities to remove the sickness. While the subduing of negative forces or the removal of spiritual pollution offers a negotiation with other beings, patients may also be directed to merit-making activities that involve no negotiation but repeated actions such as circumambulating stupas or temples, reciting prayers, attending initiations, fasting, or making donations (*sbyin pa*) to a monastic assembly. As I have described elsewhere, public merit-making rites require money, time, and social connections, while also creating significant symbolic and spiritual capital for the donor (Gutschow 2004a, 2010). Many individual merit-making practices, such as circumambulation and prayer, require little wealth, literacy, or social status, although merit making incorporates highly public acts. The public performance of purifications, ablutions, and merit making also restores social ties that may have been ruptured by illness, as patients reconnect with their communities and families. This "morally charged cosmology" (Adams, Schrempf, and Craig 2010) that encompasses both ritual healing and amchi medicine repairs ruptured bonds and restores social functioning to individuals and communities.

I argue that if one sees demons as symbolic representations of psychosocial turbulence, the exorcism is an attempt to defuse that turbulence by trying to divine what is needed and then working ritually to accomplish individual and familial or community harmony. Put another way, if the demons reflect the psychosocial stressors that have afflicted or attacked the patient, exorcisms and ablutions operate with the assumption that it is most effective to redirect these afflictions given how futile it is to destroy them in a world composed of suffering. How do the rites repair or restore individual health and the social fabric? The public performance of rites of exorcism, ablution, or appeasement offers a public atonement for the village community, which is both the audience and the beneficiary of the ritual offerings. Ultimately, the ritual is intended to benefit the wider village community by ensuring good fortune and absolving the individual inauspiciousness that has caused the sickness and disrupted the family or the wider social fabric. In Zangskari idiom, both individual karma and the collective karma of the village are improved through such public rites.

In our case study, Ngawang's family needed to restore the trust of fellow villagers after he broke the windows in the village and stole from several local households. The physical shattering of glass in this remote region represented a fracturing in the reciprocal confidence or trust that households will contain the violent tendencies of an individual member like Ngawang. The lengthy and costly ritual that Ngawang's household undertook, including a feast for the entire village and collective merit making that would benefit all the households in the village, served as a public apology and attempted restitution for the loss of the windows. While the family was not asked to pay for the broken glass, the public feast and ritual expenses served as a substitute gift to the village. Even after Ngawang had shattered all of the glass in the village during his psychotic break, the fellow villagers did not even think to call the police or demand financial compensation immediately, although gifts were accepted in due course. His family took full responsibility for his actions and tried to find medical and then ritual treatment when it emerged that this ailment could not be cured through simple medicinal formulas.

Conclusions

The logic of negotiating between human and spirit worlds is part of a broader cultural script of negotiation that is central to Zangskari healing idioms. The dialogue among the patient, their family, and healers reveals a flexible transactionalism. The transactions between family and healer are refracted by the transactions between human and nonhuman actors like demons. The interactions between patients and healers are contextual, pragmatic, and improvisational.[27] Patients and healers have considerable agency and flexibility in deciphering the causes and consequences of their ailments. It is not that the medicine is insufficient but rather that the medicine primarily addresses the humoral imbalance, while ritual healing is needed to address the karmic imbalance. For patients, efficacy is measured in both bodily improvement and moral meaning. The efficacy of treatment depends on healing the patient by reversing a transgression of physical, psychic, or social boundaries. Additionally, the efficacy of the healer is measured in terms of a broader moral framework of compassion and restitution, regardless of individual cases of success or failure. As such, the healing process both legitimates extant social hierarchies and resolves inevitable conflicts within those hierarchies.

Our case illustrates how Zangskari discourse about mental disturbances can offer a productive site for both meaning and agency. Yet this is not always the case, as the case of the young man who received shock therapy indicates. Patient and provider engage in contextual ways that require local knowledge and a specific ethical stance. For an amchi to engage with the "science of healing" (*gso ba rig pa*, i.e., Tibetan medicine) requires a deep knowledge of Tibetan medicine as well as an active ethical stance oriented toward compassion and awareness of individual and collective suffering. Although not always paragons of virtue and occasionally inclined to raucous drinking (of *chang*, or barley beer), many of the elder amchi in Zangskar that I met embody the traditional mores of reciprocity, respect, and mutuality. While the landscape of amchi medicine has changed in recent decades, many Zangskari amchi still practice within a limited rural area, where they act as village mediators, social confidants, and problem solvers on many levels. In urban Leh, Dharamsala, or Delhi, the landscape of amchi medicine and Tibetan medicine has become increasingly professionalized and globalized, and amchi are not required nor expected to act as social mediators (Pordié 2008).

In Ngawang's case, when one amchi fails to heal the patient, another is called who offers a slightly different diagnosis. Yet these multiple diagnoses are no surprise in a world where all phenomena are in constant flux, including the relationship between human selves and nonhuman selves. When a series of amchi cannot heal the patient, ritual healers are called who diagnose deeper karmic causes that require ritual healing. Because mental illness can signify both psychic and social pathology, the amchi alone may not be sufficient to heal the patient. When Ngawang's family is told to perform a dramatic exorcism that is a form of compensation for the village, this may restore some village harmony but does not heal Ngawang. After the second winter of his depression, Ngawang's family takes him further afield, where this predicament is diagnosed as a need for further ritual therapy and extensive merit making. Once Ngawang goes through a series of typical shamanic rituals and a lengthy training, he emerges as a healer himself who can now diagnose and help others. In short, his journey into the realm of spirits has brought him self-knowledge, spiritual progress, and the ability to help others in their transactions with the spirit world.

Ultimately, for the amchi and other ritual healers, the science of healing produces meaning out of individual misfortune. The amchi and other healers who repair disease and disorder engage with a philosophical system that is based on basic Buddhist truths including karma, interdependent origination, and the universality of suffering. This system transforms individual suffering into relationships of healing, help, and compassion within the Tibetan cultural realm. Karma offers a distant and indeterminate source of causality and meaning because it is mysterious and unfalsifiable, and one can always impute misfortune to prior unknowable actions in past lifetimes. The more proximate causes, however, offer negotiation and transactions with visible and invisible beings that provide meaning, agency, and restitution for ruptured relations. I argue that these by-products of the amchi system are as important as the efficacy of its healing medicines. As patients and providers cycle back and forth between healing and illness, they produce a profound response to the increasing complexity and fragmentation of modernity and structural violence within their specific local contexts that is worth further study and appreciation.

Notes

This chapter revisits early fieldwork on Tibetan medicine (1990–2003) that was part of a longer project on Buddhist nuns and social power (Gutschow 2004). I want to thank several Zangskari and Ladakhi doctors for their expertise: Lonpo Sonam Angchug of Karsha, Sonam Gyaltsan of Yulang, Jigmed Dorje of Bya, Palchug of Bagartse, Phagsang of Tungri, and Tsewang Manla of Nurla. I am grateful for conversations with Arthur Kleinman, Byron Good, Eric Jacobson, and Anne Harrington on the cultural and social constructions of illness as well as helpful comments by Fernand Meyer, Michael Aris, Geoffrey Samuel, Stephan Kloos, Laurent Pordié, and anonymous reviewers. The fieldwork was funded by the Mellon Foundation, the Jacob Javitz Foundation, and the Department of Anthropology at Harvard University.

1 The commodification of Tibetan medicine in the TAR and elsewhere is described in Adams, Schrempf, and Craig (2010); Craig (2008, 2012); Janes (2002); Kloos (2017a); and Pordié (2008), among others.

2 While Pascale Dollfus (1989, 36, 39) prefers to call amchi "secular religious specialists," this oxymoron combines somewhat separate domains, the secular and religious. I agree that amchi and other healers in Ladakh exist within a matrix of Tibetan Buddhism (see Pordié 2007; Gutschow 2010).

3 According to India's 2011 census, Leh district had a population of 147,104 (66 percent Buddhist, 17 percent Hindu, and 14 percent Muslim), while Kargil district had a population of 143,388 (77 percent Muslim, 14 percent Buddhist, and 8 percent Hindu). Leh and Kargil district were ranked first and second, respectively, in terms of India's contraceptive prevalence rate, and they share low fertility, relatively little caste hierarchy or violence, and far less socioeconomic inequality and absolute poverty than much of North India (Gutschow 2016).

4 For a discussion of the diagnosis and treatment of *smyo ba* and related wind disorders within the Tibetan exile community that discusses the biomedical categories of depression, anxiety, and psychosis, see Deane (2014) and Jacobson (2002), among others.

5 The color corresponds to the direction as the village becomes a mandala or sacred space for the purposes of the rite, and each direction is associated with specific elements, deities, and their respective colors. The exorcism rite exemplifies the

fundamental principle of microcosm and macrocosm, as both Ngawang's individual health and the wider health of the village space are healed at one and the same time.

6 Stephan Beyer (1978, 100–108, 324–55) details the generation and empowerment of ritual effigies in Tantric Buddhism, while Sherry Ortner (1978) describes in detail a Sherpa exorcism (*rgya bzhi*) that is quite similar to Ngawang's exorcism. Terry Clifford (1984, 136–45) explicitly relates exorcisms to mental illness, and Sophie Day (1989), René Nebesky-Wojkowitz ([1956] 1993), and Patrick Kaplanian (1981) offer symbolic analyses of Tibetan exorcism rites.

7 The Rinpoche, a reincarnation of the famous ninth-century Tibetan monk Lha lung dPal gyi rDo rJe, called on numerous Tantric protectors (*chos skyong*). These protectors or otherworldly gods (*'jigs rten las das pa'i lha*) have transcended the worldly cycle of rebirth, unlike demons and other lesser gods (*'jigs rten pa'i lha*), who remain trapped in the six spheres of existence.

8 Gutschow (2004b) relates the rise of oracles to the social circumstances of modern Ladakh, while Day (1989, 1990) has described the practices and training of oracles in Ladakh.

9 Day (1989, 1990) and Amelie Schenk (1994) describe the separation rite (lha 'dre phye byes) that is held during an oracle's initiation in Ladakh. The initiate's ability to distinguish good spirits from the bad may be tested by a game of dice with the officiant, calling to mind the famous dice games in the Tibetan Gesar epic and the Indian Mahabharat. Donald Lopez (1998) describes the controversy surrounding the Tibetan deity rDo rje Shugs ldan, who was one of the main deities possessing Ngawang.

10 Tibetan pulse diagnosis is summarized by Meyer (1981) and Khangkar (1982c).

11 Lobsang Rabgyay (1985a) describes the pathological urine for a wind disorder as bluish, watery, and transparent, with large bubbles that remain some time. In contrast, the urine for a combined wind-bile disorder is yellowish, light, and clear, with small to moderate bubbles that instantly disappear. There are urine patterns for specific diseases such as flu, meningitis, intestinal colic, dyspepsia, enteritis, worms, pneumonia, asthma, arthritis, and so on.

12 Philippe Cornu's (1997) succinct account of Tibetan astrology explains the origin of Tibetan divination tools such as the grid of nine squares in Chinese astrology (*nag rtsis*).

13 Rechung Rinpoche (1973, 50, 46) states that "[wind disorders] accumulate during the late spring, break out during the summer, and subside during the autumn.... Those persons born under the influence of Air [wind] have crooked bodies and are thin and bluish in complexion. Their joints produce a cracking sound during movement." Yuri Parfionovitch, Gyurme Dorje, and Fernand Meyer (1992, 1:165) translate the *Blue Beryl Treatise*, which describes the act of dressing, sleeping, and exercising appropriate to each hour and season as living "on the borderline between sun and shade."

14 Francis Zimmermann (1987, 8, 1) describes how Indian Ayurveda views "the universe [as] a kitchen," while the Chain of Being is a "sequence of foods." His analysis (viii, 9) notes that Ayurveda "presupposes a cosmic physiology: the world seen as a sequence of foods and a sequence of cooking operations or digestions at the end of which nourishing essences from the soil are exhaled in the medicinal aroma or meats...."

[In sum,] the nature of what is eaten is rendered appropriate to the nature of one who eats it."

15 Parfionovitch, Dorje, and Meyer (1992, 1:157–58) offer an illustration of the bodily points where moxa is given and, along with Lobsang Dolma Khangkar (1986, 15–16), describe the method of determining when moxibustion can occur. Out of the seventy-two points on the body available for moxibustion, six major ones are used for most wind disorders. Moxa is not given on certain days of the week or the month in order to avoid offending the planetary deities (*gza'*) who rule over these days, while the days of the month most auspicious for moxa are calculated by tracking the soul's (*bla*) monthly journey through the body. In Ngawang's case, the amchi from Bya administered moxibustion on the sixth and seventh days of the eleventh month.

16 While Pordié (2003, 2007) and Gutschow (2004b) describe the interpenetration of religious and medical discourses in Ladakh, Vincanne Adams (2001) and Craig Janes (1995, 1999a) depict the amchi in the TAR as having sanitized their medical discourse by abandoning many ritual practices and discourses.

17 Margaret Lock's (1987, 35–37) insightful essay provides an excellent discussion of the difference between biomedicine and Asian medicines using the metaphor of photography apertures. She theorizes that biomedicine captures its object with a wide aperture, focusing on the object while leaving a blurry background, while Asian medicines close the aperture, placing foreground and background in equal focus.

18 Wind disorders are classified in chapter 12 of the *Explanatory Tantra* as well as in commentaries such as the *Ambrosia Heart Tantra*, by Yeshi Donden (1977). Demonic attack is described in six chapters (73, 77–81) of the *Oral Secret Tantra*, three of which are translated by Clifford (1984). Chapter 60 of the *Oral Secret Tantra* deals with a category of central nervous system ailments known as *rtsa dkar*.

19 Khangkar (1986, 22, 23) states, "*Rlung* serves as the medium for consciousness enabling it to move from one object to another, just as a horse serves as a mount for a rider to journey from one place to another." Khangkar (1982a, 1982b) also explains how wind assists the mind's perceptive functions.

20 In Tibetan the five types of wind are *srog 'dzin, gyen rgyu, khyab byed, me mnyam*, and *thur sel*, and in Sanskrit the five types of wind are *prana, udana, vyana, samana*, and *apana*. Khangkar (1986), Jigme Tsarong (1981), and Epstein and Rabgyay (1982) describe their functions as follows: (1) Life-sustaining wind enables swallowing, spitting, sneezing, respiration, concentration, and sensory as well as mental clarity. (2) Ascending wind enables speech, breathing, salivation, good complexion, body mass, memory, and diligence. (3) Pervasive wind enables muscular movement, physical growth, lifting, walking, stretching, opening and closing of the mouth and eyes, and so on. (4) Metabolic wind enables digestion and metabolism. (5) Descending wind enables defecation, urination, discharge of semen and menstrual blood, uterine contractions, and childbirth.

21 Khangkar (1986, 29) analyzes the superior status of wind by noting, "*Rlung* is more powerful than phlegm or bile, because *rlung* makes contact with bile and phlegm. *Rlung* goes to both. Suppose we blow a fire, we cause more heat to arise." In Ayurveda, bile and phlegm symbolize the eternal oppositions of fire and water,

sun (*agni*) and moon (*soma*), lack and plethora, or dry lands (*jangal*) and wet lands (*anupa*). Even here, wind has a superior status vis-à-vis the other two humors; as Zimmermann (1987, 146–47) notes, "Wind is then introduced into this fight between fire and water, where it remains in an alternating and dominant position. The primacy and ubiquity of wind are mentioned repeatedly in the texts." Compare Shigehisa Kuriyama's (1994) description of the shifting manner in which the inner and outer wind (*qi* and *feng*) embody pervasive change, uncertainty, and disorder in Chinese medical discourse.

22   Rabgyay (1985a, 1985b), Epstein and Rabgyay (1982), and Donden and Kelsang (1977) discuss the classification and etiology of wind disorders.

23   Rabgyay (1985b, 51) analyzes the forty-eight general and fifteen specific types of wind disorder. The general types of wind disorder are classified as primary if the wind remains in its main bodily channel and secondary if it has spilled over into the two other bodily channels.

24   Donden (1986, 17) notes, "When that Karma ripens and a disease manifests in the present lifetime, it is very powerful and thus is generally fatal. In Tibet, people with this type of disease would often renounce all worldly activities and engage in spiritual practices; however, few survive this type of disorder because the disease is a ripening of a powerful action that has been committed in the past."

25   Herbert Guenther (1969, 37) notes, "All that which is not and cannot be clearly understood as it rises out of the depth of the psychic life of man, and which not only disturbs but also frequently dominates him, has been concretely formulated as 'demons.'" Clifford's (1984, 149) psychoanalytic analysis depicts demons "in the role of the Id trying to obstruct the Super-ego's higher promptings."

26   In Zangskari and Ladakhi belief, demonic spirits (gdon) are firmly located in the cycle of birth and rebirth, as detailed by Riaboff (1997), Day (1989), and Kaplanian (1981). Oddly, Ortner's (1978, 100) analysis of Sherpa culture places demons outside the transmigratory realm of existence, yet her provocative analysis defines demons as psychic projections of social hierarchy.

27   Arthur Kleinman (1980) analyzes the social and cultural construction of illness in terms of a number of vectors—including its pragmatism, flexibility, systemic nature, and ability to adapt to local contexts. This earlier and more functional emphasis on systems is repudiated in his later work on experience and social suffering (Kleinman 2006; Kleinman and Kleinman 1995).

References

Adams, Vincanne. 1996. "Karaoke as Modern Lhasa, Tibet: Western Encounters with Cultural Politics." *Cultural Anthropology* 11 (4): 510–46.

Adams, Vincanne. 1998. "Suffering the Winds of Lhasa: Politicized Bodies, Human Rights, Cultural Difference, and Humanism in Tibet." *Medical Anthropology Quarterly* 12 (1): 74–102.

Adams, Vincanne. 2001. "The Sacred in the Scientific: Ambiguous Practices of Science in Tibetan Medicine." *Cultural Anthropology* 16 (4): 542–75.

Adams, Vincanne, Mona Schrempf, and Sienna Craig. 2010. "Introduction: Medicine in Translation between Science and Religion." In *Medicine between Science and Religion: Explorations on Tibetan Grounds*, edited by Vincanne Adams, Mona Schrempf, and Sienna Craig, 1–28. New York: Berghahn Books.

Ashforth, Adam. 2005. *Witchcraft: Violence and Democracy in South Africa*. Chicago: University of Chicago Press.

Beyer, Stephan. 1978. *The Cult of Tara: Magic and Ritual in Tibet*. Berkeley: University of California Press.

Blaikie, Calum. 2009. "Critically Endangered? Medicinal Plant Cultivation and the Reconfiguration of Sowa Rigpa in Ladakh." *Asian Medicine* 5 (2): 243–72.

Blaikie, Calum. 2016. "Positioning Sowa Rigpa in India: Coalition and Antagonism in the Quest for Recognition." *Medicine, Anthropology, Theory* 3 (2): 50–86.

Blaikie, Calum. 2018. "Absence, Abundance, and Excess: Substances and Sowa Rigpa in Ladakh since the 1960s." In *Locating the Medical: Explorations in South Asian History*, edited by Guy Attewell and Rohandeb Roy, 169–99. New Delhi: Oxford University Press.

Clifford, Terry. 1984. *Tibetan Buddhist Medicine and Psychiatry: The Diamond Healing*. York Beach, ME: Samuel Weiser.

Comaroff, Jean, and John Comaroff. 1999. "Occult Economies and the Violence of Abstraction: Notes from the South African Postcolony." *American Ethnologist* 26 (2): 279–301.

Cornu, Philippe. 1997. *Tibetan Astrology*. Translated by Hamish Gregor. Boston: Shambhala.

Craig, Sienna R. 2007. "A Crisis of Confidence: A Comparison between Shifts in Tibetan Medical Education in Nepal and Tibet." In *Soundings in Tibetan Medicine: Historical and Anthropological Perspectives*, edited by Mona Schrempf, 127–54. Leiden: Brill.

Craig, Sienna R. 2008. "Place and Professionalization: Navigating Amchi Identity in Nepal." In *Tibetan Medicine in the Contemporary World: Global Politics of Medical Knowledge and Practice*, edited by Laurent Pordié, 62–90. London: Routledge.

Craig, Sienna R. 2012. *Healing Elements: Efficacy and the Social Ecologies of Tibetan Medicine*. Berkeley: University of California Press.

Day, Sophie. 1989. "Embodying Spirits: Village Oracles and Possession Rituals in Ladakh, North India." PhD diss., London School of Economics.

Day, Sophie. 1990. "Ordering Spirits: The Initiation of Village Oracles in Ladakh." In *Wissenschaftsgeschichte und gegenwärtige Forschungen in Nordwest-Indien*, edited by Lydia Icke-Schwalbe and Gudrun Meier, 206–22. Dresden: Staatliches Museum für Völkerkunde.

Deane, Susannah. 2014. "From Sadness to Madness: Tibetan Perspectives on the Causation and Treatment of Psychiatric Illness." *Religions* 5 (2): 444–58.

Desjarlais, Robert. 2016. *Subject to Death: Life and Loss in a Buddhist World*. Chicago: University of Chicago Press.

Dollfus, Pascale. 1989. *Lieu de neige et de genévriers: Organisation sociale et religieuse des communautés bouddhistes du Ladakh*. Paris: Éditions du CNRS.

Donden, Yeshi. 1986. *Health through Balance: An Introduction to Tibetan Medicine*. Ithaca, NY: Snow Lion.

Donden, Yeshi, and Jhampa Kelsang. 1977. *The Ambrosia Heart Tantra.* Vol. 1, *The Secret Oral Teaching on the Eight Branches of the Science of Healing.* Dharamsala: Library of Tibetan Works and Archives.

Dummer, Thomas. 1994. *Tibetan Medicine and Other Holistic Health-Care Systems.* New Delhi: Paljor.

Epstein, Mark D., and Lobsang Rabgyay. 1982. "Mind and Mental Disorders in Tibetan Medicine." *gSo Rig: Tibetan Medicine* 5:66–84.

Guenther, Herbert V. 1969. *Treasures on the Tibetan Middle Way.* Boulder, CO: Shambhala.

Gutschow. Kim. 1997. "A Case of Madness or 'Wind Disorder' in Zangskar." In *Recent Research on Ladakh 7: Proceedings of the 7th Colloquium of the International Association for Ladakh Studies Held in Bonn/Sankt Augustin, 12–15 June 1995,* edited by Thierry Dodin and Heinz Räther, 177–202. Ulm: Ulmer Kulturanthropologische Schriften.

Gutschow, Kim. 2004a. *Being a Buddhist Nun: The Struggle for Enlightenment in the Himalayas.* Cambridge, MA: Harvard University Press.

Gutschow, Kim. 2004b. "Shamans and Oracles in Ladakh." In *Shamanism: An Encyclopedia of World Beliefs, Practices, and Culture,* edited by Mariko Namba Walter and Eva Jane Neumann Fridman, 756–63. Santa Barbara, CA: ABC-CLIO.

Gutschow, Kim. 2006. "The Politics of Being Buddhist in Zangskar: Partition and Today." *India Review* 5 (3–4): 470–98.

Gutschow, Kim. 2010. "From Home to Hospital: The Extension of Obstetrics in Ladakh." In *Medicine between Science and Religion: Explorations on Tibetan Grounds,* edited by Vincanne Adams, Mona Schrempf, and Sienna Craig, 185–213. London: Berghahn Books.

Gutschow, Kim. 2016. "Going 'beyond the Numbers': Maternal Death Reviews in India." *Medical Anthropology* 35 (4): 322–57.

Jacobson, Eric. 2000. "Situated Knowledge in Classical Tibetan Medicine: Psychiatric Aspects." PhD diss., Harvard University.

Jacobson, Eric. 2002. "Panic Attack in a Context of Comorbid Anxiety and Depression in a Tibetan Refugee." *Culture, Medicine and Psychiatry* 26:259–79.

Jacobson, Eric. 2007. "'Life-Wind Illness' in Tibetan Medicine: Depression, Generalised Anxiety, and Panic Attack." In *Soundings in Tibetan Medicine: Anthropological and Historical Perspectives,* edited by Mona Schrempf, 225–45. Boston: Brill.

Janes, Craig R. 1995. "The Transformations of Tibetan Medicine." *Medical Anthropology Quarterly* 9 (1): 6–39.

Janes, Craig R. 1999a. "The Health Transition, Global Modernity and the Crisis of Traditional Medicine: The Tibetan Case." *Social Science and Medicine* 48 (12): 1803–20.

Janes, Craig R. 1999b. "Imagined Lives, Suffering, and the Work of Culture: The Embodied Discourses of Conflict in Modern Tibet." *Medical Anthropology Quarterly* 13 (4): 391–412.

Janes, Craig R. 2002. "Buddhism, Science, and the Market: The Globalization of Tibetan Medicine." *Anthropology and Medicine* 9 (3): 267–89.

Kaplanian, Patrick. 1981. *Les Ladakhis du Cachemire.* Paris: Hachette.

Khangkar, Lobsang Dolma. 1982a. "Breathing Exercises in Tibetan Medicine." *gSo Rig: Tibetan Medicine* 5:22–25.

Khangkar, Lobsang Dolma. 1982b. "Dr. Dolma Talking to Students of Japanese Acupuncture on 'The Five Vital Energies.'" *gSo Rig: Tibetan Medicine* 5:26–30.

Khangkar, Lobsang Dolma. 1982c. "A Talk on Pulse Diagnosis in Tibetan Medicine." *gSo Rig: Tibetan Medicine* 5:10–15.

Khangkar, Lobsang Dolma. 1986. *Lectures on Tibetan Medicine*. Dharamsala: Library of Tibetan Works and Archives.

Kleinman, Arthur. 1980. *Patients and Healers in the Context of Culture*. Berkeley: University of California Press.

Kleinman, Arthur. 1988. *The Illness Narratives: Suffering, Healing, and the Human Condition*. New York: Basic Books.

Kleinman, Arthur, ed. 1995. *Writing at the Margin: Discourse between Anthropology and Medicine*. Berkeley: University of California Press.

Kleinman, Arthur. 2006. *What Really Matters: Living a Moral Life amidst Uncertainties and Dangers*. New York: Oxford University Press.

Kleinman, Arthur, and Joan Kleinman. 1995. "Suffering and Its Professional Transformation." In *Writing at the Margin: Discourse between Anthropology and Medicine*, edited by Arthur Kleinman, 95–119. Berkeley: University of California Press.

Kloos, Stephan. 2016. "The Recognition of Sowa Rigpa in India: How Tibetan Medicine Became an Indian Medical System." *Medicine, Anthropology, Theory* 3 (2): 19–49.

Kloos, Stephan. 2017a. "The Pharmaceutical Assemblage: Rethinking Sowa Rigpa and the Herbal Pharmaceutical Industry in Asia." *Current Anthropology* 58 (6): 693–717.

Kloos, Stephan. 2017b. "The Politics of Preservation and Loss: Tibetan Medical Knowledge in Exile." *East Asian Science, Technology and Society* 10 (2): 135–59.

Kuriyama, Shigehisa. 1994. "The Imagination of Winds and the Development of the Chinese Conception of the Body." In *Body, Subject, and Power in China*, edited by Angela Zito and Tani E. Barlow, 23–41. Chicago: University of Chicago Press.

Lock, Margaret. 1987. "DSM-III as a Culture-Bound Construct: Commentary on Culture-Bound Syndromes and International Disease Classifications." *Culture, Medicine and Psychiatry* 11 (2): 35–42.

Lopez, Donald. 1998. *Prisoners of Shangri La*. Chicago: University of Chicago Press.

Meyer, Fernand. 1981. *Gso-Ba Rig-Pa: Le système médical tibétain*. Paris: Éditions du CNRS.

Moore, Henrietta L., and Todd Sanders, eds. 2001. *Magical Interpretations, Material Realities: Modernity, Witchcraft, and the Occult in Postcolonial Africa*. New York: Routledge.

Nebesky-Wojkowitz, René. (1956) 1993. *Oracles and Demons of Tibet*. Kathmandu: Tiwari Pilgrims Book House.

Ortner, Sherry. 1978. *Sherpas through Their Rituals*. New York: Cambridge University Press.

Parfionovitch, Yuri, Gyurme Dorje, and Fernand Meyer. 1992. *Tibetan Medical Paintings: Illustrations to the Blue Beryl Treatise of Sangye Gyamtso (1653–1705)*. 2 vols. New York: Harry N. Abrams.

Pordié, Laurent. 2003. *The Expression of Religion in Tibetan Medicine: Ideal Conceptions, Contemporary Practices, and Political Use*. Pondy Papers in Social Sciences 29. Pondicherry: French Institute of Pondicherry.

Pordié, Laurent. 2007. "Buddhism in Everyday Medical Practice of the Ladakhi Amchi." *Indian Anthropologist* 37 (1): 93–166.

Pordié, Laurent. 2008. "Tibetan Medicine Today: Neo-traditionalism as an Analytical Lens and a Political Tool." In *Tibetan Medicine in the Contemporary World: Global Politics of Medical Knowledge and Practice*, edited by Laurent Pordié, 3–32. London: Routledge.

Pordié, Laurent, and Calum Blaikie. 2014. "Knowledge and Skill in Motion: Layers of Tibetan Medical Education in India." *Culture, Medicine and Psychiatry* 38:340–68.

Rabgyay, Lobsang. 1985a. "A Guide to Tibetan Medical Urinalysis." *gSo rig: Tibetan Medicine* 9:28–46.

Rabgyay, Lobsang. 1985b. "Rlung Diseases and Their Treatment." *gSo rig: Tibetan Medicine* 9:47–68.

Rechung Rinpoche. 1976. *Tibetan Medicine: Illustrated in Original Texts*. Berkeley: University of California Press.

Riaboff, Isabelle. 1997. "Les *lha*, une catégorie zanskarie à géométrie variable: Ou, que sont les dieux devenus?" In *Recent Research on Ladakh 7: Proceedings of the 7th Colloquium of the International Association for Ladakh Studies Held in Bonn/Sankt Augustin, 12–15 June 1995*, edited by Thierry Dodin and Heinz Räther. Ulm: Ulmer Kulturanthropologische Schriften.

Samuel, Geoffrey. 1993. *Civilized Shamans: Buddhism in Tibetan Societies*. Washington, DC: Smithsonian Institution Press.

Schenk, Amelie. 1994. *Schamanen auf dem Dach der Welt*. Graz: Akademische Druck- und Verlagsanstalt.

Tsarong, Jigme. 1981. *Fundamentals of Tibetan Medicine according to the Rgyud Bzhi*. Dharamsala: Tibetan Medical Center.

Zimmermann, Francis. 1987. *The Jungle and the Aroma of Meats*. Berkeley: University of California Press.

7. ALLEGIANCE TO WHOSE COMMUNITY?

Effects of Men-Tsee-Khang Policies on the Role of Amchi in the Darjeeling Hills

BARBARA GERKE

This chapter explores the contemporary social situation of Tibetan amchi in the Darjeeling Hills, West Bengal, India. In particular, it demonstrates how their status in society is shaped by the rotational work scheme implemented by the Men-Tsee-Khang (MTK), the centralized institution of Tibetan medicine in Dharamsala, in the northwestern Indian state of Himachal Pradesh. The development of the MTK branch clinic in the hill town of Kalimpong (approximately seventy kilometers from the town of Darjeeling) up until 2008 is taken as an example to show how the model of institutionalized Tibetan medicine as operated by the Dharamsala MTK affects the personal lives of amchi, their place in society, and the acceptance of Tibetan medicine among Tibetans who live in a medically pluralistic, multiethnic community. In this chapter I argue that the increasingly institutionalized centralization of Tibetan medical practice at the MTK since the 1980s has changed the role of amchi and their identity in communities at the periphery where they are regularly posted. The amchi increasingly orient themselves with regard to centrality rather than locality; their allegiance is given more to the MTK center in Dharamsala and its policies than to the local communities they serve.

In referring to Tibetan medicine in the Darjeeling Hills, I am aware that the definition of "Tibetan medicine" is itself problematic. Since its boundaries are not and never have been clearly demarcated, we cannot talk about a unified system. Laurent Pordié (2008, 4, 10–17) even talks about Tibetan *medicines* and characterizes their modern globalized forms as a newly emerging "neo-traditional" form of Tibetan medicine with an urbanized and institutional character. And whereas Tibetan amchi at the MTK in India use the Tibetan term Sorig or Sowa Rigpa (*gso ba rig pa*), which means "science of healing," to describe what they view as distinctly Tibetan medical traditions, I use the term "Tibetan medicine" in its widest sense, acknowledging its heterogeneous nature with its intraregional variations and terminologies (see also the introduction to this volume).[1]

Defining who is Tibetan is equally problematic. The multifaceted identities surrounding Tibetanness found among Tibetan refugees and Tibetan(ized) communities across the Himalayas show that being Tibetan is a state of mind rather than the result of belonging to a unified nation (Gyatso 1990, 15).[2] Contemporary exile Tibetanness differs greatly from Tibetanness in Tibet both before and after 1959. We have to consider that there is nothing like a traditional Tibetan identity, since "right up until 1959, the Tibetans had very little sense of being one group" (Shakya 1993, 9). Tibetan identity was largely based on the Buddhist faith and the Tibetan language, which has many localized variants. Later developments have used the historical memory of Tibet's past to revive Tibetan religion and identity (see, e.g., Goldstein and Kapstein 1998). In the Darjeeling Hills, we deal with multiple identities and cross-border cultural affiliations among Tibetans and Tibetan groups. This makes the term "Tibetan" quite vague, and I use it while acknowledging its limitations.

The Ethnographic Setting

I lived in the Darjeeling area for long periods from 1992 until 2008 and carried out intensive fieldwork for eighteen months between 2004 and 2006.[3] This chapter was researched and written during that time.[4] Kalimpong (altitude 1,247 meters or 4,091 feet) and Darjeeling (altitude 2,042 meters or 6,700 feet) are fast-growing urban centers situated in the foothills of the Himalayas in the northeastern Indian state of West Bengal, with majestic views of Mount Kanchenjunga, the third-highest mountain in the world (8,586 meters or 28,169 feet).[5] Tibetans migrated to the Darjeeling region, locally called "the Hills," long before the Chinese occupation of Tibet in 1950. From the later part of the nineteenth century, Tibetans came as traders along the trade routes via the Jelep La and Nathu La mountain passes. Some became Indian citizens, procuring Scheduled Tribe (ST) status as "Bhutias" after India's independence. Tibetan refugees came from the 1950s onward in several stages.[6] The area of Kalimpong known as Tenth Mile, once part of the Lhasa trade route, remains predominantly Tibetan. Darjeeling has a Tibetan Refugee Self Help Centre with around 650 refugee residents (as of 2006), but most Tibetans live elsewhere in the town and are not distinguishable as such.[7] Affluent Tibetan families live outside the settlements, often run large businesses, and depend heavily on tourism. During the time I lived in the region, Tibetans in the area did not consider themselves refugees and did not use the Tibetan term for "refugee" (see Gerke 2012, 66–71; Subba 1990, 5, 75). Many of them procured the Bhutia ST status and applied for Indian citizenship.

Although the influx of Buddhist lamas from Tibet since 1959 has led to a renewal of Buddhism and the construction of numerous Buddhist monasteries in the region, Tibetan identity, especially for Indian-born Tibetans, had to be established in a multilingual, mostly non-Tibetan environment. The increasing Nepalization of the area contributed to a separation between language and identity among Tibetans. Being Tibetan no longer necessarily implied knowing the Tibetan language, and efforts made by Tibetan schools to promote studies in Tibetan did not meet with large success because they did not correspond to the needs of modern Tibetan families, for whom English was economically more valuable than an education in the Tibetan language (Gerke 2012, 71–75).

What clearly demarcates the practice of Tibetan medicine in the Darjeeling region from its practice in the Dharamsala area and amchi medicine in Ladakh is its embeddedness in a multiethnic society in which Tibetans had lived side by side and intermingled with other Himalayan communities for a long time pre-1959. The area also shows a significant medical pluralism across traditions (see next section). As we see elsewhere in this volume, amchi in Ladakh are Indian nationals and deeply embedded in enduring village and lineage ties across the region, where several hundred amchi serve the population at a village community or urban level. Although this is increasingly changing, many of them are still trained in family lineages. In Dharamsala the MTK has a strong institutional monopoly on Sowa Rigpa training in the Tibetan exile community, which is always in close interaction with the political situation of the Tibetan government in exile and is surrounded by a majority of the Indian Hindu communities of Himachal Pradesh. Sowa Rigpa practices in the Darjeeling Hills thus exemplify the unique position Sowa Rigpa can hold in interaction with multiple social ecologies (Craig 2012) at a local level.

In the Darjeeling Hills, Tibetan medical practice has been shaped by the institutionalized, Dharamsala-based MTK version of Tibetan medicine and the Chagpori tradition of the late Samphel Norbu Trogawa Rinpoche (1932–2005). I also came across a family lineage of amchi in Sikkim. All amchi basically followed the same textbooks but had different traditions of clinical practice, or *laklen* (*lag len*, the experience of medical practice through apprenticeship with a senior amchi).

In the following, I first introduce MTK and Chagpori institutions and analyze their effects on the lives of amchi within the medical pluralism prevalent in the Hills as I observed it until 2008. In the later part of the chapter, I look at how an amchi of a family lineage in Sikkim combined his lineage with the institutionalized form of his clinical practice.

Tibetan Medical Institutions in the Darjeeling Hills

The Darjeeling Hills have long been characterized by medical pluralism. During my long-term stays there I observed that laypeople from all communities tended to utilize medical and ritual specialists regardless of ethnicity.[8] Concerned less with obtaining detailed and theoretically informed explanations of illness and misfortune, they seemed more interested in practical solutions. In a multiethnic community with access to numerous health-care systems, this led to an eclectic mix of methods from which patients chose "what works." Patients used a variety of available treatment methods in pragmatic ways. This has been shown by Eric Jacobson, who writes that as soon as patients left the Tibetan clinic in Darjeeling, they "did very much whatever they believed would be most medically efficacious, including mixing the prescriptions they had received with other kinds of remedies, even biomedical ones, or consulting a different amchi, a priest or exorcist, biomedical physician or any of the many other kinds of healers which Indian society has to offer" (2000, 337).

This situation did not seem unusual for a multiethnic community with access to medical pluralist health care, in which the boundaries between the various religious and medical systems were easily crossed by patients. Like many other minorities in Indian urban settings, Tibetans chose among a variety of available healing modalities, freely mixing biomedical medications with Tibetan pills, consulting Hindu as well as Buddhist diviners, and performing rituals in Buddhist monasteries as well as in Hindu temples.

At the time, Tibetan medical institutions operated in a context in which religion and medicine were broadly intertwined. The entire picture suggested that people's sense of efficacy was also influenced by a variety of religious and economic factors, such as notions of blessing, ritual healing, the availability of subsidized medication, and the like. The method of combining religion with medicine is not unknown to Tibetan medical practice (see Pordié 2003). In fact, it is a hallmark of one of the two Tibetan medical institutions: Chagpori Medical College, established in 1696 in Lhasa, emphasized the combination of medicine (*sman*) and Buddhist dharma (*chos*). In the seventeenth century, this approach corresponded with the diffusion of the Mahayana Buddhist ideal within the medical arena, which was propagated by the Ganden government of the fifth Dalai Lama as one of many attempts "to exert direct influence over the development of learning and culture on the part of the newly formed Tibetan theocracy" (Schaeffer 2003, 621). One of these achievements, mainly directed by Sangye Gyatso (1653–1705), the regent of the fifth Dalai Lama (1617–82), was the establishment of the first medical college in Lhasa, named after the "Iron Hill" Chagpori (*lcags po ri*), on which it was built.[9] Since 1643 the fifth Dalai Lama had already attempted to institutionalize Tibetan medicine four times through the establishment of medical colleges in the areas of Drepung, Shigatse, and Lhasa, but all these attempts had failed (Meyer 2003, 103).

Sangye Gyatso intended to raise the quality of medical education and institutionalize medicine in Lhasa in an effort to establish Tibetan medicine far into the future. His efforts manifested in the founding of Chagpori Medical College, which was the first successful medical institution in Lhasa. It served as a model college and also provided trained amchi for over two hundred years to "religious hierarchs and lay sovereigns, in central Tibet and the eastern provinces, in Mongolia and even in the entourage of the emperor of China" (Meyer 2003, 117). It was destroyed by the Chinese Red Army during the Tibetan revolt of 1959. In 1992 Trogawa Rinpoche, himself trained in Lhasa by the Chagpori lineage holder Rindzin Lhundrub Paljor Nyerongshag (1889–1986?), founded the Chagpori Tibetan Medical Institute (CTMI) in Darjeeling in commemoration of the Chagpori Medical College in Lhasa. It became a recognized nongovernmental organization in 1993. Trogawa Rinpoche's early request for the status of an independent institution was declined by the Tibetan government in exile. Trogawa Rinpoche's last wish was, however, to hand over the CTMI to the private office of the Dalai Lama, following the ways Chagpori was administered in Tibet. For example, the charter of Chagpori in Lhasa had been drafted by the fifth Dalai Lama's regent, Sangye Gyatso, who also appointed the main teachers (Meyer 2003, 111). In exile, the private office of the Dalai Lama directed Trogawa Rinpoche's request to the Health Department of the Central Tibetan Administration (CTA), which was not keen to oversee the administration of the CTMI. Thus it continued operating as an autonomous nongovernmental organization now registered under the Central Council of Tibetan Medicine in Dharamsala. Until 2002 the first three batches of CTMI medical students from Darjeeling were required to take their final exams in Dharamsala and were technically treated as MTK graduates. Since the fourth batch, the final exams have been held at the CTMI. They are designed and evaluated by external qualified Tibetan doctors and supervised by the Central Council of Tibetan Medicine, but the CTMI issues its own certificates (Teinlay Palsang Trogawa, personal communication, June 2017).

The Lhasa MTK was the first secular medical institution in Tibet, established in Lhasa in 1916, and developed out of an early twentieth-century movement to modernize health care in Tibet. This was presumably partly inspired by the thirteenth Dalai Lama's encounter with British public health measures during his exile in India (Samuel 2001, 262). The MTK's first director, Khyenrap Norbu (1883–1962), published numerous medical textbooks that sought to adapt Tibetan medicine to the contemporary health-care needs of Tibetans. This trend of adaptation partly continued in Indian exile with new publications, for example, the three-volume *Textbook of Tibetan Medicine* (*bod kyi gso rig slob dpe*) and the Tibetan translation of *Where There Is No Doctor* (*sman pa med sa*) by the MTK in Dharamsala, aiming to allow easier comprehension of the classical textbooks for modern students and to teach basic modern health care.

The Dharamsala MTK was founded in 1961 under the name Institute for Medicine and Astrology for the Benefit of all Beings ('gro phan sman rtsis khang) (Kloos 2008, 20). The name was later changed to the Tibetan Medical and Astrological Institute, and in the 1990s it was changed to Men-Tsee-Khang.[10] In 1998 one senior MTK amchi told me that the eight-year course at the MTK in Dharamsala was split into two five-year courses in the mid-1960s, one on medicine and one on astrology, because the Tibetan exiled community desperately needed to train amchi to serve the suffering refugees. Moreover, students found it too difficult to memorize both the medical and astrology texts. Astrology became an independent discipline at the MTK and has been taught in a separate five-year course leading to the degree of *tsipa* (*rtsis pa*, astrologer). Compared to medicine, astrology is a less popular subject of study among young Tibetan students (Prost 2004, 122). Many amchi I spoke with, however, had a general knowledge of astrology, and interested amchi took private lessons from senior tsipa.

I found that the relationship between amchi from the Dharamsala MTK and the CTMI was collegial and not marked by competition. Many of the Chagpori amchi had their practical training in residency with MTK amchi; both followed the same medical textbooks and, at the time, sat for the same examinations. Some MTK-trained amchi also taught at the CTMI. Dharma practice among Chagpori amchi was encouraged but was a free choice. Lay as well as ordained men and women were admitted to the course. During fieldwork, I spoke with amchi from both institutions and could rely on my long acquaintance with some of the Chagpori amchi from my time as a student there in 1992.

In Darjeeling the Tibetan Refugee Self Help Centre had a visiting Tibetan MTK amchi and biomedical practitioners and a well-equipped clinic with twenty beds. The largest monastery in Darjeeling, locally called Dali Gompa, also offered X-ray and biomedical health-care facilities to local people but had no resident Tibetan doctor. The CTMI was first located at Trogawa House in North Point, three kilometers outside Darjeeling, and later opened a clinic in Darjeeling and a school in Takdah, a rural village twenty-six kilometers from Darjeeling on lower slopes with a warmer climate.[11] Chagpori amchi followed mostly the MTK curriculum with additional instructions, mainly on dharma and medicine compounding (*sman sbyor*), from Trogawa Rinpoche.[12] The CTMI prepared medicines at the Trogawa House in North Point, Darjeeling, and had its own pharmacy in Salugara, a township with about a hundred resident Tibetan families outside Siliguri, the nearest Indian city on the plains, about eighty kilometers from Darjeeling. Until 2004 the CTMI produced about seventy different medicines in its private pharmacy in Salugara as well as in Darjeeling. These were mostly made by hand with the active help of Trogawa Rinpoche's students and Indian staff. Whereas the medical education of the first three batches of students at the CTMI was centrally directed by the MTK, the pharmacy was under Rinpoche's supervision, and he was free to produce his own remedies, for which he was famous and well respected. When Trogawa Rinpoche passed away in May 2005, his funeral brought together many amchi whom I had known from 1992–93, and who were now practicing on their own or in other private clinics in Darjeeling, Delhi, Kolkata, Sikkim, and abroad (in Kathmandu and Solu Khumbu in Nepal and in Bhutan, as well as in other countries).

Rinpoche's passing initially meant a crisis of survival for the CTMI, which was entirely funded by foreign sponsors and patients abroad who anticipated his regular visits to the West. By the time I completed fieldwork in May 2006, the remaining Chagpori amchi were setting up a new clinic in Darjeeling town, since only a few patients would come all the way to the Trogawa House at North Point. With the support of foreign donors, Rinpoche's nephew Teinlay Palsang Trogawa (who was elected CTMI director), and the board members of the CTMI, the institute continued to develop, and in 2011 the first batch of female students graduated. By 2017, fifty-four amchi had successfully graduated from the CTMI (Chagpori Tibetan Medical Institute 2020).

Changes at the MTK Branch Clinic in Kalimpong

When I first came to Kalimpong in 1994, the local amchi at the MTK clinic was a senior monk, Lobsang Tashi from Dromo, briefly known as Amchi Tashi, who had been living in Kalimpong since the opening of this MTK clinic in

1985. It was the fourteenth MTK branch clinic at the time. Amchi Tashi refused to be transferred, even though he had received frequent invitations to move to Dharamsala to teach medical students. He had been trained at the Lhasa MTK. In Kalimpong he lived in an old wooden colonial cottage that housed the MTK branch clinic at the time. He also regularly visited Tibetans scattered throughout the region (in Lava, Jaigaun, and Olabari). He was assisted by two Tibetan women who gave out Tibetan pills according to his prescriptions in a small dispensary, which was part of the cottage.

I had known Amchi Tashi since 1992, and we stayed in touch over the years. I referred patients and scholars to him and went to ask questions on Tibetan medicine myself. Sometimes we exchanged literature on Tibetan medicine or Buddhism. This amchi had earned considerable respect in the community at large and among his long-term patients. As a member of the local community, he was known as the "Kalimpong amchi," and local perceptions of the efficacy of Tibetan medicine were linked to his personality as well as his good reputation. The latter was based on his diagnostic skills, especially his pulse diagnosis, and successful treatments.

When I began fieldwork in 2004, he had retired and left for Switzerland; the wooden cottage had been demolished and replaced by a concrete building with residences and consultation rooms for two new amchi. The first amchi in residence was a young layman who stayed for about two years. He married and had one child during that time. When he was transferred, a nun and a monk amchi arrived. This was the only time both consultation rooms were actually in use. The new, large dispensary was still operated by the same two Tibetan women. When I completed fieldwork two years later, both amchi had left, and a new MTK amchi—a single layman—was still adjusting to his new post. Another two-story building was under construction at the site of the old cottage to house the MTK staff and a community kitchen. When I returned in 2006, the building was completed and housed all the MTK staff and their families with children. A new amchi had arrived with her husband and their young daughter. The amchi was a newcomer from the Lhasa MTK who was still becoming accustomed to the foreign community and their languages (she spoke only Tibetan and Chinese).

I observed a similar expansion of the MTK branch clinic in Salugara. There the new MTK residence building for amchi and staff was inaugurated with a large celebration in November 2004. Three doctors were working there full-time, seeing between two hundred and three hundred—mainly Indian—patients a day. All staff lived on campus and ate together in a dining hall.

The Kalimpong branch remained small, with a maximum of ten to twenty-five patients a day, which was actually too few to employ two amchi. The Kalimpong amchi always had time to talk and often seemed bored because there was not much for them to do. The Darjeeling MTK branch clinic had between one and two amchi and more patients, some of whom were foreign tourists. The clinic setting in Darjeeling has been described in detail by Jacobson (2000).[13]

The patients using Tibetan medicines in the Hills were mostly Tibetans and Nepali Buddhist groups, such as Tamang, Yolmowa, and Sherpa. At the MTK in Salugara, as at many MTK clinics in metropolitan Indian cities, most patients were Indians from the plains. Since its introduction to India in the 1960s, Tibetan medicine has enjoyed a high popularity among Indians (Kloos 2008, 18).

I met only a few Tibetans who were taking Tibetan medicine because it was "Tibetan." The notable exceptions were some elderly Tibetans, who often felt more comfortable with Tibetan medicine and at times even linked it to their Tibetan identity. Nationalizing Tibetan medicine as a means to demonstrate cultural diversity or to strengthen Tibetan nationalist feelings in the exile community was not a major and palpable concern of Tibetans in the Darjeeling Hills. There was also no direct political need, since Tibetans could be classified under the ST status of Bhutia and had no need to join the political struggle of the other, non-ST ethnic groups; this movement had intensified during the time of my fieldwork and primarily aimed at claiming government benefits.[14]

While Dharamsala may publicize the Tibetan cause, stressing Tibetan culture through popularizing Tibetan medicine, this agenda did not penetrate to the northeastern periphery and was not evident in the way the MTK clinics were set up and operated in the Darjeeling Hills. At the center in Dharamsala, Tibetan identity, Tibetan nationalism, and Buddhist ethics are more closely interwoven with the perception and promotion of Tibetan medicine, especially since its government recognition as Sowa Rigpa in 2010 (Kloos 2010, 2012, 2015, 2016).

Isolation through Rotation

After their graduation, MTK amchi were usually transferred between the more than fifty MTK branch clinics in India and Nepal approximately every two to three years.[15] This rotation scheme seemed flexible, and I was told that once they married and had families, this period was prolonged. Postings to remote areas were shorter (six months), and requests from amchi for preferred posts were considered by the administration when possible (Stephan Kloos, personal communication, July 2006). Audrey Prost mentions that the MTK students particularly disliked being posted to the settlements in South India (2004, 239n45). The policy of rotating staff is common in the Tibetan exile administration. The school principals of the Central Schools for Tibetans rotated every five years, and Tibetan welfare officers every three years. In comparison to most MTK amchi, the Chagpori amchi achieved more stability with their patient clientele by setting up their own independent clinics or working in other private clinics in Nepal and Bhutan.

The method of rotating amchi was understandable considering the increasing number of MTK graduates who needed to be offered internships and work opportunities. Between 1961 and 2006, thirteen classes with a total of about 227 amchi graduated from the Dharamsala MTK with the degree of *menpa kachupa* (*sman pa dka' bcu pa*), out of which about 145 amchi worked at the MTK in the mid-2000s (some left or worked in private clinics; others passed away).[16] Almost thirty of them were non-Tibetan and from various Himalayan regions and other countries.[17] Most of the graduates either taught or practiced at the MTK in Dharamsala or were posted around the MTK branch clinics in India and Nepal for their practical clinical internship in the first year and then as amchi.

The rotation scheme began to affect the Hills toward the end of the 1990s. I have no official data from the MTK Dharamsala or other MTK branch clinics, but both the Darjeeling and Kalimpong amchi, who started the branch clinics in 1975 and 1985 respectively, had been there continuously until the middle to end of the 1990s. Amchi Tashi stayed fifteen years in Kalimpong; amchi Keyzom Bhutti worked as the MTK amchi in Darjeeling for twenty-five years. Moreover, Trogawa Rinpoche practiced in Darjeeling for several decades. These continuous presences provided opportunities for stable, long-term doctor-patient relationships.

Amchi Tashi and Trogawa Rinpoche have already been introduced. In 1975 amchi Keyzom Bhutti set up the first MTK branch clinic in Darjeeling in her one-room apartment, which required a lot of personal sacrifice at the time (Jacobson 2000, 134). In 1998, when we met in the United States (to which she had recently migrated), she recalled in an interview:

> At that time there was no Tibetan medicine at all in Darjeeling, but there were many Tibetan refugees there. So I set up that clinic and worked there for twenty-five years. . . . I was the only Tibetan doctor there. Also

it was very difficult to get a license to open the clinic, even though I had a degree from the Tibetan Medical College [i.e., the MTK in Dharamsala]. The local people, the Indians and Nepalese, and even the Tibetans, didn't know anything about Tibetan medicine. So at first it was very difficult to get patients, because the people just didn't know anything about it. After a while, however, I was seeing fifty to sixty patients a day. (in Gerke 1999, 56)

As this large patient clientele testifies, Keyzom Bhutti, one of the first female MTK-trained amchi, was clearly able to establish Tibetan medicine in Darjeeling before she moved to the United States. In 2000 Trogawa Rinpoche was the only Tibetan medical practitioner left in the Darjeeling Hills who had a strong and long-term reputation, and Tibetans would travel far to receive a consultation. The late Dr. Pema Dorje (1950–2015), a senior MTK physician who worked as the chief medical officer in the area for five years in the 1990s and was based in Salugara, also had a good reputation and a long waiting list of patients (about eighty per day) whenever he came to visit the region thereafter. Over the years I observed that whereas previously people would go to a particular amchi for a medical consultation, now they went "to the MTK to get medicine." Patients using Tibetan medicine increasingly expressed their medical beliefs more in terms of "Tibetan medicine works" than "I go to amchi X because he/she is really good."

Between 1998 and 2007, five amchi were posted in Kalimpong; in Darjeeling the postings lasted slightly longer. As of 2007, the Darjeeling MTK amchi was an exception and had been there for six years because he had a family. My discussion is therefore mainly based on Kalimpong and explores the question of how the rather frequent turnover at the Kalimpong MTK has affected the status of the amchi in the local community.

In Kalimpong several Tibetans I spoke with gave as one of their reasons for not using Tibetan medicine the fact that there was always a different amchi, and they did not know the current one and whether he or she was experienced or not. Previously, trust in the efficacy of the Tibetan medical system in the region had been linked to the long-term resident amchi.

Based on my observations, I concluded that this MTK rotation scheme led to a depersonalization of Tibetan medical practice, a loss of status of the amchi in the local community, and a change in amchi identity. It was certainly also a contributing factor for Tibetans using less Tibetan medicine, although in this context the growing influence of biomedicine has to be taken into account as well.

In Kalimpong the MTK amchi on rotation did not have much time to build up a reputation in the community. In addition, most of them were below thirty and considered inexperienced. Most of the young MTK amchi I spoke with did not have much contact with the local population outside their working hours and often used their weekends or holidays to visit their colleagues in other MTK branch clinics. There was always the thought of being posted elsewhere soon, and they preferred to spend their free time chatting with their ex-classmates across India and abroad via the internet; these friendships were more enduring than new local contacts. There were obviously exceptions among the amchi who were married and had children and had to deal with local schools, teachers, and their children's peers.

For some amchi, the rotation scheme led to experiences of isolation and loneliness, as in the case of the young Tibetan amchi who had come to Kalimpong toward the end of my fieldwork. He told me that only elderly Tibetans came to his clinic—most of them because once they reached the age of seventy, they got free medicines from the MTK. He hardly had any young Tibetan patients and had trouble finding friends in the multiethnic community of Kalimpong town. In May 2006, three months after his arrival, he complained, "When I go to the market, I cannot make out who is Tibetan. They all look the same; they all speak Nepali. It is difficult to make new Tibetan friends here."

The heterogeneous character of the Tibetan community was often difficult for newcomers. The new amchi did not want to join a *kidu* (*skyid sdug*), the main community and self-sufficient welfare networks of Tibetans in the region.[18] He saw no sense in becoming a kidu member since he would be transferred again in a couple of years. The Tibetan community, itself heterogeneous in nature, did not take much notice of him or his knowledge, since he was one of the many amchi passing through. Since the MTK provided him with accommodation, he hardly left the compound, except occasionally in the evenings and on Saturdays and Sundays, when he used internet cafes to be in touch with his MTK colleagues. He knew some Hindi but only a little Nepali and often felt homesick. He had fled his village in Tibet at the age of twenty-one to go to India to "see His Holiness and receive education." Both objectives had long been fulfilled, but there was no way back home. The institutional rotation scheme intensified his experience of displacement and did not provide an opportunity to settle down in a new community. His friends were thus mainly colleagues from the MTK in Dharamsala, the only place in India where— during his medical education—he had spent five years without interruption.

Professionalization and Control

The Central Council of Tibetan Medicine in Dharamsala, under which the majority of amchi are now registered (462 medical practitioners as of 2016; see Central Council of Tibetan Medicine 2018a), was set up in 2004 to "control fraud" of counterfeit medicine production and sales and to keep track of "how many amchi there are," I was told by a governing member–cum–officer in charge in 2005.[19] One of the council's main aims is to "protect patients, public and professionals by ensuring standards [for] medical education and training" (Central Council of Tibetan Medicine 2018b). With the growing number of professional amchi, the need for external control and standardization arose. The MTK amchi I spoke with looked at it as an additional security scheme. But amchi also admitted that it presented yet another mechanism of control that made it more difficult for them to set up independent clinics. For many reasons, it has been professionally much easier for amchi to work within the MTK system.

The MTK branch clinics are often situated close to Tibetan settlements, although many can also be found in non-Tibetan Indian metropolitan areas. They have been built as residence-cum-clinic compounds and, among other reasons, are needed to employ the increasing number of MTK-trained amchi who have not received enough training to open independent clinics and produce their own medicines. Working independently would either require additional training in pharmacology or an arrangement with the MTK to buy drugs from the MTK's pharmacy in Dharamsala, which has been restricted.

After the first few classes of amchi graduated from the MTK following its founding in 1961, the then-standard additional three-year training in making medicines was taken off the curriculum and turned into additional education at the MTK pharmacy for selected amchi. The amchi training was shortened to five years of theoretical training and one year of clinical practice. The intention was to supply amchi for the large, suffering Tibetan refugee community as quickly as possible. The pharmacy was enlarged with the incentive to make the MTK financially independent.[20] Today the number of amchi far exceeds the health-care needs of the Tibetan communities, and the earlier, well-intentioned policy has long achieved its aim. The continuous growth and expansion of the MTK pharmacy has turned the MTK in Dharamsala into a centralized monopoly and a profitable institution that supplies and funds all branch clinics, exports abroad, and has valuable charitable programs.[21] Amchi are dependent on this system and face difficulties when they want to practice independently. Nevertheless, the MTK amchi respect those amchi who work independently.

Compared to the previous hardships of this profession, the MTK employment schemes with a stable income, social benefits, housing, and so on have made the lives of amchi easier. But this has come at the cost of professional independence. I do not argue that the division between pharmacy and clinical practice in Tibetan medicine is in itself negative or hegemonic. Rather, in this chapter I explore some of its consequences for the local relationships and identity of amchi in the periphery.

In the Darjeeling Hills, Tibetan public health issues were mainly directed to the respective Tibetan welfare officers, who subsidized biomedicine for economically underprivileged Tibetans. However, in Kalimpong the Tibetan welfare officer did not collaborate with the MTK or provide any guidelines or information on Tibetan medicine for Tibetans (as one would expect, since both bodies come under the Department of Health of the CTA). This was surprising considering that in Dharamsala collaborative efforts were made between the biomedical Delek hospital and the MTK. According to Prost (2004, 124), Delek physicians and MTK amchi referred patients to each other, and both took part in selected therapeutic management schemes.

The enlargement of the MTK branch clinics in predominantly Indian areas (as my example of the Salugara MTK showed) reveals that the MTK was gearing itself toward the much larger number of Indian patients using Tibetan medicine (see Kloos 2017, 145), who brought more economic benefit compared to the minority of Tibetan patients. Overall, the MTK pharmacy was "by far the most profitable enterprise under the Tibetan Government in exile" (Kloos 2008, 37), which itself was heavily involved in the MTK administration from 1975 to 2004 (22–23).

Despite the MTK's rapid growth and success, many Tibetans themselves were not convinced of the efficacy of Tibetan medicine. In fact, young Tibetans in the Darjeeling Hills had very little awareness of Tibetan medicine. In 2004 I questioned twenty-one grade 12 students at the Central School of Tibetans in Kalimpong using bilingual questionnaires (Tibetan and English). Seven students had never taken Tibetan medicine, nine "once or twice," and four "occasionally." For none of them was Tibetan medicine the regular choice of medication when ill. Those who had taken Tibetan medicine thought that the advantage was what they called "the lack of side effects." When I spoke informally with middle-aged Tibetans in Kalimpong and Darjeeling, they would generally talk positively about Tibetan medicine; when questioned in detail, it became clear that many had never used it or did not have in-depth knowledge of it.[22]

In Dharamsala the MTK stressed appearing "scientific" in its research outlook (Gerke 2011; Prost 2006). The research focus was largely on clinical trials for treatment of cancer, non-insulin-dependent diabetes mellitus, and hypertension, in an attempt to "legitimate the status of Tibetan medicine by proving its curative efficacy clinically with the use of Western scientific randomised controlled trial procedures," with the aim of gaining "credibility vis-à-vis biomedicine and in the scientific community at large" (Prost 2004, 129).

In the following section, I consider an amchi from a family tradition in Sikkim who was trained at the MTK in Dharamsala and worked in a government hospital in Sikkim, to elucidate the ways in which a family tradition can be combined with institutionalized amchi training.

Having *Jinlab*, or How to Carry On an Amchi Family Lineage in an Institutionalized Profession

In 2005 I came across one family lineage of amchi in the neighboring state of Sikkim, which illustrates the changes faced by a family lineage of amchi at a time of increased institutionalization and regulation of Tibetan medicine in India. At the time, one family-lineage amchi, whom I will call Amchi Passang, worked at a government-sponsored department for Tibetan medicine at a Sikkim government hospital. The government clinic itself had a unique status. It did not operate under the MTK in Dharamsala, even though it received medicines from the MTK and employed MTK-trained amchi. It did not follow the rotation system of the MTK branch clinics. Two amchi worked from 9 a.m. to 1 p.m. and saw about twenty to thirty patients a day. They worked closely together with the biomedical departments of the hospital, and they and the biomedical doctors referred patients to each other. This kind of collaboration led, in the eyes of one of the amchi, to the Tibetan clinic receiving the chronic cases where biomedicine had failed to achieve a cure. All medicines were given to patients free of charge. Therefore, they gave only seven to ten days of medication and requested that the patients come for a follow-up consultation. The MTK branch clinic at the other end of town received only a few patients (sometimes only five a day), because their medicines mostly had to be paid for by the patients.[23]

Amchi Passang was in the sixth generation of an amchi family lineage, which had been passed on to him by his father, who had established a private clinic in Sikkim. He was the fifth amchi in the lineage, was in his late sixties when I met him in 2005, and specialized in *tarsek* (*gtar bsreg*, bloodletting and moxibustion) and also used cupping. A booklet published privately by the family describes the history of the lineage, which began in the early nineteenth century with an amchi who lived southwest of Lhasa. The third amchi in this lineage treated the Chögyal of Sikkim and was consequently exempt from paying taxes.

Amchi Passang was the first of this family lineage educated at the MTK in Dharamsala. He said he needed a MTK degree to legally practice as an amchi in India. He was recommended by the Sikkim government for admission to the MTK and thus did not have to pass the admission test. There were three hundred applicants for twenty seats at that time, and it was difficult to get admission. He thought he was lucky to get into the MTK. However, he had to pay the fees himself.

In 2005, when I met Amchi Passang at the government hospital during an informal visit, he told me that he preferred to work at the hospital with its short working hours and no worries about procuring medical supplies, rather than joining his father's clinic. Unlike Passang, who relied on a regular supply of drugs from the MTK pharmacy in Dharamsala, his father spent a large amount of his time preparing about seventy types of medicines on his own. The benefits that came along with Passang's post at the government hospital included a regular monthly salary, free accommodation, allowances, and automatic promotions with increasing years of service. Since he had officially left the MTK, he was not allowed to sit for further MTK exams to obtain higher degrees, such as the *menrampa* (*sman ram pa*) degree.[24] However, he traveled to Dharamsala occasionally to participate in amchi seminars and conferences.

Amchi Passang was married and had a five-year-old son. For him, the combination of the MTK training, the government post, and his family lineage proved to be a suitable blend. I noted the following conversation in my field notes after a short chance encounter on May 28, 2005:

AMCHI PASSANG (AP): It was hard to study only with my father. Until grade ten I was not interested in medicine. If you study in your family, you are less motivated. Sometimes my father was moody; I also got moody; the discipline was not there. So I went to MTK after grade ten.... I don't like the hard life of an amchi, collecting plants, making medicines, being independent like my father. Here, I only see patients from 9 a.m. to 1 p.m., afternoons are free, and I can go to the gym, read, and enjoy life.

BG: Did you get any additional training from your father?

AP: MTK only gives theoretical training, but the practice is important; the experience, laklen. I only had a one-year internship in Orissa, then two years at Bilbao in Spain, then eight years in Sikkim at the hospital. I did not study much with my father.

BG: Will your son become an amchi as well?

AP: Yes.

BG: Will he have a choice?

AP: Not really. We have a family lineage of amchi. I am in the sixth generation. The lineage makes the practice more powerful. Even though I have not learned much from my father, I have the lineage.

BG: What does that mean, "having the lineage"?

AP: The *jinlab* [blessing] is there.

BG: Does this require any special practice?

AP: No, I read the prayers in the morning before starting my work.

Amchi Passang's situation highlights some of the changes that a lineage amchi may go through when confronted with the centralized MTK medical education and the offer of a stable government post. This situation forms an attractive blend for the "modern" version of the amchi profession: fixed working hours and other conveniences (social security, automatic promotions), the institutionalization of training (with an employed teacher in a classroom setting instead of his father teaching at home), and a guarantee of having the jinlab of the family lineage.

The Tibetan concept of jinlab (*byin rlabs*, Sanskrit *adhiṣṭhāna*), which is often translated as "blessing," deserves a closer look since it is an intrinsic aspect of Tibetan ideas about a lineage. Jinlab is quite complex, probably of pre-Buddhist origin, and involves concepts of power. *Jin (byin)* is one of the attributes associated with the old Tibetan kings. The pre-Buddhist divine king possessed jin as "a personal property or quality of his physical body" in the sense of "splendour" and "glory" (Huber 1999, 90). Jinlab literally means "wave of *byin*" (Samuel 1993, 450). In Tibetan dictionaries, we find jin translated as "pomp, splendor, magnificence, blessing, and resplendence" (The Tibetan and Himalayan Library 2019).

Jinlab is generally understood as the blessing power inherent in sacred sites, objects, and landscapes, which can be exploited through a ritual engagement by a lama. Jinlab is in fact one of the prerequisites for a lama to "claim to be an effective supplier of magical power" (Samuel 2005, 70–71). Its underlying relationship with power makes it a source of protection from harm and increases auspiciousness for people and their communities. Moreover, jinlab is considered important in the transmission of a lineage.[25]

The notion of having jinlab from a family lineage is probably also related to the concept of having the right *dungrü (gdung rus)*, which in this context refers to a lineage or descent line. Bone, in Tibetan *rü (rus)*, is a patrilineal and primary kinship-forming factor in many Tibetan groups (see, for example, Aziz 1978; Diemberger 1993; Levine 1981). Hildegard Diemberger (1993, 91–96) analyzed the patrilineal "bone" versus the matrilineal "blood" lineage among the Tibetan-speaking Khumbu in northeastern Nepal. She explains how for a male, the patrilineal transmission by bone is also something one *has* and does not need to acquire. This is similar to jinlab. Further research is required here on how rü and jinlab are related in explaining amchi family lineages, especially when they are passed on from father to daughter, or mother to daughter. If the passing on of jinlab is not linked to "bones," which is patrilineal, female amchi would also be able to pass on the lineage to their daughters. If the lineage conception is based on "bones," daughters can receive the lineage from their fathers, but they cannot pass it on. However, as Heidi Fjeld and Theresia Hofer have shown (Fjeld and Hofer 2010–11; and, more recently, Hofer 2018), medical lineages were transmitted to and by female amchi outside patrilineage, especially through medical houses, pointing to a variety of ways in which a lineage can be passed on. Amchi Passang did not particularly talk about rü. It is, however, clear that for him the family lineage implies that he *has* the jinlab, whereas the rest of the amchi's theoretical knowledge and the practical laklen need to be acquired through training.

Did the new institutionalization of the amchi profession affect the jinlab he received from the family lineage? Amchi Passang felt that the jinlab was there automatically, even without receiving his father's training. Undergoing years of apprenticeship and receiving his father's special laklen of bloodletting and moxibustion were not required to have jinlab. The laklen, in fact, was not so important in his clinical practice at the hospital, which was based on dispensing Tibetan medicines. The MTK's main therapeutic focus is on using pharmaceutical products. Additional therapies, such as bloodletting and moxibustion, are covered in their theoretical training, but only a few amchi who manage to acquire additional training from senior amchi with practical knowledge specialize in these methods. The institutionalization of Tibetan medicine in this case did not affect Amchi Passang *having* the jinlab. He, however, chose to distance himself from what usually comes along with a family tradition—the laklen of his father.

The son received very little from his family lineage in terms of practical medical knowledge. He felt that the jinlab was affected by neither the absence of intensive religious practice (which his father still engaged in) nor the fact that he had received very little in terms of oral transmission concerning medical procedures or preparations of medicines from his father. Separating the jinlab from the rest of what it would have entailed to carry on his family tradition led him to reinvent his status to the point that the family lineage could easily continue and coexist with a socially secure position as a MTK-trained amchi at a government hospital.

Conclusions

This chapter explored some effects of the institutionalization of Tibetan medicine by the Dharamsala MTK on the amchi in the Darjeeling Hills and analyzed one example of a family-lineage amchi from Sikkim. The material presented demonstrates a certain monopoly by the MTK pharmacy and a loss of amchi agency through the MTK rotation scheme as I observed it between 2004 and 2006. The status and potential professional independence of amchi at the time were shaped and controlled by the MTK's economic strategies and its centralization of institutional management. This, along with the policy of rotating amchi through the more than fifty MTK branch clinics in India and Nepal, meant that those amchi who rotated frequently experienced a loss of social status and sometimes feelings of isolation in the communities in which they were assigned to work. Moreover, the rotation scheme seemed to be a contributing factor to the lack of knowledge and limited use of Tibetan medicine within Tibetan communities themselves. More research is required to see whether this still persists today and also applies to other MTK clinics situated in Tibetan communities in other regions across India and Nepal.

To conclude, during the period under investigation, MTK amchi on frequent rotation aligned themselves more with the center than with their locale. Their identity was increasingly shaped by the MTK at the center; they identified more as MTK amchi than as amchi of a particular region or community. Fieldwork carried out in Kalimpong between 2004 and 2006 showed that for patients in the community, the reputation of a particular amchi acquired less importance, since the amchi were perceived to be "only passing through." The relationship of Tibetan patients to Tibetan medicine consequently changed into a more formalized relationship with the MTK as an institution, "a place to get medicines." This was supported by institutionalized benefit schemes, such as free medicines for Tibetans aged seventy or above and subsidized prices for students and ordained monks and nuns. Kalimpong, as an example of the periphery of the MTK establishment, showed that Tibetan medicine was not used or promoted to strengthen Tibetan national feelings or express Tibetan identity. This seems different at the center in Dharamsala, where Tibetan identity, Buddhist ethics, and the promotion of Tibetan medicine have been more closely interwoven (Kloos 2008, 2017).

In Dharamsala the MTK administration tended to impose a uniform, centralized model of Tibetan medicine. Individual amchi, however, often held different views and admired their hardworking colleagues who manufactured their own medicines or who ran their own clinics and bought medicines from private Tibetan pharmacies. Still, Amchi Passang's example points to a trend toward giving up clinical independence in exchange for regular and shorter working hours. Amchi Passang's example also shows how the institutionalization and licensing of amchi in India have affected the ways amchi from family lineages who hold a MTK degree value and negotiate their relationship with their lineage. A new generation of institutionally trained amchi, who also come from traditional family lineages, seem to perceive the transmission of lineage through jinlab in innovative ways. In the case described, lineage did not require the studying and acquiring of practical expertise, or laklen, that was particular to the family lineage, nor the use of therapeutic tools traditionally passed on from father to son.

Today, with the number of female amchi increasing to more than half of all institutionally trained amchi, further research could focus on how patrilineal conceptions of lineage transmissions might change among male and female amchi when Sowa Rigpa knowledge is passed on in institutional settings. Will amchi identity be shaped more by medical institutions than by lineage, thus giving less prominence to patrilineal transmission?

The overall picture in the Darjeeling Hills of that time reveals that the expertise of the MTK amchi was underutilized and confined to the MTK institution. At the time of my fieldwork, amchi in Kalimpong, for example, were neither empowered nor encouraged to work with the local Tibetan welfare officer, Tibetan social networks (kidu), and other Tibetan organizations, all of which could have offered opportunities to spread general knowledge of Tibetan medicine and public health care.[26] If the MTK developed more decentralized, community-based approaches to health care, allowing amchi to stay longer in one community, amchi knowledge could be better utilized for the benefit of local communities, even outside the MTK consultation rooms.

The data presented here also raise broader questions regarding the role Sowa Rigpa could play in the health care of Indian Himalayan societies in the long run. The dynamics of centralized control and professionalization underscore the potential of Sowa Rigpa practitioners working in the peripheries. Its transformation at the local level sheds light on how the increasingly institutional employment schemes of amchi might curtail the individual agency of amchi practice and move practitioners away from traditional forms of practice in which amchi still have a defined role in the community they serve, as described by Kim Gutschow (this volume). While the professionalization of Sowa Rigpa in many cases has led to a better income and legal status for amchi across the Himalayan range, the challenge remains to find ways to integrate practitioners well into the communities they serve.

Notes

I am grateful to Sienna Craig, Stephan Kloos, Alex McKay, Audrey Prost, Charles Ramble, and Geoffrey Samuel for their helpful comments at various stages of this chapter. The writing of this chapter was completed during the FWF project P30804, funded by the Austrian Science Fund (FWF) through the University of Vienna.

1 The official website of the MTK defines Sowa Rigpa as "the ancient Tibetan system of medicine, astronomy and astrology" (Men-Tsee-Khang 2017d). The use of the term *Sowa Rigpa* has more recently been discussed by Sienna Craig and Gerke (2016).

2 See also Klieger (2002) and Diehl (2002), which discuss Tibetanness in the diaspora as an "imagined" identity that is constructed from Tibetans' own imaginings of the homeland as well as Western projections of Tibetan identity.

3 For other publications of this research material, see Gerke (2010a, 2010b, 2011, 2012).

4 References to websites have been updated for this publication.

5 According to the 2001 census, Kalimpong had a total population of 42,980 and Darjeeling a total population of 106,257 (quoted in Fareedi and Lepcha 2002–3, 4). These figures are low estimates, focus on urban centers, do not include villages, and have continued to increase with intense and uncontrolled migration into the area.

6 Tibetan refugees in the Darjeeling and Sikkim regions have been studied by Tanka Subba (1988, 1990, 1992, 2002). For a brief summary of existing literature on Tibetan refugees in India until the end of my fieldwork in the region, see Prost (2008, 8–10).

7 According to a 1998 survey by the Planning Council of the CTA in Dharamsala (CTA 2000), 85,147 Tibetans were living in India (48,005 males and 37,142 females) at that time. In West Bengal, Darjeeling and Kalimpong were the urban areas with the largest groups of Tibetans: 2,455 in Darjeeling and 2,141 in Kalimpong; the total Tibetan population in West Bengal numbered 6,455 (CTA 2000, 36). Smaller Tibetan settlements of a few hundred people were located near these main urban areas. The actual figures were no doubt higher since only Tibetans in the settlements or families that were in touch with the CTA were taken into account in this survey.

8 For an example of medical pluralism among Nepali groups in the Darjeeling Hills, see Strässle (2007). For a more recent study on medical pluralism and mental health among Tibetans in the Darjeeling Hills see Deane (2018).

9 For details on Chagpori Medical College in Tibet, see Gerl and Aschoff (2005) and Meyer (2003).

10 For details on the history of the Dharamsala MTK, see Kloos (2008, 2011, 2017).

11 By 2017 the CTMI operated five clinics in the Darjeeling region. See Chagpori Tibetan Medical Institute (2020).

12 See Jacobson (2000, 137–47) for a detailed description of some of these spiritual practices, which he observed both in Dharamsala and Darjeeling.

13 See Samuel (2001) for a description of a MTK branch clinic in Dalhousie and Prost (2004, 2008) for details on the MTK clinics in Dharamsala.

14 See Shneiderman and Turin (2006) for a succinct summary of this issue.

15 For a list of these branch clinics see Men-Tsee-Khang (2017c).

16 The first class, in 1961, had six students graduate (Gerke 1999, 55).

17 Amchi Wangdu, personal communication, September 2009.

18 The kidu was a lower- and middle-class social welfare system in the larger urban areas of Tibet (Miller 1956, 165). In Darjeeling many kidu started as transport syndicates and later became mutual aid societies for Tibetans in the Hills to compensate for the absence of health insurance and social security.

19 Fraud of producing and selling counterfeit "precious pills" known as *rinchen rilbu* (*rin chen ril bu*) was a serious problem at the time (see, e.g., Men-Tsee-Khang 2002, 2; or Prost 2008, 77).

20 According to Jigme Tsarong, who was the director of the MTK from 1975 until 1980 and also headed the Research and Development Department (established in 1980) for several years, the MTK pharmacy started with a budget of 3,000 Indian rupees (Kloos 2008, 24). It reached an annual turnover of 39,900,000 rupees and a profit of about 20,000,000 rupees by 2007–8 (Kloos 2010, 171).

21 As of 2017, the MTK pharmacy produced 172 types of medicines (Men-Tsee-Khang 2017b). Sorig herbal health-care products (supplements, health drinks, skin and hair care, and incense) are advertised on the MTK website (Men-Tsee-Khang 2017a) and through their export branch (Men-Tsee-Khang Exports 2009).

22 In the absence of any detailed study on how many Tibetans use Tibetan medicine, these are only general observations.

23 As in all MTK branch clinics, however, medicines were discounted for monks, nuns, and students and were free of cost for the underprivileged and patients above seventy.

24 Other MTK amchi take exams every five years to renew their license and have the opportunity to obtain higher degrees. These exams are demanding and require a lot of preparation on the part of the amchi, since they include the oral recitation of large parts of the Gyüshi (*rgyud bzhi*) from memory as well as written tests.

25 Tibetans have conceived of three types of lineages: the family lineage, or *dung gyü* (*gdung rgyud*), the transmission of tantric teachings or empowerments to disciples called *lop gyü* (*slob rgyud*), and lineages of "emanations" of incarnate lamas known as *ku gyü* (*sku rgyud*; for details, see Mills 2003, 125).

26 One has to acknowledge here the benefits of free medical camps and outreach programs regularly organized by the MTK, which provide health care to Tibetans in remote areas and introduce Sowa Rigpa to new rural and urban patients, who are mostly Indians.

References

Aziz, Barbara. 1978. *Tibetan Frontier Families: Reflections of Three Generations from Dingri*. Durham, NC: Carolina Academic Press.

Central Council of Tibetan Medicine. 2018a. "Detail List of Registered Practitioners." Accessed April 30, 2018. http://tibmedcouncil.org/registered-medical-practitioner.

Central Council of Tibetan Medicine. 2018b. "Introduction." Accessed April 30, 2018. http://www.tibmedcouncil.org/introduction.

Chagpori Tibetan Medical Institute. 2020. "Tradition in Transition." Accessed March 19, 2021. https://chagpori.org/tradition-in-transition/#chagpori-trained-amchis.

Craig, Sienna R. 2012. *Healing Elements: Efficacy and the Social Ecologies of Tibetan Medicine*. Berkeley: University of California Press.

Craig, Sienna R., and Barbara Gerke. 2016. "Naming and Forgetting: Sowa Rigpa and the Territory of Asian Medical Systems." *Medicine Anthropology Theory* 3 (2): 87–122.

CTA (Central Tibetan Administration-in-Exile), Planning Council. 2000. *Tibetan Demographic Survey 1998*. Dharamsala: Central Tibetan Administration, Gangchen Kyishong.

Deane, Susannah. 2018. *Tibetan Medicine, Buddhism and Psychiatry: Mental Health and Healing in a Tibetan Exile Community*. Durham, NC: Carolina Academic Press.

Diehl, Keila. 2002. *Echoes from Dharamsala: Music in the Life of a Tibetan Refugee Community*. Berkeley: University of California Press.

Diemberger, Hildegard. 1993. "Blood, Sperm, Soul and the Mountain: Gender Relations, Kinship and Cosmovision among the Kumbo (N.E. Nepal)." In *Gendered Anthropology*, edited by Teresa del Valle, 88–127. London: Routledge.

Fareedi, Mashqura, and Pasang Dorjee Lepcha, eds. 2002–3. *Area and Issue Profile of Darjeeling and Sikkim*. Darjeeling: R.C.D.C. Hayden Hall.

Fjeld, Heidi, and Theresia Hofer. 2010–11. "Women and Gender in Tibetan Medicine." *Asian Medicine: Tradition and Modernity* 6 (2): 175–216.

Gerke, Barbara. 1999. "From Tibet to Massachusetts: The Journey of a Tibetan Lady Doctor; Interview with Dr. Keyzom Bhutti." *AyurVijnana* 6:54–59.

Gerke, Barbara. 2010a. "The Multivocality of Ritual Experiences: Long-Life Empowerments among Tibetan Communities in the Darjeeling Hills, India." In *Ritual Dynamics and the Science of Ritual*, vol. 2, *Body, Performance, Agency, and Experience*, edited by Axel Michaels et al., 423–41. Wiesbaden: Harrassowitz.

Gerke, Barbara. 2010b. "Tibetan Treatment Choices in the Context of Medical Pluralism in the Darjeeling Hills." In *Studies of Medical Pluralism in Tibetan History and Society; PIATS 2006: Proceedings of the Eleventh Seminar of the International Association for Tibetan Studies, Königswinter 2006*, edited by Sienna Craig, Mingji Cuomu, Frances Garrett, and Mona Schrempf, 337–76. Andiast, Switzerland: International Institute for Tibetan and Buddhist Studies.

Gerke, Barbara. 2011. "Correlating Biomedical and Tibetan Medical Terms in Amchi Medical Practice." In *Medicine between Science and Religion: Explorations on Tibetan Grounds*, edited by Vincanne Adams, Mona Schrempf, and Sienna Craig, 127–52. Oxford: Berghahn Books.

Gerke, Barbara. 2012. *Long Lives and Untimely Deaths: Life-Span Concepts and Longevity Practices among Tibetans in the Darjeeling Hills, India*. Leiden: Brill.

Gerl, Robert, and Jürgen C. Aschoff. 2005. *Der Tschagpori in Lhasa: Medizinhochschule und Kloster*. Ulm: Fabri.

Goldstein, Melvyn C., and Matthew T. Kapstein. 1998. *Buddhism in Contemporary Tibet: Religious Revival and Cultural Identity*. Berkeley: University of California Press.

Gyatso, Losang. 1990. "Tibet: A State or a State of Mind?" *Himal*, January/February 1990, 15.

Hofer, Theresia. 2018. *Medicine and Memory in Tibet: Amchi Physicians in an Age of Reform*. Seattle: University of Washington Press.

Huber, Toni. 1999. "Putting the *Gnas* Back into *Gnas-skor*: Rethinking Tibetan Pilgrimage Practices." In *Sacred Spaces and Powerful Places in Tibetan Culture: A Collection of Essays*, edited by Toni Huber, 78–104. Dharamsala: Library of Tibetan Works and Archives.

Jacobson, Eric E. 2000. "Situated Knowledge in Classical Tibetan Medicine: Psychiatric Aspects." PhD diss., Harvard University.

Klieger, P. Christiaan, ed. 2002. *Tibet, Self, and the Tibetan Diaspora: Voices of Difference; PIATS 2000: Proceedings of the Ninth Seminar of the International Association for Tibetan Studies, Leiden 2000*. Brill's Tibetan Studies Library. Leiden: Brill.

Kloos, Stephan. 2008. "The History and Development of Tibetan Medicine in Exile." *Tibet Journal* 33 (3): 15–49.

Kloos, Stephan. 2010. "Tibetan Medicine in Exile: The Ethics, Politics, and Science of Cultural Survival." PhD diss., University of California, San Francisco and Berkeley.

Kloos, Stephan. 2011. "Navigating 'Modern Science' and 'Traditional Culture': The Dharamsala Men-Tsee-Khang in India." In *Medicine between Science and Religion: Explorations on Tibetan Grounds*, edited by Vincanne Adams, Mona Schrempf, and Sienna Craig, 83–105. London: Berghahn.

Kloos, Stephan. 2012. "Die Alchemie exil-tibetischer Identität: Anmerkungen zur pharmazeutischen und politischen Wirksamkeit tibetischer Pillen." *Curare* 35 (3): 197–207.

Kloos, Stephan. 2015. "Impotent Knowledges: Preserving 'Traditional' Tibetan Medicine through Modern Science." In *Fugitive Knowledges: The Preservation and Loss of Knowledge in Cultural Contact Zones*, edited by Andreas Beer and Gesa Mackenthun, 123–42. Münster: Waxmann.

Kloos, Stephan. 2016. "The Recognition of Sowa Rigpa in India: How Tibetan Medicine Became an Indian Medical System." *Medicine Anthropology Theory* 3 (2): 19–49.

Kloos, Stephan. 2017. "The Politics of Preservation and Loss: Tibetan Medical Knowledge in Exile." *East Asian Science, Technology and Society: An International Journal* 11 (2): 135–59.

Levine, Nancy E. 1981. "The Theory of *Rus*: Kinship, Status and Descent in Tibetan Society." In *Asian Highland Societies in Anthropological Perspectives*, edited by Christoph von Fürer-Haimendorf, 52–78. New Delhi: Sterling.

Men-Tsee-Khang. 2002. "Caution." *Men-Tsee-Khang Newsletter* 9 (4): 2.

Men-Tsee-Khang. 2017a. "Herbal Health Care Products." Accessed June 20, 2017. http://men-tsee-khang.org/hprd/product.htm.

Men-Tsee-Khang. 2017b. "Medicine." Accessed June 20, 2017. http://men-tsee-khang.org/dept/pharmacy/med-precious.htm.

Men-Tsee-Khang. 2017c. "Men-Tsee-Khang Branch Office." Accessed June 20, 2017. http://www.men-tsee-khang.org/branch/index.htm.

Men-Tsee-Khang. 2017d. "Mission." Accessed June 19, 2017. https://www.men-tsee-khang.org/mission/mission.htm.

Men-Tsee-Khang Exports. 2009. "Our Products." Accessed June 20, 2017. http://www.men-tsee-khang-exports.org.

Meyer, Fernand. 2003. "The Golden Century of Tibetan Medicine." In *Lhasa in the Seventeenth Century: The Capital of the Dalai Lamas*, edited by Françoise Pommaret, 99–118. Leiden: Brill.

Miller, Beatrice D. 1956. "Ganye and Kidu: Two Formalized Systems of Mutual Aid among the Tibetans." *Southwestern Journal of Anthropology* 12 (2): 157–70.

Mills, Martin A. 2003. *Identity, Ritual and State in Tibetan Buddhism: The Foundations of Authority in Gelukpa Monasticism.* London: RoutledgeCurzon.

Pordié, Laurent. 2003. *The Expression of Religion in Tibetan Medicine: Ideal Conceptions, Contemporary Practices, and Political Use.* Pondy Papers in Social Sciences 29. Pondicherry: French Institute of Pondicherry.

Pordié, Laurent. 2008. "Tibetan Medicine Today: Neo-traditionalism as an Analytical Lens and a Political Tool." In *Tibetan Medicine in the Contemporary World: Global Politics of Medical Knowledge and Practice,* edited by Laurent Pordié, 3–32. London: Routledge.

Prost, Audrey G. 2004. "Exile, Social Change and Medicine among Tibetans in Dharamsala (Himachal Pradesh), India." PhD diss., University College London.

Prost, Audrey G. 2006. "Gained in Translation: Tibetan Science between Dharamsala and Lhasa." In *Translating Others: Translations and Translation Theories East and West,* edited by Theo Hermans, 132–44. Manchester: St. Jerome.

Prost, Audrey G. 2008. *Precious Pills: Medicine and Social Change among Tibetan Refugees in India.* Oxford: Berghahn.

Samuel, Geoffrey. 1993. *Civilized Shamans: Buddhism in Tibetan Societies.* Washington, DC: Smithsonian Institution Press.

Samuel, Geoffrey. 2001. "Tibetan Medicine in Contemporary India: Theory and Practice." In *Healing Powers and Modernity: Traditional Medicine, Shamanism, and Science in Asian Studies,* edited by Linda H. Connor and Geoffrey Samuel, 247–68. Westport, CT: Bergin and Garvey.

Samuel, Geoffrey. 2005. *Tantric Revisionings: New Understandings of Tibetan Buddhism and Indian Religion.* Delhi: Motilal Banarsidass.

Schaeffer, Kurtis R. 2003. "Textual Scholarship, Medical Tradition, and Mahayana Buddhist Ideals in Tibet." *Journal of Indian Philosophy* 31:621–41.

Shakya, Tsering. 1993. "Wither the Tsampa Eaters." *Himal* 6 (5): 8–11.

Shneiderman, Sara, and Mark Turin. 2006. "Seeking the Tribe: Ethno-politics in Darjeeling and Sikkim." *Himal Southasian* 19 (2): 54–58.

Strässle, Susanne. 2007. *Biomedizin im Kontext: Medizin, Glauben und Moderne in den Darjeeling Hills, Indien.* Züricher Arbeitspapiere zur Ethnologie 17. Zürich: Argonaut.

Subba, Tanka B. 1988. "Social Adaptation of the Tibetan Refugees in the Darjeeling-Sikkim Himalayas." *Tibet Journal* 13 (3): 49–57.

Subba, Tanka B. 1990. *Flight and Adaptation: Tibetan Refugees in the Darjeeling Sikkim Himalaya.* Dharamsala: Library of Tibetan Works and Archives.

Subba, Tanka B. 1992. "Tibetans in Exile: Economic Pursuits and Ethnicity." In *Ethnicity and Politics in Central Asia,* edited by K. Warikoo and Dawa Norbu, 204–15. New Delhi: South Asian Publishers.

Subba, Tanka B. 2002. "One or Many Paths: Coping with the Tibetan Refugees in India." In *Dimensions of Displaced People in North-East India,* edited by Joshua C. Thomas, 131–48. New Delhi: Regency.

The Tibetan and Himalayan Library. 2019. "THL Tibetan to English Translation Tool." http://www.thlib.org/reference/dictionaries/tibetan-dictionary/translate.php.

Afterword
When "Periphery" Becomes Central
SIENNA R. CRAIG

It is ground I solicit to keep balance,
to memorize the contrariety of a journey
in a sequence of form, of history.
—TSERING WANGMO DHOMPA,
My Rice Tastes like the Lake

In Tibetan religious traditions, a *terma* (*gter ma*) is a "hidden treasure." Although terma are sometimes described in material terms—a text or ritual implement ensconced in rock, buried under earth, hidden in sky or water—these precious resources are also forms of intention, teachings to be revealed when a practitioner is primed to receive their wisdom.

Without stretching the spiritual analogy too far, the body of work represented by this volume feels a bit like a terma. At once rich and meticulous in its rendering of village-level realities and attentive to the larger social and structural forces shaping local lives in the Indian Himalayas, this book has been nearly two decades in the making. The pace and exigencies of academic publishing notwithstanding, this is a long time. However, what has emerged through this liminal period, itself one of major social, economic, and medical transformation in the subcontinent and the world, is a text that teaches us about many things, including, but certainly not limited to, the state of Sowa Rigpa in India.

The case studies in this volume ground crucial components of what Stephan Kloos (2017) has, elsewhere, described as a "pharmaceutical assemblage" shaping the Sowa Rigpa industry. Also, perhaps more important, this book has shown the social antecedents and political-economic inflection points that have given rise to this assemblage in the first place. This work from the periphery helps us to understand some of the stakes involved in the pharmaceuticalization and commercialization inherent in the expanding Asian medicines marketplace—itself at once a diffuse center of global capital and a network of authority and influence tied to specific nodes of production and modes of regulation. As Tibetan poet Tsering Wangmo Dhompa (2011, 8) describes, the book reads as "a sequence of form, of history." Without this sense of locally grounded history, we are unable to fully grasp the present moment, let alone imagine possible futures for Sowa Rigpa.

Said another way, the whole of this book is more than the sum of its parts. As Stephan Kloos and Laurent Pordié note in their introduction, this text is not merely a collection of social science cases. Rather, taken together, these individual chapters form a coherent meta-ethnography that reveals different layers of socioeconomic and medical transformations at work across the Indian Himalayas. Through detailed treatments of specific times and places—a birth in Shun-Shade, an episode of madness in Zangskar, crises of moral authority in Hanu and medical authority in the Darjeeling Hills, the collective ache caused by the absence of amchi on the Changthang—readers come to see how and why the periphery matters. Indeed, one might argue that only by attending to that which is small in scale can we conceive of the changes and mark the points of continuity that define Sowa Rigpa in national and global contexts.

These chapters also cohere into *one* story when it comes to considering the dynamic tensions between "mainstream" Tibetan medicine as it is practiced in India, and its "others." The former can operate as an orthodoxy whose rays of power and influence radiate out from Dharamsala, strong and single-pointed like the sun. In contrast, the heterodox vitality of places like Ladakh feels more lunar. Consider the moon's capacity to illuminate—as in the brightness that comes from the successful reimagining of amchi's abilities to support themselves in Lingshed—and the moon's propensity, by casting shadows, to at once reveal and obscure, as the authority of the state in shaping what or who a government amchi is, or the slippery nature of an amchi's recruitment of healing power for political ends.

The social ecologies of health and illness, medicine and development, described in this book illustrate some of the most formative *and* resilient theories in medical anthropology and related disciplines. Here I am thinking particularly of medical pluralism and illness narratives but also of the ways that medicine operates as a form of social knowledge—at once authoritative and contested.

These chapters elucidate themes about the nature of labor, money as a social institution, and reciprocity, as well as about the relationship between ethical ideals and local moral worlds. In their introduction, the editors sketch uniting points of inquiry for the volume. These include the role Sowa Rigpa plays in maintaining health and addressing suffering in Indian Himalayan societies and the unifying concerns—such as access to good amchi and good medicine, or the interplay between Sowa Rigpa and biomedicine—that cut across social and therapeutic landscapes. The structure of the book further reinforces the conceptual axes on which this intellectual project hinges: individual amchi, on the one hand, and the communities of which they and their patients are a part, on the other.

In the chapters by Fernanda Pirie and Stephan Kloos, we come to appreciate the importance of scale and the enduring value of village-based ethnography. With both positive and negative examples at play (the "good" amchi and the "bad" amchi), we are reminded that these authority figures are villagers first and that their capacity to maintain their medical or religious influence depends on maintaining interpersonal relations. Scale remains a theme, but in a different way, in Calum Blaikie's chapter on Ladakh's nomadic communities that are struggling with the loss of amchi, owing to source forces of migration and attendant social change. Here we see the challenges associated with remoteness, but this chapter also disabuses the reader of any easy parsing of "rural" and "urban." In considering where there is no amchi, we cannot help but see Leh and the Changthang as linked, just as the social and geographic manifestations of center and periphery are interconnected.

While Blaikie's chapter introduces us to some of the points of ambivalence about development as a social category, the story told by Florian Besch and Isabelle Guérin about public health and development, nongovernmental organizations, and the meaning of community does an excellent job in showing the sedimented nature of power and authority at the local level—how it can be an intervention's downfall or the fulcrum on which its success may hinge. Building on these currents of ambivalence, the chapter by Laurent Pordié and Pascale Hancart Petitet further instantiates ideas about power, control, and authority through the prism of childbirth. This vulnerable time brings into focus both the value of amchi medicine and the potential for its ongoing marginalization in contemporary India. As something of an antidote to this view, Kim Gutschow's chapter has a recuperative effect: it shows the value of Sowa Rigpa diagnostic practices and links the inner social worlds of (mental) illness with the outer social worlds of money and modernization. Here, health hangs in the balance between individual and collective. These themes flow smoothly into the final chapter, Barbara Gerke's study of Men-Tsee-Khang branch clinics in Darjeeling and Sikkim. The institutional amchi we meet in this chapter provide a perfect counterpoint to the embeddedness of the healers we have encountered in earlier chapters and, as such, show the value and the limits of individual and institutional forms of authority.

Finally, this book exemplifies the forging of scholarly community. The authors of these chapters are not simply researchers whose work is presented side by side. Rather, they have cocreated a body of knowledge; they have openly and ethically navigated the waters of so-called pure and applied social science; and, in many cases, they are friends. This book acknowledges enduring connections between people and places. Why does this matter? It matters because, all too often, we hear about the same micropolitics that plague someone like Tashi Bulu, or that mire the good intentions of programs like the ones rolled out by Nomad RSI, playing out among academics. We, too, can be territorial—despite the urgency to decolonize scholarly fields, despite collaborative turns. We, too, can become overly invested in singular analysis—despite disciplinary training to the contrary. We, too, can forget the importance of intimate portraits in our effort to render broad pictures. We, too, can overlook the tentative nature of social change in our efforts to craft solid social theory. And so I hold this collection as an effort that pushes against what modernity forgets and, as Paul Connerton (1989, 2009) describes, toward what society and human relationships can help us to remember.

References

Connerton, Paul. 1989. *How Societies Remember*. Cambridge: Cambridge University Press.
Connerton, Paul. 2009. *How Modernity Forgets*. Cambridge: Cambridge University Press.
Dhompa, Tsering Wangmo. 2011. *My Rice Tastes like the Lake*. Berkeley, CA: Apogee.
Kloos, Stephan. 2017. "The Pharmaceutical Assemblage: Rethinking Sowa Rigpa and the Herbal Pharmaceutical Industry in Asia." *Current Anthropology* 58 (6): 693–717.

Contributors

FLORIAN BESCH is an anthropologist and has conducted research on the modernization of Asian medicines, alternative medicines in Germany, and healing aspects in martial arts. He works as a coach and facilitator at NEVO, a human resources agency based in Göttingen, Germany, focusing on organizational and personal change processes, mindfulness and embodiment trainings, integral development, conflict resolution, and health prevention.

CALUM BLAIKIE is a senior researcher at the Institute for Social Anthropology, Austrian Academy of Sciences (ÖAW). His research explores the interface of the medical, economic, pharmaceutical, and political fields, focusing on Sowa Rigpa in Himalayan India and Nepal. He has published articles in numerous journals including *Anthropology and Medicine*, *Current Anthropology*, *Social Science and Medicine*, and *Asian Medicine* and is coeditor of the forthcoming volumes *Asian Medical Industries: Contemporary Perspectives on Traditional Pharmaceuticals* (with Stephan Kloos) and *Building Craft Traditions in Tibet and the Himalayas* (with Hubert Feiglstorfer). He currently leads a research project investigating the implications of the recent official recognition of Sowa Rigpa (Tibetan medicine) by the government of India, and its subsequent integration into national governance structures and public health-care programs.

SIENNA R. CRAIG is an associate professor of anthropology at Dartmouth College. Her research interests circle between high Asia and North America and focus on experiences of health and illness, medicine and science, across cultures, as well as on the dynamics of migration and social change. Craig is the author of *The Ends of Kinship: Connecting Himalayan Lives between Nepal and New York*; *Mustang in Black and White,* with photographer Kevin Bubriski; *Healing Elements: Efficacy and the Social Ecologies of Tibetan Medicine*; and *Horses Like Lightning: A Story of Passage through the Himalayas,* as well as a coeditor of *Medicine between Science and Religion: Explorations on Tibetan Grounds* and *Studies of Medical Pluralism in Tibetan History and Society; PIATS 2006: Proceedings of the Eleventh Seminar of the International Association for Tibetan Studies, Königswinter 2006,* among other publications. Craig enjoys writing across genres and has published poetry, creative nonfiction, fiction, and children's literature in addition to scholarly works in medical and cultural anthropology.

BARBARA GERKE is a medical anthropologist and currently the project leader of the Austrian Science Fund (FWF) research project "Potent Substances in Sowa Rigpa and Buddhist Rituals" at the University of Vienna. She works across the disciplines of medical anthropology and Tibetan studies, and her research focuses on medico-religious interfaces in

Sowa Rigpa pharmacology with ethnographic fieldwork in Nepal and among Tibetan and Ladakhi communities in India. Her monograph *Taming the Poisonous* (2021) examines the use of refined mercury in Tibetan medicines and related safety and toxicity debates. Her first monograph, *Long Lives and Untimely Deaths* (2012), analyzes long-life rituals, as well as vitality and life-span concepts among Tibetans in the Darjeeling Hills.

ISABELLE GUÉRIN is a socioeconomist, a senior researcher at the French Institute of Research for Sustainable Development (IRD), and a research associate at the French Institute of Pondicherry. She specializes in the role of debt and credit in the dynamics of poverty and inequality and combines ethnography and statistical analyses in her interdisciplinary and comparative work. She publishes in journals of development studies, anthropology, political economics, and geography. Some of her coedited works include *Randomized Control Trials in the Field of Development: A Critical Perspective* (2020, with Florent Bédécarrats and François Roubaud) and *The Crises of Microcredit* (2015, with Marc Labie and Jean-Michel Servet).

KIM GUTSCHOW is a senior lecturer in the Departments of Anthropology and Religion at Williams College, where she is affiliated with Public Health, Environmental Studies, Science and Technology Studies, Asian Studies, and Women's, Gender, and Sexuality Studies. She has worked in the Indian Himalayan region of Ladakh since 1989, publishing over thirty-five articles on Tibetan medicine, maternity care and maternal mortality, Buddhist monasticism, and community-based irrigation and land-use practices in the Indian Himalayas. She is the author of the award-winning monograph *Being a Buddhist Nun: The Struggle for Enlightenment in the Indian Himalaya* (2004) and editor of *Sustainable Birth in Disruptive Times* (2021). She received a Humboldt Fellowship for Experienced Researchers in 2009 for *Birth: From Home to Hospital and Back Home Again* and a National Geographic Award in 2019 for *Climate Change Adaptation: By the People, For the People.*

PASCALE HANCART PETITET is a medical anthropologist and senior researcher at the French Institute of Research for Sustainable Development (IRD–TransVIHMI). Her research in India and Cambodia explored the historical constructions, the production and the circulation of ideologies, norms, and practices in the field of human reproduction and reproductive health. Since 2013 her transdisciplinary research in Laos explores the intersections of reproduction politics, national and transnational migrations, and infectious vulnerabilities. She is the author of fifty articles and book chapters and experiments with various innovative approaches for scientific mediation (radio programs, films, and theater).

STEPHAN KLOOS is an anthropologist and serves as the acting director of the Institute for Social Anthropology at the Austrian Academy of Sciences (ÖAW). His research explores the larger sociocultural, political, economic, and public health role of Sowa Rigpa (Tibetan medicine) and other Asian medicines in India, China, Mongolia, and Russia, with a particular focus on their transformation into Asian health industries. He is coeditor of the forthcoming book *Asian Medical Industries: Contemporary Perspectives on Traditional Pharmaceuticals* (with Calum Blaikie) and has published articles in numerous journals, including *Current Anthropology, Social Science and Medicine, Medical Anthropology*, and *EASTS.*

FERNANDA PIRIE is a professor of the anthropology of law at the University of Oxford. Specializing in Tibetan societies, she uses ethnographic and historical methods to study and compare legal practices and texts. Fieldwork in Ladakh led to the monograph *Peace and Conflict in Ladakh: The Construction of a Fragile Web of Order* (2007). She followed this with fieldwork in Amdo, and she has conducted research into Tibetan legal history, funded by the United Kingdom's Arts and Humanities Research Council, Legal Ideology in Tibet: Politics, Practice, and Religion (2016–18). This has led to a series of publications and a website containing source material (tibetanlaw.org).

LAURENT PORDIÉ is an anthropologist and a senior researcher at the French National Center for Scientific Research (CNRS-CERMES3) in Paris. His current work examines the industrial production of herbal medicines, the global circulation of pharmaceuticals, and heterodox pharmaceutical practices. His recent works include *Global Health and the New World Order* (2020, with Jean-Paul Gaudillière et al.) and *Circulation and Governance of Asian Medicine* (2020, with Celine Coderey).

childbirth, amchi roles in: overview, 120; and abnormalities, 124–28; butter fish, 126–31, 138n24; disapproval of, 129; gender, 122; government recognition, 129–30; impurity protection, 125; knowledge of, 121–23, 125, 135n4, 136n10, 137n23; Leh, 128–31, 133; meanings to patients, 130–31; modernization impacts, 132–34; reincarnation beliefs, 121; training, 132–33

childbirth in Leh: amchi involvement, 128–31, 133; biomedicalization, 128–31, 138n30; delivery, 131

childbirth in Shun-Shade: Buddhist contexts, 121, 135n3; butter massages, 123, 126, 136n9; delivery, 123, 136n10; and the klu, 128; male involvement, 123; placenta rituals, 123–24, 136n13; pollution concepts (*drib/grib*), 123–24; pregnant women, 122–25; *rlung* (wind), 125, 137nn21–22; Sonam Thundup, 121. *See also* childbirth, amchi roles in

childbirth practices: biomedical approaches, 130–31, 133; biomedicalization of, 119–20, 131, 133–34, 138n30; birth attendants, 124–25, 137n18; contexts, 119; and fish, 138n28; Hindu contexts, 135n2; male involvement, 123, 136n11; manuals, 132; placenta rituals, 136n15; pollution concepts (*drib/grib*), 123, 136n14; pregnant women activeness, 135n6; pregnant women's responsibilities, 137n20; prior scholarship, 119; temperature associations, 127; in Tibet, 138n31. *See also* childbirth, amchi roles in; childbirth in Leh; childbirth in Shun-Shade

Chonglamsar, 90n23

Clifford, Terry, 157, 164n6, 166n25

Commons, John, 96

community health centers. *See* Lingshed village community health center

Cornu, Philippe, 164n12

Craig, Sienna, 159, 162

Darjeeling Hills amchi: Amchi Tashi, 177–78, 180; astrological knowledge, 176; Darjeeling town MTK branch, 179–81; and Delek hospital, 184; family lineages in Sikkim (Amchi Passang), 185–90; geographic allegiances, 171, 189; interschool relations, 176; isolation, 182, 189; Kalimpong MTK branch, 177–79,
181–82, 190; Keyzom Bhutti, 180–81; long-term, 180; MTK-affiliated versus independent, 183–84, 190; professionalization and control, 183–85; on rotation, 180–82; Salugara MTK branch, 178; Sikkim government hospital, 185; social status, 171; training, 173; Trogawa Rinpoche, 175, 177, 181

Darjeeling Hills area: Darjeeling town, 171–72, 191n5; Kalimpong town, 171–72, 184, 191n5; *kidu*, 182, 192n18; medical pluralism, 174; Sikkim government hospital, 185–86; Tibetan identity, 173, 179; Tibetan public health concerns, 184; Tibetan residents, 171–72, 191n7. *See also* Darjeeling Hills amchi; Darjeeling Hills Tibetan medicine

Darjeeling Hills Tibetan medicine: Chagpori Medical College (1696–1959), 174–75; Chagpori Tibetan Medical Institute (CTMI), 175–77, 191n11; Dali Gompa monastery, 177; influences on, 173; institutions, 174–77; Kalimpong MTK branch, 177–79, 181–82, 189–90; MTK branch clinic enlargements, 184; patients, 179; pluralism, 174; religious elements, 174; Salugara MTK branch, 178–79; social contexts, 173; Teinlay Palsang Trogawa, 177; Tibetan awareness of, 184; Tibetan Refugee Self Help Centre, 176–77. *See also* Darjeeling Hills amchi

Day, Sophie, 164n6, 164nn8–9, 166n26

demons: descriptions of, 157, 166n25; and karma, 158, 166n26; as psychosocial stressors, 160; rites of appeasement, 159; and wind disorders, 148–50, 163n5, 164n7

development projects as political arenas, 103

Diemberger, Hildegard, 188

dietology, 153, 164n14

Dollfus, Pascale, 163n2

Donden, Yeshi, 165n18, 166n24

Dorje, Gyurme, 164n13, 165n15

drib (*grib*), 136n14

Epstein, Mark, 156–157, 165n20

equality-hierarchy tensions, 35

exorcisms, 148–50, 159–60, 163n5, 164n7

family associations (*pha spun*), 59n3

fish consumption, 127, 138n26

Fjeld, Heidi, 188

Rindzin Lhundrub Paljor Nyerongshag, 175
rlung. See wind disorders
Rozario, Santi, 136n11
rü, 187–88
Rupshupa: overview, 65; biomedicine versus
   Tibetan medicine views, 81–82, 86; complex
   medicine use (*rinchen rilbu*), 84; Medical
   Aid Centre (MAC), 80–81, 86; therapeutic
   pragmatism, 82, 86. *See also* Rupshupa
   amchi
Rupshupa amchi: access difficulty impacts,
   81–84, 86–87; biomedical training, 79;
   community ideals, 73–74, 77–78, 85, 87;
   controversial, 77–78; long-distance treatment practices, 83–84, 86; need for, 85–86;
   NGO funding, 77–79; payment systems
   and problems, 75–76, 78–79, 86–87;
   reintroduction difficulties, 86–87; ritual
   specialists, 76–77; symbolic roles,
   85; Tibetan refugees, 74–75; unpopular,
   77–79. *See also* Rupshupa amchi
   out-migration
Rupshupa amchi out-migration: overviews, 65,
   73; community impacts, 70, 80–85; factors
   influencing, 79–80, 87, 90n24; individual
   examples, 74–79
Russell, Hazel, 132

Sahlins, Marshall, 52
Samad. *See* Rupshupa
Samuel, Geoffrey, 7, 35, 86, 123, 136n11
Sangye Gyatso, 175
Sangye Smanla, 55
Schenk, Amelie, 164n9
Schrempf, Mona, 159, 162
Sherab Singe, 76–77, 84
Shneiderman, Sara, 4
Shun-Shade, 120–21, 124, 137n17. *See also*
   childbirth in Shun-Shade
social power: Hanu Gongma village examples,
   47–52, 53, 56–58; medical power links, 57;
   urban contexts, 60n16
Sonam Paljor (Photoksar village amchi): am-
   bitions for sons, 32–33; amchi practice, 31;
   avoidance of politics, 26; conflict resolution
   role, 24; as headman's assistant (*membar*),
   24–26, 30; household, 24, 31–32; modesty,
   33–34; religious study, 31, 38n13; resentments

toward, 32–33; road connection views, 37;
   social status, 23–25, 31, 33–34, 36; training,
   31; village meetings, 30
Sowa Rigpa. *See* Tibetan medicine
Stein, R. A., 35
sustainable livelihoods framework: overview,
   67; Changpa nomads analysis, 67–70;
   limits, 70; migration forms, 88n6;
   Rupshupa amchi out-migration analysis,
   79–80, 87

Tashi Bulu (Hanu Gongma amchi): ambition,
   33, 51–52, 60n15; biography, 45–46; death,
   58; government position, 46, 51; on ideal
   amchi qualities, 53–54; on modernization,
   50; NGO benefits, 60n14; reputation, 46,
   54, 56; social and medical power, 46–48,
   51–52, 56–58; status, 45–46, 51, 60n11; training of students, 45, 57–58, 59n10; wealth,
   46, 51–52, 60n11
Tenzin Sherab, 74–77, 83–84
terma (hidden treasure), 197
therapeutic pragmatism, 82, 86
Tibetan identity, 172–73, 179, 189
Tibetan Medical and Astrological Institute.
   See Men-Tsee-Khang
Tibetan medical practitioners. *See* amchi
Tibetan medicine: biomedicine encounters,
   72–73; Buddhist institutionalization
   attempts, 175; Buddhist monk training in,
   89n21; Central Council of, 183; changes in,
   42; definitional difficulties, 171–72, 191n1;
   dietology, 153; exile communities developing, 2; feminization, 10; Hanu Gongma
   village, 44; history of, 1–2; humors, 153,
   156–57; industrialization, 3, 5; Ladakh, 10,
   70–73, 134; legal recognition, 2–4, 114, 130,
   139n32; Lingshed village, 100–101; moxibustion, 154, 165n15; pharmacological theory,
   138n25; prior scholarship, 5–10, 15n4; pulse
   reading, 122, 151–52; social ecologies, 3;
   standardization, 71–72, 89n18; terminology for, 4–5; urine analysis, 152, 164n11;
   wind, 155–56, 165nn19–21. *See also* amchi;
   Darjeeling Hills Tibetan medicine; Gyüshi;
   medicines; reciprocity systems; wind disorders; Zangskar Tibetan medicine
Tibetans living in India, 171, 191n7

Trans Singe-la Local Doctors' Association (TSLDA), 102
trims, 89n14
Trogawa Rinpoche, 175, 177
Tsering Phuntsog, 129–30
Tsering Wangmo Dhompa, 197–98

Union Territory of Ladakh, 145–46
urine analysis, 152, 164n11
Uyanga, Joseph, 88n2

village-based ethnography, 199. *See also* Hanu Gongma village; Photoksar village

Wiley, Andrea, 131–32, 138n30
wind, 143, 155–56, 165nn19–21
wind disorder case study (Zangskar): amchi diagnoses and treatments, 147, 151–54, 158–59; background, 146–47; Buddhist monk ordainment, 150; Dragom Rinpoche's involvement, 148–50, 158, 164n7; exorcism, 148–50, 163n5, 164n7; familiar responsibility, 161; karma explanation, 150, 158; merit-making, 150, 158, 161; oracle training, 150, 162; pulse diagnosis, 151; symptoms and mania, 147–49
wind disorders (*rlung*): childbirth complications, 125–27, 130; and class, 145; in classical texts, 165n18; contributing factors, 145, 153, 164n13; diagnosis and treatment, 150–55, 164n11; in the Gyüshi, 137n19, 150–51, 155–57; as mental disturbances, 155–59; symptoms, 156; types of, 137n21, 156, 166n23. *See also* wind disorder case study
witchcraft treatments, 159

women: Hanu Gongma village, 45; health-care decisions, 45; and the klu, 128; Lingshed village, 107; Photoksar village, 25, 29, 33, 37n5, 38n10, 38n17; pregnant, 122–25, 135n6, 137n20. *See also* women amchi
women amchi: Darjeeling Hills, 180–81; Hanu, 59n5; historical, 15n3; lineages, 188; Nomad RSI training, 9–10; numbers of, 9–10, 59n5, 134, 190; Zangskar, 152

Zangskar: overview, 145–46; Buddhists, 145–46; health concerns, 144–45; health facilities, 155; income rates, 147; wind disorders, 150–55, 164n11
Zangskari amchi: Buddhist philosophical contexts, 162; decline in numbers, 152; diagnostic methods, 151–52, 162; dietology, 153; exorcisms, 159–60; karma considerations, 157–58, 160–62; knowledge of patient's family, 152; Lonpo Sonam Angchug, 144; medicines, 144, 154, 161; Meme Palchung, 152; mental disturbance understandings, 155, 158; merit-making prescriptions, 150, 154–55, 158, 160–61; purification rites, 160; and religion, 144, 163n2; rites of appeasement, 159; virtues, 162; wind disorder diagnosis and treatment, 150–55, 164n11; witchcraft treatments, 159; women, 152. *See also* wind disorder case study
Zangskar Tibetan medicine: medicine production, 144; modernization, 143–44; ritual healers, 162; social hierarchy maintenance, 161; transactionalism, 161, 163. *See also* Zangskari amchi
Zimmerman, Francis, 164n14, 165n21